I, THE WRITER

114 Essays About Being A Writer Written by Modern Writers Worldwide

D1113497

A Sweetycat Press Publication

Cover design by Priti J
Book formatting by Pam Van Allen

This is a Steve Carr/Sweetycat Press Publication

DEDICATED TO:

Jai Mehta, a great poet, our friend. R.I.P.

ABOUT SWEETYCAT PRESS

Founded by author Steve Carr, Sweetycat Press has one mission: to elevate in the world of publishing the status of the best emerging writers and authors on the writing scene today. An emerging writer is defined as someone who has produced some high-quality work but isn't yet well-known.

The 114 essays in this volume were written by emerging writers worldwide, many who are in the *Who's Who of Emerging Writers 2020*, also published by Sweetycat Press

Sweetycat Press has a Facebook Group that has over 400 members, all who are published authors, poets, songwriters or journalists. Sweetycat Press has also published *The Book of Books* which includes 129 novels and books in a one-of-a-kind catalog that represents the best in modern literature by writing talents on the cusp of fame.

The Sweetycat Press series *In A Flash* narrated by author Dave Gregory and The Poetics series narrated by author Wendy Vogel can be found on YouTube under Sweetycat Press.

THE WRITERS

iv

I, TRINITY ADLER

Building fantasy worlds, publishing stories and poetry, for a writer these are daring acts of exposure. Once my work takes form to enter the world, there I am, naked on the page. I've tried to disguise myself from the real world in fantasy pieces. It isn't possible. Every experience of my life infuses my characters, shapes their existence, dictates the rhythm of the prose and poetry typed onto the page. I unwind my soul, turn by turn, within my story arcs. Events I witness become the spark to give my characters a truthful voice. There is no way out of that bargain.

As a child I watched my dad live with a disintegrating spine. Over time, that injury incurred a plane crash, destroyed his career. Before he lost his ability to work, my mom plowed her way through college earning advanced degrees in Library Science to support us. Reading, education, and creativity always carried value at our house. I published my first poems in my teens.

I finished college to find my literary education wouldn't earn much of a living, but I had the good fortune to find a job in the medical field. The medical center at my college needed a person to translate the collected notes of doctors from their worldwide field trips. I begged for that job and got it.

My work translating those documents into family histories and patient pedigrees thrilled me. A writer couldn't have a better training ground. It paired with my writing talents just as a new study of human genetics hit its stride. The Human Genome Project was absorbing researchers in a quest to map the secrets of DNA's influence over disease.

At the lab I'd unpack blood samples along with the copious notes the doctors brought back with them. I sorted that blood for the first experimental stages of separating out DNA, the map of life. Next, I documented the stories of survival, loss, and exclusion by disease from across the globe to fill our patient files. People came to

1

our clinic for a lifeline in their suffering. Then a new pandemic coursing through the world adding an uncomfortable edge that altered their medical care.

HIV infections transformed our hazardous materials proto cols in the labs. At first, none of us thought it too difficult to handle. We treated all our samples as contagious. Because no one knew the method of transmission, blood banks had no way of screening for HIV infections and no reason to do so. It was considered an STD.

When a little boy with hemophilia became the first case of a child contracting AIDS, his tragedy marked the start of a disaster for our hemophilia patients. Because all hemophiliacs needed regular blood transfusions, the disease swept over that patient community and ended all questions about the method of transmission. It brought our lab into pandemic studies and put an intimate face on the suffering, or so I thought, until I moved West.

It's one thing to read about victims of a disease, or meet those patients in a hospital setting, it's another to confront the reality of it in your day to day life. When I arrived in California, AIDS was ravaging the gay community. The news agencies of the world didn't show its devastation.

Once settled into our new home and jobs, my husband and I began a tour of our state. We wanted to visit San Francisco. Nothing could have prepared me for my first trip to the city. I wanted to explore the legendary places authors like Dashiell Hammett and Mark Twain described in their work. A stroll into the park in front of Ghirardelli Square opened my eyes to the full scale of the HIV pandemic in the most affected city for the disease on earth.

At that time, doctors often refused to treat those carrying the virus. Nursing homes wouldn't take victims. Medical care bankrupted patients. Landlords evicted them. Significant others died or deserted their partners. Because a majority of the infected were gay men, many of their families already rejected them and they had nowhere to turn. Hospitals weren't set up for long term care of such a large population. Once given an AIDS diagnosis, the victims had no chance of support. There, in the park, on blankets laid out under trees, we saw crowds of weakened, dying men.

At first, you might assume it was a busy public venue, filled with tourists enjoying the day, until they saw you and approached. The advance of the illness left dark patches of cancer on their faces and emaciated their bodies. The dying had no other choice but to beg for money to eat, or get meds, if they still had the strength to walk. The desperate men who approached us asked for anything we could spare. Some offered sex acts in return for cash. It was shocking and heartbreaking.

We arrived at the height of the pandemic. After our trip, the gay community rallied and began fund raising for research and care programs to improve treatments and change attitudes towards HIV patients. This visit profoundly altered my view of the world. They say you write what you know. I ran from my knowledge. I thought submerging in fantasy worlds created escapes from reality. Instead, I found it provided avenues into reader's minds for acceptance of truth.

If our lives are an ongoing learning experience, it's a writer's obligation to share that education. My given name is common among published authors so I work under the pen name Trinity Adler. Not to hide, but to draw attention. I have stories I want discovered.

Trinity Adler lives and works in Carmel, California. Her poems and stories are featured in Written Across the Genres, Clockwork Wonderland, Cairn Terriers in the Movies, Life in Pacific Grove, and on numerous blogs and websites. Trinity's story "Oracle at the Delphi" won a placement in the *Faultline anthology* of the SF Chapter of the California Writer's Club. Her poem "Twenty Capitol Crimes" was featured in the 2019 Harvey Milk Pride celebration in honor of Gilbert Baker. Her poem "Friends" was featured in the Harvey Milk Photo Center 2020 Online Pride Artists and Authors show. She writes a column for the Central Coast Writers Branch of the California Writer's Club. She's a filmographer and curates a history of Cairn Terrier films at www.cairnterriermovies.com.

I, FAREED AGYAKWAH

A poet is as good as his ears and eyes. To be a poet, one must be all ears; and have eyes that never weary in seeing well. A poet can be anything - the charm is in his vision. If he is a worm, he must be a book worm burrowing and pouring perpetually over the written word.

I developed my love for books at an early age - say six or seven. My Papa was such a prodigious influence. He used to bring big books from the University of Cape Coast, where he worked as a laboratory technician. *Golden Voyages* and *Time to Read* are examples of such books. The illustrations in them were always lively. Trying to draw or trace a thing or two was a new-found joy. On one particular occasion, my Papa soaked up plain sheets of paper in kerosene. We dried them under a bright day sun. When we all agreed that the sheets had dried up well, we placed one of them on a beautiful spread of illustration in one of those books. By Jove! The beautiful illustrations appeared- the plain paper shone like a sky beneath a rainbow. What a resplendent new way to trace it was to me!

Practice after practice made me a better artist amongst my contemporaries. I remember at the age of eight or nine I used to draw the key players in the Ghana Black Stars squad of 1992. They had won the African trophy. The arts I did were not exact likenesses of the players. But I always knew that to draw the squad's skipper, Abedi Pele, I needed to complete the work by leaving a twisted strip of plaited hair behind the back of his head - what distinguished him as a brand, then.

A food vendor in our primary school became the target of such drawings. I was her great fun. Whenever I drew, she would send the drawings around the school compound telling all the other food vendors what a wonderful artist I was. Often times, my art work won me food or peanut from the sellers.

Although I was not a bad student, what stood out was my ability to read widely and write better. I never enjoyed reading for long hours. But my elder sister, Naa Dedei, did; she was only in Primary six while I was in Primary four. From Primary four on up through Basic School and beyond, she had already garnered admiration from her teachers and even people in Senior Secondary School. By age eleven, I had already started wondering if I could ever read or write like her. When she was in Junior Secondary School (JSS) her teacher would mark her essay scripts with a high score, and draw a befitting trophy underneath. I remember stealing those papers and showing it to my close friends at school. Her performance in English Language made me hungry for success in writing. Eventually, reading and writing won out over my love for drawing.

My major encounter with reading and appreciating poetry started in Senior Secondary School (SSS). For the first time, as an adolescent, the clock within ticks by, reminding you of the need to further your education, land a good job, fulfill tax obligation, rent an apartment, buy a car, marry and what have you. The question of how to achieve all these can make a young boy forget to write.

My muse sank into oblivion for quite some time. But something happened which would lead to a rediscovery of my muse. I was going home to my lunch one day when I noticed a little orange book on my compound. This naturally should come to me as a surprise. But what surprised me most was the fact that my compound had been swept by an unknown, if not unseen hands- a hand other than mine! My mood was one of stony silence, as I picked up the book wondering from where and who it had come to me. Yet, hitherto, I search for both the sender and the sweeper.

But he is no writer who picks up a book without opening. Two poems in the book namely "Lucy" and "Abou Ben Adhem" struck the lyrical cord within. The former was written by William Wordsworth, and the latter, Leigh Hunt. Reading them made me feel like a poet. These poems sounded to me like something I had written by myself. From that moment, it felt like Israel suddenly waking up to freedom. I began to write, for keeps. All these experiences have given impetus to my craft, making me grow mellower and assured in the face of the tides of life.

Through 2007 to date, I have dedicated myself to reading, writing, getting published. These opened me up to more international collaborations and recognition/awards hitherto.

The mighty spider who has cast wide His web to cover the corners of this world has been faithful. The spider stays faithful and true to His calling. Why did the spider weave such a web? Answer- to reveal His glory. Why do I write? Answer- to reveal the glory of God in me. Through woven words, I trap the ills, be it political, economical, social, technological, environmental, or legal, in the fabrics of society. These ills are what give me sleepless night, as a writer- the motivation! The penchant to sacrifice my personal comfort through my feelings, thoughts, ideas, qualia and unique voice to inspire the change we desire to see in our world is wholly mine. To do this job well, as a writer, the ears and eyes must always be on the ground.

Fareed Agyakwah, a prolific writer from Ghana, conventionally educated at the University of Cape Coast - the same university whose hospital saw his birth. Several magazines, reputable journals, ezines and anthologies have seen his works appear in them. A favorite few among these are *Setu Bilingual, Cajun Mutt Press, Wreaths For a Wayfarer,* Nationalism: (Mis)understanding Donald Trump's Capitalism, Racism, Global Politics, International Trade and Media Wars, Vol 2. (Africa Vs North America), Best New African Poets (2019), and the World's Biggest Anthology on Contemporary Literature- Songs of Peace (2020). Agyakwah is a recipient of "Temirqazyq-The Best Poet/ Writer of the World (2019)".

I, MEHREEN AHMED

I don't know if anyone believes in the power of place. What it is, is that every place has a spirit, a soul of its own which renders influence over people and controls them in a peculiar sort of way. Power which can shape a character, mold a mind, and provide poetic inspiration. Yes, that's the kind of place I am talking about. A unique place which may have molded me, I, the writer since inception.

I remember sitting in my garden as a child and watching the peaceful river flow by.

*

I want to find out, not about its source, but about what stories its sonorous waves have carried for millions of years now. The debris it has collected on its way. Each has a story to tell. The bark of a tree must have come from someplace where a tree stands. It may have had a love heart etched on its skin and names of innumerable lovers over many past years, until the bark snaps off one day, and is swept away by a storm along with dry leaves into the depths of this river.

*

Then one day, I discover Virginia Woolf, James Joyce, Tagore, and Nazrul Islam. Their works expand my horizon, and fill up my mind with music, style, mood, tone, and emotions, pouring into the fount of adulation for them. I find my niche in maturity. I know that I want to be like my masters. My pot of gold, my imagination has been eluding me all this time, but now the time has come to explore it.

*

My dairy slowly begins to reshape into something else, something worth noting. I realize nature alone isn't sufficient. I need to add more to it, another organic world, the living world of humans where the two meet and dance the tango in my imagination. Creativity takes place. That is the beginning of something new, but raw. Something which transpires into more significance at a later date. I start to write. But did not publish until much later, "A Winter's Tale" came out in *The Sheaf* in the winter of 1987 in Canada, University of Saskatchewan.

This is followed by more journalistic write-ups published in subsequent issues of the same newspaper. However, I find myself drawn to this raw and grittiness of life rather than its polished facade. I want to delve deeper into the core. This, the core of human nature, which Joseph Conrad defines as innate (*Lord Jim*). My writings find a new wave of nuanced expressions in a stream-of-consciousness style. I start to publish books, short stories, flash fiction and so on. But, I also publish academic articles and book reviews at the same time.

*

In the same vein, I reflect that there may be a deep dilemma hidden to this premise. Where a latent talent may exist in the heart of it, is still hard to decipher. True to everything else which finds their way into this world, be it a blade of grass, or a nightingale, or even the sirens of the ancient seas. A writer's connection to fertile imagination, which is must in this business of creation, is this an innate gift unlocked by the power of place? Or is it borne out of sheer hard work only, the much cliched idea that perspiration does it somewhat? Or maybe it is both. I can't really tell.

*

Although I do believe that in my case the fact that I went through the many developmental stages incognito which I have mentioned above. Like a telltale bark of tortured human skin, the dilemma still stands, is this innate after all? Perhaps, it is for imagination to be fertile enough to give birth to the many sirens, it has to be designed in that manner. A gift, a talent that people are born with. Such an imagination which is unlocked at the right time and place. The life of a mind that I, a writer, have no choice but to think of the impossible, fairies, elves or life on Mars which no science can prove of their existence anywhere, except in one place — the mind, the poetry of imagination when put in words makes me what I am. I, the writer.

Me. Yes, I visualize myself, often, I really don't think, I had any plans of becoming a writer ever. I am clueless as to what brought me here. Thus far. Ah! But, something stirs within when I see the trembling of a leaf. A gnawing pain in the gut without reprieve, as I sit by a river trying to understand its tales of a meandering journey. This journey, I began as a child like the river flow, like the ocean full of surprises, surprised myself, when I put down the first two words on white paper with fresh ink. Sirens called in celebration. Nightingale screeched and a night owl starred down in awe. That I imagine, therefore I am. Descartes summed it up so brilliantly and concisely, "I think, therefore I am." A natural process, how do we think? Nobody knows, they just do. Just like the many constellations in the celestial, the far-fetched big bang. What precipitated all this? How did it all come about? Who could have predicted them?

*

That I have written my first few words. Autumn leaves lay scattered, dry and crunchy on a wet path by the cafe I went every morning for a caffeine shot. There, my first story was born. It took off. It has happened. But I will say this, if all those readings, hard work and the sum of the unseen spirits have guided me, my guardian angel, I wouldn't know. Because I couldn't tell for sure or predict its beginnings or endings of this journey, its various developmental stages. For I never planned to become a writer. I became one.

Mehreen Ahmed is an award-winning author, internationally published and critically acclaimed by Midwest Book Review. She has written Novels, Novella, Short Stories, Creative Nonfiction, Flash Fiction, Academic, Prose Poetry, Memoirs, Essays and Journalistic Write-Ups. Her works have been podcast, anthologised and translated in German, Greek and Bengali. She has two masters' degrees and a bachelor's (Hon) in English Literature and Linguistics from the University of Queensland and Dhaka University. She was born and raised in Bangladesh. At the moment, she lives in Australia.

I, WARREN ALEXANDER

From the time I wrote my first ransom note I was hooked. But as beginning writer, I did get a lot of rejections, but I also received a number of inquiries from the police.

I did not like children's books because, well, they were written for children. And while others were watching unrealistic TV shows such as *Leave It to Beaver* and *Father Knows Best,* I watched TV shows like *Ernie Kovacs, That Was the Week That Was,* and *Jack Paar.* Paar had a frequent guest named Oscar Levant, an actor, pianist, and wit with a twitch who sported an 'I don't give a shit' attitude. I loved Oscar; there was an unapologetic authenticity to him. Kovacs did comedy bits which I did not understand which indicated I had much to learn.

My entire world view changed when I read *Lysistrata* by Aristophanes in college. Every generation thinks they invented sex and the right to be self-righteous about the world they inherited and I propagated this arrogance to the fullest. *Lysistrata* demonstrated with great majesty, that these problems were 1000's of years old.

I was an editor of the college newspaper from which we were thrown off, because what we thought was funny and what the administration thought was funny were three different things. They became particularly annoyed when we ran a drawing on the front page of a barroom brawl with the headline, *President Drops Quarter at Faculty Meeting.*

I received an MA in Creative Writing from NYU where my teachers included Tom Keneally, E. L. Doctorow, and Peter Carey. My personal essay for admission included passages about looking at people's shoes while riding the subway and creating stories about them and that I wanted to write like J.D. Salinger. Although Salinger wrote about alienation, everyone identified with that. But by definition, how could everyone be alienated? This proved that Salinger was a most able writer. In grad school, I finally found a profitable use for the trait that was first observed by my kindergarten teacher. She said that I was the first five-year-old cynic she ever met. In grad school, I learned how to round my cynicism and observations into characters, dialogue, and themes.

I am a royal pain in the ass and that is essential for any writer or person in the arts to be successful. You must tell the world to "go to hell" and do what you want. BUT it must be well-crafted, thoughtful, creative, and represent on the page what the brain thought. Being an idiot without producing the best work possible, is a double failure.

Among the writers I admire are Saul Bellow, Paul Beatty, Elena Ferranate, Flannery O' Connor, Delmore Schwartz, Billy Collins, Oscar Wilde, Elmore Leonard, Aristophanes, and Laurence Sterne. If I continued on for my PhD, my dissertation would have been about Sterne and the intellectual freedom with which he wrote in the time he wrote.

One writer who I love and should not is Pedro Carolino. Pedro wrote a Portuguese-English phrase book, even though he did not speak English. He used a Portuguese-French phrase book and then French-English phrase book. Mark Twain wrote the introduction for the first American edition and could not decide whether it poetic or idiotic. His book is currently called *English As She Is Spoke* and my favorite phrase is "To craunch a marmoset." I do not know what it means nor do I care to. A fictionalized version of his life is in my queue of future works, as he deserves recognition for his single-mindedness and not let his ignorance or naivete get in his way. Lessons for us all.

I live by Chuck Close's admonition, "Inspiration is for amateurs. The rest of us just show up and get to work. If you wait around for the clouds to part and a bolt of lightning to strike you in the brain, you are not going to make an awful lot of work. All the best ideas come out of the process; they come out of the work itself."

So do not whine and sit your bony ass down and do the hard work if you want to be writer and write, write, write and read, read, read. And shun all the romance and stereotypes about writers and writing, they become built-in obstacles and excuses.

Now get back to work, I've wasted enough of your time.

Warren Alexander, was born and still lives in New York City. His satiric novel, *Cousins' Club,* was a semi-finalist for 2017 BookLife Award for General Fiction. He was the April 2019 *Spillwords* Author of the Month and the featured writer for the July 2020 edition of *Inner Circle Writers' Magazine.* He has also participated in over two dozen photographic exhibits including one where his work was chosen by a curator from the Guggenheim New York. He and his wife have visited over 45 countries and returned from most of them. He is currently working on a satiric novel about business and otherwise writes poems, an occasional short story, and essays for which he has no expertise.

I, PETER ASTLE

For a number of years, I taught on a new A-Level Creative Writing course at Burton and South Derbyshire College. Although I was technically qualified to teach it – having studied creative writing as part of my degree – I wasn't sure I was up to it.

Fifty-percent of the Writing Portfolio was a thing called The Commentary, in which students had to analyze their "Approaches to Writing," their "Literary Influences," and their "Experience of being a Writer."

This would challenge many professional writers, let alone a group of sixteen to eighteen-year-olds.

Many students claimed to have no 'literary influences' and the question about their 'experience of being a writer' just confused them. To be honest, it confused me too.

In the end, I encouraged them to think about their early experiences of writing and the pleasures of creativity. When that didn't work, I brought in a pile of comics I'd created myself when I was eleven years of age.

As a kid, I'd loved *The Beano, The Dandy* and *Whizzer and Chips*, and decided to create my own comic. I called it *Jester*. It contained about a dozen comic-strip stories in each issue. I was no artist and the felt-tip drawings, with speech-balloons, were crude to say the least. But each badly drawn strip cartoon had a story with a start, middle and an end.

I explained that I actually sold these comics to school friends for two pence and was enormously proud when my friends forked out some of their pocket money to buy the next edition.

Okay, the total readership of *Jester* was just three people, but that didn't stop me.

In fact, it was a good thing. I had to produce each issue by hand, copying from the master copy, and if I had any more customers I would never have kept up. These were the days before computers and I had no access to a photocopier.

Even though it cost me more in felt-tip pens, paper and staples than I was making from sales, I carried on churning out issue after issue because I just loved writing the funny stories. Why? Because I was creating story worlds and characters that belonged to me.

Clearly, there were *similarities* with the characters in *The Beano*, *The Dandy* and *Whizzer and Chips*, but there were also *differences*. Enough differences to make each story unique. This led to a discussion about genre, the idea of *similarity* and *difference*, and before long the students were able to list authors they'd enjoyed and how their own stories were influenced by the writers they admired.

On a roll, I went on to explain how I'd been influenced by writers like Roald Dahl, Stephen King, Alan Bennett, Agatha Christie and Harlan Coben.

Pacing the classroom, I rattled on about intricately woven plots and the pleasure of the perfect twist ending. It was enough to get them thinking about the stories they liked to write, which was generally vampires. By the end of the second semester, they just about had The Commentary licked.

The AQA guidelines encouraged students to explore online writing groups, so I decided to check them out for myself.

I rarely used social media at the time, but it wasn't long before I was hooked. Buoyed by the support of members in the Facebook writing groups, I started submitting my own short stories to various anthologies and competitions. With every acceptance my confidence grew. I was under no illusion that I would make much money through these groups, but I was heartened by the feedback and the competition wins.

In 2018, I won a short story competition in the Inner Circle Writing Group. The prize was a book contract for a collection of short stories. The task of putting together around eighty-thousand words of short stories was daunting, but I was confident I had enough material to adapt, rework and polish to fill the book.

Since leaving school, I had never really abandoned writing. I was a musician for ten years, a teacher for eighteen, but always a writer at heart. I dabbled in writing a novel, which I never finished. I wrote several shorts that were published in the local newspaper. I got paid for a couple of stories for *The People's Friend*. I got a pitiful royalty payment for a comedy story for a Young Adult anthology. Yet, I carried on.

But now the time was right.

My college decided to close the A-level department and all sixth-form staff were all offered redundancy payments. In 2018, I took my cheque, sold up, bought a motorhome (RV) and headed off – jobless and homeless – to a campsite in Benidorm, Spain.

For me, this was the perfect environment to finish the collection and to work on other new writing projects. I loved the community and plenty of ex-pats were happy to read my stories and offer encouragement and advice. This was the first time I had the freedom to write without the burden of a full-time job. I used the time to write as much as I could and nudged the niggling concerns about employment to the back of my mind. It was quite a productive time.

Covid-19 turned the world upside-down in 2020, but even that provided new ideas for me and other writers. In recent times, the pandemic has been a springboard for creative writing projects across the globe, and a constant reminder that ideas and influences always come from somewhere other than just the authors' head.

Without *The Beano, The Dandy* and *Whizzer and Chips, Jester* would not have been born. My comic might not have reached a huge audience, but *Jester* was my creation and I was proud of it.

I've still got a few copies, if anyone's interested.

Peter Astle is a former Media and English Teacher from Derby in the UK. He has had many short stories published in a range of magazines and international anthologies. He recently won two book contracts with Clarendon House Publishing to publish collections of his short stories. Peter enjoys writing stories with surprise or twist endings. His first collection is entitled *Twists and Turns* is set to be published in 2020. He's currently traveling Spain in a motorhome (RV) along with his faithful dog, Joey.

I, GABRIELLA BALCOM

Unimaginable—that's how I'd describe the power and impact of words, and they've been as important to me as breathing throughout the majority of my life. This may sound exaggerated, but it isn't.

My father was a teacher and linguist; my mother taught before I was born, working in a library after. Books surrounded me from my earliest memory. My mother began teaching me to read and write when I was a year old, and my father introduced me to other languages at the same time. However, these things alone didn't make words important to me.

I was an only child, and other than my mother "playing school" with me, I spent my time alone. Once I'd mastered reading and writing, she turned her focus elsewhere. My father spent his spare time on his hobbies. My parents never bought a TV, but loved movies, so we went to theaters a lot. They routinely took me to libraries, where I checked out dozens of books each time (I read fast). Although my parents participated in events at work, they isolated themselves in their personal lives. We visited very few people, and my father didn't allow anyone in our home. In a similar vein, I wasn't permitted to visit classmates, and none could come see me.

A tabby cat took up residence under an old car my father had when I was three or four, and gave birth shortly after. She was my first friend. I remember crawling underneath the car to pet, talk, and read to her. Sometimes I fell asleep there.

But my connection to words was truly solidified by something else, the thing that had the greatest impact on me. Abuse.

My father came from another country, was much older than my mother, and had a dominant personality; my mother was passive. He emotionally abused both of us, but I alone was battered physically. Once, when I was two, he raged in the front room, smashing and demolishing things, while my mother sat nearby eating a snack and tuning him out. I ran to my room at the far end of our home, and heard him stomping down the hall in my direction. My room was tiny, the closet full, and the one hiding spot was under my bed, positioned in a corner. I crawled underneath, scooting as far back as I could—up against the wall. If I could've escaped *into* the wall, I would have. My father didn't find me, and I stayed hidden for hours while his rampage continued. The next morning, he acted as if nothing had happened.

However, his "explosions" usually led to different endings. My belongings were destroyed. I was beaten with pieces of wood, his hands, his long metal key chain, or whatever he found at hand, occasionally knocked flying. I could've died several times. When I said my mother was passive, I meant *passive-passive.* She never intervened, usually reading and eating throughout everything. Despite my father's behavior, I know he loved me, but he believed violence was acceptable and his right.

His physical abuse stopped when I was ten. One evening, he walked over to hit me, and I went to meet him. I'd had enough. He saw that in my eyes and never struck me again. In a twisted way, my actions won his respect.

I didn't share the above to horrify, provoke, or garner sympathy. I did it to show why I desperately needed an escape. Something to give me hope for the future. Something to hold onto and provide warmth. Stories did just that, lifting me straight out of hell, transporting me to magical kingdoms, places where people laughed, were happy, triumphant over evil, and heroic. I experienced kindness, friendship, wonder, and learned of individuals enduring misery, how they survived, and countless other things. Need I say more?

My first "writing" was listing animals that began with the letters of the alphabet, but I moved into creating stories. Needless to say, cats figured into many of them. I won a writing contest when I was six for my composition about animals who met, became friends, and moved in together. I began journaling when I was eight, writing poetry at thirteen, and I read and wrote constantly.

17

Once I finished high school, I stayed busy with college, work, marriage, and children, later with divorce and single parenthood. I stopped writing but read voraciously whenever possible. I wrote work-related articles for my job, but nothing for myself. Overall, my family and I endured ups and downs, happiness and shattering grief, but we survived.

I felt prompted to write many times, but didn't until 2012, when I couldn't hold back the words anymore. They poured out of me as if a floodgate had opened, and I wrote a *lot*. My first writing was cathartic, but it turned creative. I never thought of submitting anything, but someday I'll go back and revise my early works.

In 2018, I had an idea to do something with my writing and joined a Facebook writing group. I noticed a submission call, wrote two stories, and hired my first editor. My "Bobby-You'd Never Guess" was accepted and published in *A Contract of Words*. (Eventually, I submitted the second story, "Suzie's Wish;" it was published in *Athena*.) More of my works have been published since, as well as my first book, *On the Wings of Ideas* (Clarendon House Publications). My novella, *The Return*, is currently pending publication by Black Hare Press in their *Deep Underground* series. Each acceptance has thrilled me, and I've dreamed of my tales having a strong impact on others.

Everybody's values and life experiences are unique, and each person has a different opinion about words. As for me, I view them as much more than shapes on a page. They brought me company when I was alone, warmth in the midst of coldness and cruelty, hope when I was in despair, and I can truly say they saved me.

Gabriella Balcom lives in Texas, works in a mental health field, and writes fantasy, horror/thriller, romance, sci-fi, and more. Her interests include traveling, music, good shows, genealogy, and photography. She says she's a sucker for a great story, loves forests, mountains, and back roads, and she has a weakness for lasagna, garlic bread, tacos, cheese, and chocolate. Gabriella has had 210+

works accepted for publication, and was nominated in 2020 for the Washington Science Fiction Association's Small Press Award. Her book, *On the Wings of Ideas*, came out recently, with another pending publication.

I, IRENE BARON

Who am I? I am an award-winning artist, writer, and author. I have one adult daughter whom I love very much.

My sincere interest in writing began when I learned my 10th grade English teacher read my essays aloud as good examples to all her classes except mine. With that endorsement, my confidence in writing grew.

My family paid little attention to my writing. I sold my first oil painting at age 12 but never sold written work until I published books after the age of 50. Unpaid, I wrote for and edited many newsletters and journals for over 20-years. When unannounced awards would appear in the mail, my parents would be quietly pleased.

My life has been guided toward religion and science. A high school counselor called my parents to tell them they must send me to college. They did, demanding a science degree. It was difficult and rewarding. I would not have made it without my parental support.

When I later received 68 astronomy programs from NASA JPL, persons I contacted there didn't know the DVDs had existed or who sent them. I used the programs nightly over several years to find and document the Christmas star. Using inter library loans, my local library located almost 100 requested books that I used to learn Babylonian symbols and symbolism still used by astronomers at the time of Christ's birth. That investigation resulted in the award-winning illustrated book, *Unraveling the Christmas Star Mystery*. It was named the best Christian education book of 2013. Readers ages 13 to 93 told me how much they loved it. Such comments helped my self-confidence in making it easy to understand.

I believe my Heavenly Father wanted mankind to know that the Christmas star did exist. It was a position marker like a GPS for the birthplace of Jesus Christ. There were nine additional celestial events in the few months prior to his birth announcing who was being born and how important He would be to mankind. My work validates the Bible story of His birth which should make persons of all religions sit up and take notice.

I studied all fields of science during college and graduate school, including astronomy. I loved learning about the universe. That background enabled me to become an Information Specialist with Battelle Memorial Institute. They sent me to London to train with the World Engineers Council for coursework dedicated to technical writing. It was fascinating as were the sightseeing trips. In SE Asia I worked with ARPA during the Vietnam War. As Director of Aerial Photography, I contributed to the top-secret counter-insurgency book for the military. Those four+ years provided experiences most people have no idea even existed. I used some of them in *Mindreacher*, the first thriller in the psychological & geopolitical sci-fi series.

Authors are told books should be written for understanding by a typical 5thgrader, I tried to simplify my work. Always excited about new discoveries, I wanted readers to experience wonder and excitement. The first *Mindreacher* has some science. The first sequel contains less science and more action. Readers of all ages will love it. I learn as my writing evolves.

During my sophomore year in high school, I wanted to become a nun. I took catechism and spoke with pastors and priests. An angelic visitor let me know I didn't need to be in a convent to do God's work. My first two books are partial proof that visitor was correct. More such books are in the process of using ancient scriptures.

"Mary, Did You Know?" was a song that made Mary sound like a common teenager off the street. She was not. The song gave me the impetus to use the eyewitness accounts of Apostle James, Joseph's youngest son, to write the true story of Mary. I did so using the historical narrative method. Her parents were informed by angels that Mary was named and dedicated to be the mother of Jesus Christ before her conception. The book, *Mary Knew – A Biography of Mary from Ancient Scriptures* is an award-winning book. Readers say, once started, it consumes their life until they finish it.

As a teen, I lived for sports, especially tennis, swimming, water/snow skiing, jogging, rappelling, and so on, not knowing each endeavor added damage to joints. I have a reconstructed shoulder which impacts typing, artwork and my life. Constant pain impedes feeling like typing

I am the mother to an exceptionally wonderful and brilliant adult daughter who, while finishing her doctorate, became ill with undiagnosed C-difficile for over 3-years. Each coma was death-defying, one of them lasting over a month. That still impacts our lives.

When informed that authors were to spend 50% of their time marketing, I became frustrated trying to fit everything into my life. I drool over offers by public relations firms.

Much quiet time is spent in a small office researching, writing, and marketing using the Internet. My rescue terrier is always by my side letting me know when to take breaks.

I enjoy my writing friends and authors on social media who give excellent advice.

Irene Baron is an award-winning author, artist, aerial photographer, and teacher. She completed 4 years of top-secret work in Thailand for a classified government counter-insurgency book. She lived in Germany and had unique experiences in 27 countries. She uses those experiences in writing her *Mindreacher* psychological thriller series. A professional Information Specialist, her hobby is researching science topics. A graduate of Hiram College & Ohio University, she also participated in National Science Foundation-sponsored studies. Irene has one daughter. They reside in Ohio. Her *Mindreacher* thriller series and other books are available on Amazon.

I, JIM BATES

For the last eight months of her life, I had the privilege of being the primary care-giver for my mother. We spent many hours talking and reliving our past, looking at photographs, going for short walks and sometimes just sitting together enjoying each other's company. Mom was a single parent and I was her oldest son. We were close. We were friends.

Mom never asked much of me. "Just be the best person you can be," she told me. "Don't get a big head and always look out for your younger brothers. Think of others before you think of yourself."

"I'll try, Mom," I told her many times as I grew up. "I'll try."

"There's one thing, though," she often said, "you should be a writer. You're good with words."

So, while I was caring for her, I started to seriously write. I started writing a poem a day, while I was caring for her, and I continued writing a poem a day after she passed away. Four years later, I had accumulated over one-thousand four hundred poems. Almost all of them were crap, but that experience taught me one thing: it taught me discipline. I still make it a point to try to write every day.

Mom instilled in me a love of reading. I was never a good student in school. I graduated from high school in the middle of my class, with no honors at all. I was just average. But I liked to read and I loved to escape into the world created on the page. In fact, I began writing a story when I was in fourth grade only to grind to a halt when I realized I didn't really have anything to write about. Mom said that maybe when I got older, I'd have more life experiences. By the time Mom had died, I'd had those experiences. In spades. I also had something to prove: to myself. I wanted to prove that I could write stories that were intelligent, interesting, and, more accurately, stories that I enjoyed reading. I started writing short stories.

A friend of mine suggested that I start a blog. "Do the best work you can. Write your best stories and post them," she said. She didn't say that I should judge myself on what other's thought, which I really appreciated. She said that I should judge myself against myself; advice I still follow today. Between you and me, I love it when people like my stories, but I don't really care if they don't. I write to write what I consider good stories. We are all adults. If someone doesn't like my work, that's fine. The important thing is that I do.

So how does this get back to my mom? Well, she died before I ever had anything published. She wanted me to write, she believed that her oldest son, this average student who wasn't much good at book learning, had a way with words. Her opinion of my stories would have been the only one that mattered.

With that being said, as I contemplated what to say as a dedication to my first collection of stories, coming out in late 2020, I didn't have to think too long or too hard. I dedicated it to my mom. It reads "Dedicated to Betty Ann Cory, who taught me to believe in myself, to care for others and to appreciate the beauty found in nature." I think, even if it embarrassed her, which I know it would have, she would have liked it because it came from me, and it came from my heart.

You know what? I think she would have liked a lot of the stories, too.

Jim lives in a small town twenty miles west of Minneapolis, Minnesota. His stories and poems have appeared in many online and print publications. His collection of short stories, *Resilience,* is scheduled to be published in 2020 by Bridge House Publishing.

I, ROBERT LEE BEERS

Piracy is a way of life for an author. Sometimes piracy, the intentional theft of your book with no way to collect what is rightfully due you for the time involved in creating the tale, can be both infuriating and rather funny. The sixth volume of the Tony Mandolin series is my example of such piracy.

The book is titled The Clone in the Closet. Frankie, Tony's partner in the PI business is cloned without his knowledge. The reason for that comes clear about three-fourths of the way into the book. I had no idea that particular story would be so popular, especially with a Chinese audience, and as the Bard said, there's the rub.

Every author checks out on what their work is doing online. Come on, admit it. We are an egotistical lot. Well, about two years ago I was doing that and came across a retailer I was unaware of selling The Clone in the Closet. Not only that but the book had about 50,000 ratings, most of them 4 and 5 stars. Cool, I thought, now where are those royalties? Even at e-book rates that would be a nice check. No dice.

I found the email address of the retailer and asked that question. When I checked back later that day, the listing was gone. A day later the website was gone. Since then I've wondered, what would it take to get my series translated into Cantonese?

For the author, writing is not just a job, it is the act of creation. Those words become your baby, your child, your young adult you send off into the world by hitting the Send button. There is far more than just effort instilled into those words, there is emotion, passion, grief, and in my case, a massive dollop of sarcasm and irony.

I have been writing for nearly three decades now, and even though I have achieved some success, I really have yet to be discovered. There is an ambivalence within me now about the perceived injustice of seeing what I know to be a far lesser writer achieve worldwide fame. For me, it has now become the continuing creation and maintenance of my "family". You see, I now am there when I write a scene. I see the buildings, the landscape, and I hear the voices of those speaking the dialogue I type down. That is what the ongoing creation of characters a writer has come to love for nearly thirty years. But that is also where the ambivalence comes into play because all artists want accolades for their effort in creating what they consider to be beautiful. We are not satisfied with a few passersby sneaking a glance. We want a stadium filled with cheering fans. And, a nice royalty check now and then wouldn't hurt.

Mister Beers is the author of 17 novels, four of which were produced into full-cast audio dramas. He has a Master's degree in Graphic Design but prefers writing, cooking, and attempting to sound like Chet Atkins on his Taylor guitar.

I, ANDREW BIRCH

It would be easy to begin this with a reference to my primary school English teacher that claimed that I would never amount to anything. It'd be a good opener, and somewhat cathartic. But in all honesty, there are many more positive things that outweigh this memory from when I was six years old. She doesn't deserve a reference, nor will she get one. And so these are the positive things that have affected me, driven me and guided me on my journey to find my author's voice, and become a storyteller and poet.

Firstly, my home city of Manchester, and the people in it, are a major driving force in both my art and my writing. Not the rich folks in their offices with their expensive designer suits, but the homeless guys on the street corners, each one often with a bedraggled but loyal dog in tow. Or the overweight security guard in the high visibility vest and the tie that looks like it's strangling him and forcing all the blood into his face. The junkie begging for scraps in the bus station who can't walk straight. The middle-aged woman with heavy shopping bags who stopped wearing make-up ten years ago, and whose idea of a good time is to sit down for a half hour without the kids screaming at her. Those are my people, my inspiration. Those are the people I grew up with on the streets of South Manchester, the people that inspire my writing and the people that my stories are aimed at. They're just everyday people who want a good book to read on the beach, or on the train and to enjoy it.

When I was younger, I was a city bus driver on the streets of Manchester, and the fierce camaraderie between my colleagues and I inspired my Travels with a Barbarian stories, and the fiercely loyal warrior race contained within the pages of those tales. My friends here in the north would help each other with anything. We might be downtrodden, but we're fiercely loyal and proud. If it wasn't for my upbringing in the down-at-heel north of England, I wouldn't be the kind of writer I am today.

I think that the mentality that we have here in Northern England helped shape me as a writer somewhat. The idea that we usually do whatever we're told we can't possibly do. I've always been told that I'm too stupid to be a writer, or that writers have to have some kind of deep higher purpose, or an increased intelligence. My natural northern awkwardness decided that I didn't have to have some deep higher purpose, or to have to contribute to some cultural zeitgeist. In fact, all I had to do was to entertain people, and tell stories. It's that cussedness that has spurred me on, to fly in the face of the Starbucks cultural elite and to be a working-class author, that just wants to write normal stories for normal people.

Of course, I can't write about what shaped me as a story teller without speaking of dear Helen. She was to have been my twin sister. She died shortly before my birth. In fact, were it not for her death, neither of us would have lived. In fact, it could be said that Helen is my driving force in life, the reason I strive to do well and continue to pick myself up when life knocks me down. You see, she gave me the gift of life. Her life. And until I began writing as The Birch twins, the one who laid down her life for me was merely a name recorded in a single book in a forgotten place. Now every single piece of work I produce bears her name so that it can be remembered and known. If I have a reason to succeed at writing, then it is to share that name.

But her influence is more than that. I could always hear her voice in my head from a young age. To this day, I write female characters better than male ones. I believe that it's the part of her that still exists within me. Knowing of her presence has shaped the way that I write, and the subject matter. When she is involved, the writing is ethereal and wistful. Our relationship is somewhat unusual and symbiotic. I am the instrument, but she the musician. She is the center of all my worlds, and the architect of them.

The story that she inspired and "wrote" *Poohsticks Bridge*, was a turning point for me. An independently published novel, it was my second full length book, and is a story about a young boy and girl.

It's a blueprint of how my life would have been with her, had she lived. It was cathartic to write, and terribly difficult at the same time. I didn't consider myself a true writer until the release of that book. It was this novel that gave me a knowledge of marketing, of the importance of having editors, cover artists and beta readers - in fact a team of people that cared enough about my characters and, more importantly, caring about my sister's voice as much as I did. During *Poohsticks Bridge*, I acquired a contact list of people that I could trust, and would wish to work with again. People who cared, and were as passionate about my work as me.

The production of *Poohsticks Bridge* opened doors a tiny crack, and that led to short stories, and more things being published. A confidence grew within me that told me that I was a writer of worth. Little by little the mountain is being climbed, and the list of contacts and fans is growing. I learn new things every single day. Every day, I develop my style a little more. Every day I have a new story to tell. And every single day, that forgotten sister that gave her life for her brother is becoming more and more known.

Andrew R Birch, Manchester, UK. Graduated with a degree with honours in Literature. Has independently published two novels, *The Life of Lol* and *Poohsticks Bridge*. Short stories published at The *Literary Yard* include "Stranger on the Line," "Dragged up," "The Coyote" and the three-story series: "Travels with a Barbarian." His poem, "When I was Nine," features in *Poetica*, published by Clarendon House.

I, BRANDY BONIFAS

I grew up on the edge of Appalachia, nestled amongst the gently rolling foothills of southeastern Ohio before they fade into the flat land to the north. As an only child, I explored the hill where I lived, my imagination running as wild as the flowers growing along our gravel road. Indoors, I could be found with a pencil and notebook in hand, filling pages with loops and swirls, pretending to write in the pretty cursive style my parents used, or sitting cross legged at my mom's feet, dictating the stories I'd made up so she could write them down for me on pages I'd pre-illustrated.

I can't say what first made me want to write. The urge was always there, bubbling below the surface like a pot about to boil over. Maybe it was the mystery of the written language, the way adults could read words on a page, deciphering secrets that remained elusive to me. I remember how impatient I was to learn those secret combinations of letters and words until that hidden world opened itself up to me. At last, I could read…and better yet, *write* the stories I wanted to read.

I recall perusing the dusty books stored in an upstairs bedroom of my grandparents' old farmhouse, relishing the sweet, organic smell of their yellowed pages. That's also where I found my grandpa's old army chest from WWII. I opened the lid like a window through time, the writer in me drawn to the hand-written letters tucked inside.

I spent most of my weekends at that farmhouse, whiling away afternoons in my grandpa's workshop, revived by the fresh scent of oak shavings as he handcrafted his locally famous chairs. Or I would daydream during long walks through the wooded hills behind the house to the spot where I carved some of the memorable dates of my youth into the bark of an old beech tree. Or I would drink in the earthy aromas of canning season as the women in my family made efficient work of the harvest in the big kitchen.

That kitchen bore witness to countless tales, and it was no secret that I wanted to become a writer. Inevitably, someone would look my way and tell me I should write down all these stories into a book. But being young, I had no interest in them then. I would smile and say, "Maybe, someday." As a teenager, I couldn't fathom writing a book about something as mundane as kitchen table conversations when my head was full of epic fantasies and edge-of-your-seat adventures. I wrote to escape reality not to revisit it.

In my twenties, I became a closet novelist, bringing my fantasy worlds to life at the edges of the day after college or work. I seldom revealed my secret dream of becoming an author to anyone because when I did, they would take one look at me and say, "Oh, you should write children's books!"

By then, I had perfected my polite smile. "Maybe, someday," I would say again while secretly cringing inside. How could they think I should write children's books? If only they knew the war-ravaged worlds I'd built in my mind, complete with detailed histories and religions, heroines and zealots. I worked feverishly towards my goal. I couldn't explain why but I felt time ticking away, my intuition telling me that if this novel was going to happen, I needed to finish it…and fast.

I almost made it, too.

I was in my thirties when I met and married my husband, and a few years later, welcomed my son into the world. It was an amazing time in my life, but also one in which I felt the rug yanked from beneath my feet. Suddenly, I was pulled from my fantasy world and planted firmly in reality. We moved for my husband's work and I sadly left my rolling Appalachian foothills behind for the flatter land of northern Ohio where the trees are sparser, the winters colder, the winds fiercer, and the pace of life faster.

I stopped writing for seven years—an eternity in my mind. I began to wonder if I would ever write again. I made a few feeble attempts, but it wasn't until my son started school that I could finally catch my breath and try to put my thoughts in order again.

When I sat down at the keyboard this time, so much had changed. I was homesick for my hills...and for my words. My grandparents' old farmhouse was gone, lost in a fire. And the novel I'd spent so many years writing had blown away like so many ashes as well. Suddenly, those stories I'd once listened to around the kitchen table came back to me and poured onto the page with a passion different from the kind that drove me twenty years prior. I can't claim that the stories came out the way people intended I write them. The memories are melded instead with the magic of my childhood, the truth embedded in each story like a hidden treasure for those who know where to look.

Even my son became an unexpected muse, and yes, to my surprise, even children's stories started running through my head demanding to be written. I'd come full circle, despite my own best efforts. I admitted defeat...and found my voice.

Life still steps in and takes control. My son is only young once, and it's my job now to make the world magic for him. My stories are the ones that must be patient, waiting for me to find the time and energy to give them the attention they deserve. But if there is anything the slower pace of life amidst the rolling hills of my home has taught me, it is patience and to trust that wherever I am on my path in life and as a writer, I am right where I need to be to prepare for the next leg of the journey.

Brandy Bonifas lives in Ohio with her husband and son. Her speculative fiction has appeared in anthologies by Clarendon House Publications, Pixie Forest Publishing, Zombie Pirate Publishing, Black Hare Press, Blood Song Books, Reanimated Writers Press, and Dastaan World, as well as the online publications *CafeLit, Spillwords Press,* and *Mercurial Stories.* Her short story "The Clock Struck Twelve" was voted readers' favorite in *Fireburst: The Inner Circle Writers' Group Second Flash Fiction Anthology 2018* and was selected to appear in *Gold: The Best from Clarendon House Anthologies Volume One 2017/2018.*

I, GARY BONN

I'm about to take you on a journey. You may have made a similar one before.

But first...

There is a game, possibly thousands, maybe *hundreds* of thousands of years old. It is played on the west coast of Africa where Namibia and Angola meet. The nomads there tie a ball of grass tight and bind it again with hand-made string. Leaving a tail with which to throw it, they cast the whole thing high in the air and whoever is playing races to grasp the ball so they can throw it next.

Knowing indigenous people, who lack any medical aid whatsoever, this game is played gently.

Not so here in the UK where competition, murderous aggression, rugby and other forms of abuse are publicly condoned. I hit the ground spinning, which was precisely what I'd done earlier to Aiden my friend. He did it back harder.

So ... then I was laid up for two weeks with a sprained everything and on painkillers which made the world vague.

But I spent the fortnight elsewhere – another world I'd stumbled upon as my eyes closed in pain.

Cold and dark, the place seemed desolate and uninhabited until I heard voices: arguing. Four female faces glowed as candles spluttered into life. Narrowed glances interrogated each other's eyes.

Over several days I recognized this as preparation for trading by headset and phone line, part of the morning routine in which yesterday's treasure (a metal dust?) is exchanged for money.

I spent my two weeks rest in this imagined but unrelentingly severe environment, getting to know the people, why they were in such a dangerous place, what made them as they were.

I learned their personal likes and dislikes, their routines and how far they would go to help each other (hardly at all).

One of the first surprises was these people have striking skin when they move from this gloomy echoing cavern to the outside. Silver or gold, this skin reflects the savage sunlight. Without even sunglasses or cream the women seem to cope as if evolved for this ferocious radiation and searing heat. That's intriguing. Their first daily task outside is to clear the area of dangerous animals, there are always some, and then remain vigilant all day for more.

These animals float, buoyant on hydrogen-filled papery bodies. They are all nightmarish but the most common species is a dipsomaniac's vision of hades. Insubstantial, about the size of a dog – and delicate – these carnivorous creatures carry the authority of their stings and the terrible death they offer.

The people here work hard, though it's difficult to know what they collect … definitely some sort of dull dust which can be separated from desert sand using water and sieves. They avoid each other, working as far apart as possible. Cooperation occurs only when they all team up to clear the area they work in. That makes sense – those lethal animals can come silently from anywhere.

There's a child here, willful and independent, but she stays close to her mysteriously elegant and athletic mother and never speaks to the other women as if warned away.

There's another mystery here too. In the two weeks I've spent exploring this place, getting to know the people, their routines, overhearing conversations I've never heard the words man or men mentioned. I'm probably being over-dramatic but it does seem strange.

There's a test I do when in other worlds, trying to measure tension among people. It's generally high here which explains why the dust-collectors avoid each other. I get the feeling conflict must carry a higher price outside and is strenuously avoided.

There's a bizarre thing that happens every morning. One of the cavern walls changes. I can't explain how because I fail to understand what I'm seeing. Whatever it is I must perceive it differently to these people; they can actually look at it directly. Whatever, it's how they obtain their food and send produce away.

Today a new person came with the supplies. A tiny slip of a girl, the sort you can miss in a crowd – even a very small crowd – arrived on a box but fell off when a switch was pressed.

Since that moment tension has soared far too high for people to suppress. Something is going to happen, something extreme – and I'm here to record the story.

And I did. Two weeks of enforced rest drew me harder into a new world than I had ever gone. Of course, readers will more readily lose themselves in a world a writer has spent time in, felt, smelled and heard, than one he or she creates as they write. But that's not just why you go. Certainly, your journey is to map it out, meet the people: get inside their heads, find what led to their present situation etc. and bring all that to the reader. Your detail will be coarse, "Eve, the tall one with the ragged hair," and fine, such as Eve watching light refracted in drops of water as they fall from her finger – and the impenetrable expression she wears as it happens. Water, for her, holds secrets and qualities her peers are missing.

But just now this is about you – your journey. You will become fascinated and immersed yourself as, despite its exotic nature, the world you view begins to hang together in the *coherent and believable*. See it, grasp it and bring your tales back with you.

I mention this journey in particular for something someone said. An almost impossibly tall woman walked close to me. She was watching that world but, like me, invisible to it. She touched my shoulder, and said, "You're from another world too. Good for you: good for us both. If we do not force back the boundaries of our realities, everyone we know will remain trapped."

Gary is Scottish and writes a lot. Very early in his career he was challenged to write in a variety of genres. Now he can work in all but romance and erotica – his wife suggesting he sticks to what he knows. He has work traditionally, hybrid and self-published, producing young adult, science fiction and fantasy in novels and short-story collections. Currently he's attempting to edit novels nearly ready for publication but set aside as ideas and muses clamored for attention. When not writing he does what he can to help other writers and artists.

I, DAVID BOWMORE

My desire to create light has always found an outlet. But I didn't understand about darkness until recently.

Let's start at the beginning.

I wanted to write from a young age. No one tried to dissuade me, although my mother kept saying, 'Get a trade first, David. You can always fall back on a trade.'

In my family, some of us read and some of us didn't. Nan read westerns and *True Crime* magazines, my aunt read me *The Hobbit*. My Mum was always telling people I could recognize 200 words before I was two years old. I was destined to be a reader. My father lost fingers; being a cabinet maker in the 1960s and '70s was a dangerous occupation. This put me off the idea of getting a trade.

However, an erratic home life and poor education meant I entered adulthood with no idea of how to pursue my half-arsed dream of being a writer. A need to earn money forced me into kitchen work. Oh dear, a trade beckoned. I clawed my way from pot-wash boy in a pub to head chef of a renowned restaurant before escaping the darkness to become a teacher of young wannabe Gordon Ramseys.

The person who gave me the encouragement to teach was my wife, Jai. A qualified teacher herself, she saw in me a natural need to inform, demonstrate and educate.

*

Before I started writing, some ten years ago, I took up photography for a short time.

Click, a candid street scene.

Click, a perfectly composed reflection of ancient architecture.

I preferred working with film than digital technology – more thought goes into each photograph. This was my first taste of creating something that wasn't edible. An artistic pursuit for pleasure alone. However, emerging from the dark room with captured light wasn't creative enough to quell my imagination.

*

Over the course of twenty years, I would often say to Jai, "I must be able to write better than this tosh." Then toss the tiresome book in the charity pile for someone else to endure.

After having heard this for the umpteenth-millionth time, she said, 'Go on then.'

"Go on what?" I said.

"Write something.'

"What?"

"Find out about it and write something."

So I bought Stephen King's *On Writing…*

A hundred thousand words of experimenting, a patient editor pointing out my schoolboy errors, and six months later, I had my first story published.

Most days I try to write something. I used to follow King's advice and shut the door on all distractions by sitting at a dedicated writing desk. I still do this, but now I can write on an iPad almost anywhere. The lightbulb flickers to life, ideas start to flow, and they must be written.

Since my first submission in 2018, my stories have appeared in more than fifty publications. I've written a book of connected short stories that won't be found anywhere else, released a best of collection, and, as if that weren't enough, actors of stage and screen have performed my work.

If, three years ago, you'd have said that this was going to happen to me, I'd have said you were talking complete rot. Who is their right mind would be interested in my scribblings? But it has and I'm overjoyed, not to mention honored, that so many people seem to admire and enjoy my writing.

So I write, while trying not to be distracted by other ideas, projects or calls – but I'm only human, and sometimes the temptation is too great.

Before I submit the story, I give it to Jai to cast her eye over. After all, she's the one with an English degree. I used to have a problem with partial sentences and split infinitives. Now it's the odd spelling mistake or misplaced comma. I must be getting better.

If it's accepted, happy days. These people like my stuff, remember them for future subs.

If it's rejected, never mind. The story will always find a home somewhere else.

*

But why do I write?

Escapism. Simple as that.

Or is it? What am I escaping from? Not my wife or dog (a miniature poodle, goes by the name of Floyd). They are my entire world. So, it must be something else. Something that's been there for a long time, hiding in the shadows. On days when writing does not occur, I hear it growling in the recesses of my subconscious.

Despair, Self-Hate, Self-Destruction and Worthlessness.

Depression is a bitch - a black dog nipping at my ankles that sometimes wrestles me to the ground. I have smelled her rancid breath and felt her jaws around my throat often. For me, the whole process of writing is like shining a super-bright torch in the black dog's face.

I remind myself that without darkness we cannot experience light.

*

Jai, always encouraging and supportive, has been a constant in my growth as a human being. Without her, I am nothing. I would certainly never be able to describe myself as a writer. I'd still be Kitchen Swelter. On days when I don't feel like sitting at my writing desk, she says, 'Go down and get on with it, even it's only for an hour.' So I do and it usually turns into a good two- or three-hour session.

Jai has a special person in her life, a speech and drama tutor who gave her an appreciation of the arts that she would never have received from anyone else as a child living in Doncaster, in the 1960s. Recently, I met this incredible lady – she's 92 and still teaching.

God bless Miss Barton. Without her influence, Jai wouldn't be who she is today. Without Jai, I wouldn't be a writer.

Jai tells me that my writing is special. I tell her that she is beautiful, and precious too. The most special thing in my life.

I love her to distraction.

I love her more than words.

David Bowmore lives in Yorkshire with his wonderful wife and a small white poodle. He has worn many hats in his time; chef, teacher and landscape gardener. Since 2018, David's stories have been published in more than fifty anthologies. His book of connected short stories, The Magic of Deben Market, and his best of collection, Tall Tales & Short Fiction, are available in paperback and Kindle through Amazon.

I, BELINDA BRADY

My love of reading and writing has been with me for as long as I can remember. As a kid, I simply adored reading, and could often be found hidden away, nose buried in a book. I loved the different worlds stories could transport you to – from kids running their own babysitting business to supernatural thrillers with ghosts and vampires – anything and everything was possible and I lost myself completely in these tales. I so favoured these worlds to my own. I tried my hand at writing here and there, and I remember penning my own 'Choose Your Own Adventure' type story (based on vampires, of course) that was well received by my family, but I never thought much about it. I kept diaries for years, the entries both cringe-worthy and descriptive and when I read them back, I'm transported to that very moment I wrote those words and what I was feeling or experiencing at the time. And though I loved it dearly, writing was something I never thought I could do. It was something I did for myself, in private, in the form of diary entries or long-winded letters to my best friend. Going further with it was never thought of.

I thought about studying journalism when I was in high school, and this briefly gained momentum after I was pulled aside one day. My English class had been asked to write a story based on a writing prompt for a competition and my story got a special mention. I think it may have even placed third? I remember the teacher telling me it was good, but that was about it. No encouragement to maybe peruse this path…. nothing. I was a bit of a rat bag in high school – talkative, distracted, distracting – so I think that stopped any kind of overly enthusiastic reaction. Eventually, I left school, got a job…. and well, we know how it goes. Life happened and the thought of becoming a journalist went out the window. That urge to write never went away though, but it was something I just didn't think I could do. I didn't have the right education; I wasn't smart enough, good enough. The list went on. So I just pushed it away and got on with things.

41

The moment where things changed was one New Years' Eve a few years ago. I was talking New Years' resolutions with a friend over several glasses of bubbly, and she asked me what mine was. What was my dream? At this point, the urge to write was overwhelming. Like a scratch that needed to be itched – only this time it wasn't going away with just keeping my words to myself. I wanted to get them out there. Telling my friend this, she told me to go for it. What did I have to lose? So, the next day, with a slight hangover, and before I could lose my nerve, I wrote my first ever blog entry. I remember hitting 'submit', flinching in terror from the computer screen as I did, and seeing my words go live. And although that post didn't set the world on fire, it did open up a whole new world to me.

Things moved pretty quickly after that. I wrote about anything and everything and became acquainted with some awesome like-minded writers along the way. I enjoyed blogging, but when I started writing fiction again, with some encouraging feedback, I knew I had come home. I wrote the genres I adored as a kid, and still adore today, with varying degrees of success. I've had acceptances that never cease to amaze me. I still remember screaming at five am one morning when I opened an email advising me a story I had submitted was going to be published in a book, my first ever. I've had many, many rejections that feel like a gut punch regardless of how expected the rejection was. I've had great feedback; I've had lousy feedback. I question what I write every single time, the self-doubt and criticism just waiting to crash any writing session, or acceptance celebration, like an unwanted party guest. Via social media, I've landed some wonderfully supportive writer friends, whose words of congratulations, commiserations and advice are appreciated more than I could ever express.

We all want our words to touch someone, to leave a mark, and we will, in our own way, be it good or bad. The writing world is huge and fierce and competitive, but it's also a world full of opportunities. You just have to be open to them and not be afraid to put yourself out there. Join writers' groups. Write a little; write a lot. Embrace your words when they flow; ride it out when they don't. Submit to every publisher, magazine, e-zine, etc. you can find that appeals to you.

Just put yourself out there.

I am so grateful for the opportunities I have been given, and hopefully, continue to be given. I have learned so much and I will continue to do so. I have grown so much as a writer and for that, I am forever grateful.

To anyone reading this who is contemplating a leap into the creative unknown, whatever that may be, I say go for it. You have nothing to lose and everything to gain. I am so happy I took a chance on that overcast New Year's Day and published those words. I'm only sorry I didn't do it sooner.

Life is simply too short for 'what ifs?'

A bookworm since childhood, Belinda is passionate about stories and after years of procrastinating, has finally turned her hand to writing them, her preference for supernatural/thriller themes often competing for her attention. She has had several stories published in a variety of publications, both online and in anthologies. Belinda lives in Australia with her family and has been known to enjoy the company of cats over people.

I, M W BROWN

In 2014, when I was comfortably nestled in my 40s, I happened to turn on my satnav one day; for those outside of the UK it's better known as a GPS, but in our household, it's called the sticky map, so named by my daughter because it's a map and it sticks—simple five-year-old logic. I was puzzled because the sticky map was having trouble searching for a location. After a few choice words and thumps on various buttons I discovered it was trying to search for the town of IUAOHUH, thanks to my daughter playing with it when I wasn't looking. Little did I know that those random letters would set in motion a chain of events that would change my life forever.

I began wondering how strange it would be if IUAOHUH existed. My imagination started whirling. What if the sticky map could take me there in an instant? What if it could take me *anywhere* I wanted in the blink of an eye? What if I entered a place like Atlantis or Heaven or the Underworld?

The idea kept growing, picking up elements of my favorite genre—horror, until finally, after reading a mediocre book that had managed to become a best seller, I thought, "Even I can do better than that. I'm going to write a book."

At school, I'd loved writing stories, but creative writing was not something considered as a career by my teachers, especially with my love of all things horror. So, after decades in finance and after being unable to shake my sticky map idea, I finally picked up a pen and started writing again.

Six months later I joyfully typed "The End" and excitedly sent off my manuscript to twenty or so agents. I sat back waiting for the replies to come flooding back with dreams of bestsellers and giving up my day job to become a full-time writer. My inbox had as much activity as a thermal underwear shop in Hell. Perhaps my first draft was not as great as I had thought. I spent the next year devouring articles on writing techniques and editing then revised and revamped my manuscript.

Excitedly, I again sent my manuscript to agents and indie publishers. Another six months passed, and I was getting used to "Thanks but no thanks" emails. I had just about given up on ever becoming a published writer when I came across an open call for a science fiction anthology. I rattled off a short story and submitted it. To my surprise, I received an email saying my story had been accepted. I was over the moon. In 2017, I officially became a published author. With my confidence restored, I started to look into self-publishing my novel but then received a reply from a small publishing company. Instead of the stock rejection reply, I was amazed to find they wanted to publish my book! After a few hectic months of editing and rapidly learning about pimping, street teams, social media platforms, book launches etc., in 2018 my first novel, *Portraits in Flesh*, was published.

It's not been an easy path. There have been rejections, my first publishing company closed, and writing time can be hard to find. I'm constantly learning my craft, but there is so much more than simply writing. I have had to learn all about marketing and designing. I spend more than half my "writing time" not writing but on promoting my books.

It's been a long journey but now I've had close to twenty short stories, six novels published and can add International Bestseller to my name. Don't let anyone tell you it's an easy life but if like me, you discover writing is your passion, don't give up. Keep learning, keep writing, and remember it's never too late to start.

Looking back, I'm glad I didn't venture into the book world when I first discovered my love of writing because of the life lessons I had yet to learn, but I do wish I hadn't left it quite so many decades!

M W Brown is from England and has penned *Portraits in Flesh, The Lingering Taste of Salted Chocolate, Reality,* and co-written *The Broken Mirror Series*, as well as over a dozen short stories.

I, NATALIE BROWN

I was first published at 15 years of age in the Pedro Menendez High School's *Ascension* literary magazine. Creative Writing taught by Mr. Rick Ryan was one of the elective classes that I was required to take to avoid PE courses, so I took it without question. That class would go on to form everything that I am as a writer and author today.

Over a decade later, I was pregnant with my third son and got a job working overnight at a gas station across the bridge from where I lived. The radio station that was programmed was a mix of 80's, 90's and today, but played the same ten songs repeatedly all night long. My mother used to listen to old horror radio shows to calm herself for sleep at night (The Shadow was her favorite). So I took a note from her book and began listening to the modernized version, horror podcasts.

Chilling Tales for Dark Nights, Creepypod and the *NoSleep Podcast* were my very favorites, and they got me through a lot of long and mentally arduous nights. I fell in love with their storytelling and the way the narrators brought the situations to life.

I left that job to go on a semi-permanent state of maternity leave, but the horror podcasts were a part of me by then. I listened to them at night after my two older children would go to sleep, in my husband's arms at night while we drifted off to sleep, and even in the hospital after I had my son.

Before long, my therapist said something that really stuck with me. He's like, "The situations in your head are always way more terrifying than they are in reality. Have you ever thought about being a writer?" At the time it barely even took up more than a single thought's worth of space in my mind, but after I got home from my session it really kicked in. What if... what if I *could* do the same thing that these authors do for the podcasts? What if I tried to write something of my own?

That was over a year ago now, and since then I've been included in over 50 anthologies, published 8 horror anthologies under Nocturnal Sirens Publishing as well as retained jobs for the podcasts I fell in love with in the first place. I am a story scout for *Creepypod*. That means I work in author relations, arranging payment for stories, asking for permissions, etc. I'm also on the writing team of *Chilling Tales for Dark Nights* as well as a voice actor, writer and media director of the *Scarecrow Tales Podcast.*

Specializing in domestic horror, I love to write about situations that can actually happen in everyday life. You won't find many ghosts or demons in my stories, but there are plenty of haunted hearts and minds.

My husband and 3 sons are extremely supportive about my work and I'm super lucky to have them.

N.M. Brown is an international best-selling author from Florida. She's a happily married mother who sheds light on the dark corners of the mind that we like to keep hidden. Her other publications include stories in *Sirens at Midnight*, the recent award-winning series *Calls from the Brighter Futures Suicide Hotline*, the *Scary Snippets Collections, Mother Ghost Grimm Children's Horror Anthology, Dark Xmas*, along with several others. Her passions include soap making, publishing and spending time with her horror loving friends and family.

I, ELAINE MARIE CARNEGIE-PADGETT

My Mama read to us every day. I usually held the baby, (whichever it may have been) and Mama read stories I can still recite today from memory. The first volume of the *Childcraft Encyclopedia*. I wanted to tell stories like that... I was probably four years old. Then we graduated to the *Time-Life Nature Encyclopedias*. This was our daily routine from my earliest memory until I started school. My Mama has always been my greatest fan.

I didn't think of being a writer, I loved to tell stories. I made them up and my siblings, cousins, and friends would gather round. When we congregated at my grandparents, I helped care for the children. I told them stories. I listened to stories too. My Maw-Maw told ghostly stories and my daddy told funny ones. Daddy had a quirky sense of humor and he loved to debate a point and so did Maw-Maw. I sat at their knee many a Sunday afternoon in my childhood while they solved the problems of the world.

I only remember wanting to be three things in my life, besides a mother. A football player, a ballerina, and a writer. At eight years old, I was terribly disappointed to find out I *could not* be a football player like my brothers. I thought it was unfair, and I campaigned against it, but ultimately lost that battle. So, I decided to be a majorette instead... We're from Texas so... the whole "Friday Night Lights" thing. We lived it. My brothers still hold records at the 6A High School we attended. It's like a feeling you never forget, a moment that remains a part of you...

I competed and performed in dance, twirling, ballet, modeling, and gymnastics since I was nine years old. I was terrible at ballet, but I persevered. I struck out at football because of my gender and ballet since I *hated* it... but I learned discipline and the value of working for what I wanted. I learned to have confidence in my writing, public speaking, and showmanship. I was a weird adolescent. I wouldn't dare go to a party. I was shy. One on one conversation, or a book report in front of the class handicapped me with fear; but put me in an auditorium to make a speech or perform in front of 3,000 nameless faces, and I'm your girl. I told you I was weird!

Both of my parents wrote poetry. My daddy authored essays and articles, not for publication, just to write them. My mother is a painter and a rather good one. Those creative gifts go back through the generations on both sides of my family. When I was about eleven, I began reading the bible to my brothers and sister every night and we prayed together. Sometimes I would write the prayers and lessons. I took it seriously because I was teaching them, and I loved them so much.

I began writing down my stories at 12 years old. I have always written in some form since that time. My mind went places my vocabulary could not yet go at that age, and it frustrated me because when I read what I had written... it was terrible. When I was fourteen my sweet Aunt Patsy, (my Mama's sister) helped me with my writing. She wrote vivid, twisted poetry, and it enthralled me. I began by writing verse that copied the emotion her poems made me feel, and soon I was writing decent poetry.

My daddy, a strict disciplinarian, believed we should not have one idle second with which to get up to mischief. So, the five of us were an accomplished bunch. You name it, at least one of us tried it! We played every sport, band, choir, drill team, cheerleader, and pep squad, and we hunted, fished, camped, boated, swam, and attended humongous family gatherings regularly. Friday nights (not counting football season) were family nights and if we didn't pile our station wagon full of friends and go to the drive-in, we built a fire and roasted hot dogs and marshmallows and yep... you guessed it, told stories. It was a wonderful childhood, and my parents worked hard to give us the life and memories they did not have. That love and sacrifice are the steel of my personal foundation.

I went on to raise a bucketful of children to responsible adulthood. Beautiful, contributing members of society and excellent parents. *Possibly a little on the wild side...* They are the best of me. I thank God every day for that dimension in my life. To love another human soul unconditionally is a humbling and transcendental experience, but that story is too long to explore in this essay.

I was already working as a paralegal and when the kids flew the coop, I went to work as a Private Investigator. I had so much fun and learned so much, and that experience is also too long for this essay. I took a second job for a weekly Newspaper and covered many important issues, and sometimes the paper and the PI crossed paths on subjects such as human trafficking and politics.

In 2014, I met *the wind beneath my wings...* my significant other, my partner in crime and love, work and life... my soulmate. He offered support and constant encouragement for "The Book" I always wanted to write.

I started seriously writing fiction in 2016 (with the intent to publish) and I have *almost* finished my second novel, along with many short stories, poetry, articles and essays, although this is the first one I have written about myself.

I have a love affair with the written word and the emotion it evokes in the human spirit. I am a writer, and in the words I record are bits of who I am, where I have been, and where I am yet to be.

Elaine Marie Carnegie-Padgett worked as a Paralegal, and PI, has written for *Discovery ID*, the Texas Legislature, and worked with the FBI and Texas Rangers. As a side gig she worked as a journalist, history and foodie columnist before accepting a publishing partnership; then opening her own SPPublishing and Author Services. She is published in print and online venues, anthologies, charity and collaborative projects. She is the author of *The Gaia Factor*. Elaine makes her home in the East Texas Piney Woods... doing what she loves and living her best life!

I, STEVE CARR

"I'll never understand it or approve of it."

My mother said that to me when I was age 46. She wasn't talking about my writing. She was talking about my sexual identity. I've been really lucky as a gay man. She is the only person who since I came out openly as gay at age 22, during my second year of a four-year enlistment in the Navy, that has said anything even remotely negative to my face about that aspect of my personality. By the time I admitted to the world that I was gay, I had already spent three years in the Army as a military journalist, having been trained at the prestigious Defense Information School, and the prior two years in the Navy as an instructor in the Psychiatric Technician Program at the Portsmouth Naval Hospital. I came out in 1977, before gays were even allowed to serve in the military, at least not do it and anyone know it. From the moment I came out I never kept it a secret that I was gay and no one seemed to care. Again, I was lucky.

I have no doubts that we don't choose our sexual identity, we're born with it. Other than those few lucky ones like me who came out before being gay started being more socially accepted, no man or woman would have deliberately chosen to be gay. It could have gotten you killed. In many parts of the world it still can. Possibly writers are born to be writers also. There was nothing in my environment, other than school, that would have led me on the course to be a writer.

While time may pass in a linear, chronological order, how we remember it happens in a much different way, at least for me it does. The events of my life, from the first time as a young boy I realized I was attracted to other boys, to the first time I realized I could put my vivid imagination to work as a writer, the events of times past bounce around in my head like ping pong balls. But while my self-discovery as a gay male has always been on a forward trajectory, my path to being a full time, frequently published author, has been as erratic as the ping pong balls. It's not that I didn't enjoy writing, I simply was never committed to it. For me, it came too easy. In school and college, I got excellent grades in writing classes. In the Army, writing articles for newspapers was easy. My plays were well-received and garnered good reviews. At age 62, the first short story I wrote just to show a college student I was mentoring how it was done, was quickly accepted. Four years later and with over 440 stories accepted for publication or published since 2016, writing is a snap.

What I lack is what I call the *angst factor*. I've never felt the need to drown my sorrows in drinking or drugs and despite growing up in really crappy, poverty-level conditions, my childhood memories are almost all good ones. I was an easy-going kid with lots of friends, an average student through most of school except in English and Science where I excelled, physically active, and blessed with what I assume were fairly good looks that attracted girls and other boys alike. I went to Sunday school and church every Sunday morning, Sunday evening, and on Wednesday nights, for most of my young life and don't remember once ever hearing a lesson or sermon where my sexuality was condemned, and it was a Baptist Church that I went to. I learned a lot from the Bible, especially how to write good stories. I was taught young to care about others and to help others when I can. I also have a really big soft spot for animals and wildlife in all its varieties. I lived near a museum when I was a youngster and visited it frequently so I acquired early a taste for good art. The zoo was also nearby and I spent more hours there than I can recount.

Am I boasting about my life or my writing? Possibly, but the only true thing that stands out about me, that I would hope others hear, is it's okay if you're gay, and it's even better to be able to say out loud if it applies to you, "I am a gay writer." It doesn't mean the stories you write have to have gay themes or characters, most of mine don't, but there's something truly liberating and self-defining in being okay with who you are and then setting it aside and giving it no more or no less importance than anything else that makes you who you are.

Ask David, the most important person in my life for the past 22 years what I'm like as a writer and he'll most likely tell you I'm insufferable. I spend long hours at the computer, revel with every short story acceptance, complain loudly with every rejection, and protect the short story as an art form with every fiber of my being.

What my mother said to me, "I'll never understand it or approve of it" was meant to devalue me as a person, but it could have just as easily been said to me about my writing, but she never said a word about my writing, yet I'm very proud of my accomplishments as a writer, and proud to be gay.

Steve Carr, from Richmond, Virginia, has had over 440 short stories published internationally in print and online magazines, literary journals, reviews and anthologies since June, 2016. He has had seven collections of his short stories, *Sand, Rain, Heat, The Tales of Talker Knock* and *50 Short Stories: The Very Best of Steve Carr,* and *LGBTQ: 33 Stories,* and *The Theory of Existence: 50 Short Stories,* published. His paranormal/horror novel Redbird was released in November, 2019. His plays have been produced in several states. He has been nominated for a Pushcart Prize twice. He is the founder of Sweetycat Press.

I, ALDO CERNUTO

I, a writer.

No, sorry. Something is not working in this opening line. Let me edit it.

I, a writer?

Ah, right, that's much better.

That question mark is my muse, my mentor, my main source of painful—yet effective—inspiration. It instils in me the harshest of anxieties—that I can indeed be a writer. It surreptitiously elicits answers that no spoken words can possibly articulate. Only those I put down on paper can do that. And, quite often, even they struggle to make it.

Depriving me of that question mark is evil—it is criminal. It's like brutally yanking the pen from my hand and snapping it in two.

If I am a writer, in fact, it's only because I obstinately and constantly doubt it.

I doubt that I will be able to write one more word, one more sentence, one more chapter, one more book.

I doubt, therefore I am (a writer). And I was quite precocious in realizing my limits, as I have doubted it forever, even as a child.

I remember my first day at school when I took pen in hand in my first attempt to make my mark on literary history. Except it was the wrong hand. Or, more precisely, it wasn't the right hand—it was my left one.

Well, the concept of left and right wasn't so clear to me at that time, but a flash of lucidity suddenly hit me in the shape of my teacher's cane. It landed on my poor left hand with such brute force that left it paralysed for a few hours—the middle finger rigid, unable to bend. From that moment on, every time I thought of becoming a writer, I was reminded of that image—my own left hand giving me the finger. How could I possibly develop a glimmer of self-confidence, as a writer, after such a non-starter?

From that day on, I was forced to write with my wrong hand. That is, my right one.

Decades of diabolical scrawl followed; kilometres and kilometres of trembling calligraphy that have accompanied each and every attempt to create. Zillions of uncertain and crooked words that, besides their literal meaning, say it all about me as an author. "Are you sure you've got what it takes?" they insist.

Yet these doubts bring with them some benefits. That special sense of reward that I feel when I happen to alight upon the jewel that is the perfect word in a morass of synonyms. Or the unfathomable happiness of composing a string of words that sound like music to my ears. Sometimes even the simple joy of constructing a decent workmanlike paragraph. Not to mention the triumph of penning "The End" after months of toil.

Such felicity doesn't last long, though. It's just momentary; then I reach for my beloved question mark and put it where it belongs.

I, a writer? (seriously?)

Great.

Now I can start writing again.

Aldo Cernuto (Turin, 1955) developed his career in the advertising industry. First as a copywriter, then as an executive creative director, he has worked in some of the major international networks, including McCann Erickson, Lowe Group and Y&R, winning several international awards. He loves his job to the point that he has dedicated a non-fiction book to creative ideas: *Il Mal d'idea* ('Aching for Ideas', 1999), written in Italian. *The Curse of Knowing* (14 July 2020), which he wrote in English, is his first work of fiction.

I, N.D. COLEY

I sit down to write and ask myself, "Can I do this again?"

It's a fair question, seeing that there was a time when I didn't know that I was a writer at all. I knew that I enjoyed reading. As a kid who did not see himself as an acceptable part of the scenery in junior high, I read the works of Stephen King with ferocity—I started with *The Talisman* and moved on to *The Shining* and *The Stand,* books that almost certainly shaped my appetite for wanting to read about the paranormal and the end of the world. Kids were trying out cigarettes or making it to second base for the first time, while I would fan my fingers over the worn, yellowed pages of a hardback library book.

It was almost certainly the time in which my creative nucleus—that part of me that wants to create things that have never been said before so that other people can read them and decide that getting up in the morning isn't such a bad idea after all—was shaped.

Writers are often thought of as creatives, right? And there I was, most fascinated by stories that bottled up Armageddon and destruction and gave them to me in the course of a one-thousand-page monster. Books about the end of the world seemed so big to me in those days, but now they strike me as a set of Cliffs Notes to the eschaton. If one could truly imagine the end of the world, it certainly wouldn't fit into a novel.

And here I already stand corrected: Cormac McCarthy, author of *The Road* (my favorite novel and arguably favorite piece of literature), seems to have captured the sense of it in about 300 pages.

Years later, it makes sense that my aesthetic is rooted in cosmic issues—fear, illness, loss, existential crisis and the heat death of the universe and the meaning of life. If I can reduce the wonderful complexities of all of the sonnets and plays and stories and poems of the universe, I'd say with equal parts confidence and sadness that all writing is a response to that unavoidable truth: Things break down or

56

they die, and often without an extended warranty. Writing is our means of coping with this or, in more delusional moments, trying to solve the problem.

But perhaps we have solved the problem, or at least arrived at the next best thing. We write stories about our first loves and our lost loves because there is something in those experiences (however distant and separated by time) worth preserving. We speak of struggles so that our own histories can live vicariously through the page and perhaps inspire someone else. When there is nothing someday and the sun is cold and the Milky Way has long had its collision with Andromeda, I hope that the collective writings of humanity have a home in a transmission, sent barreling towards some distant galaxy to other living beings who have either cheated death or, like us, become immortal a story at a time.

This leads me to the ultimate 64,000-dollar question — is it better for one to earn fame while alive and fan out quickly, or to pass on in obscurity and become the substance of legend? Edgar Allan Poe, who died broke and in almost total obscurity (at least compared to his current fame) is tattooed on my left arm. He remains iconic among gothic writers, and is often credited with giving the detective short story its identity. I wonder, in those moments equally punctuated by hope and delusion, if I can be an author who lives on and ends up as a tattoo design or a beer cozy or a bobblehead doll. Most days I think I would be satisfied with a positive Amazon review and enough in royalties to upgrade the size of my morning coffee.

And to return to the beginning of this essay—I would not have become a writer had not a high school teacher of mine (who tragically passed away at the young age of 47 in 2019) scribbled a single note in the margin of a descriptive essay in freshman English. To paraphrase: He said that I had a writer's voice, and that he loved it.

Huh. Who knew?

And that was all it took. I didn't fully realize it then, but that is when I became a writer. On some level I started to see myself as a person who could say things, and in such a way, that I could have conversations with other great writers and not blush. I started devouring literature of different genres and discovered a love for satire and dystopian fiction. I dedicated myself to the study of Vonnegut as an undergraduate and laid the groundwork for my future as a graduate student of literature. I discovered what I love and who I am because I am a writer, and I am grateful for that identity.

And for all of my platitudes about being true to my aesthetic, I cannot say that I don't dream of a house so big I'd never visit all the rooms, of having my books sell on the currency of my name as movie studios purchase them without any clue as to what they're about. I cannot say that I don't want to be loved and be a household name—to see my literature pass the hands of Midas and literally turn to gold. This is all true. Money may not buy happiness, but it does make misery a more attractive prospect.

But mostly I just want to write and have someone say, "I really enjoyed that, Nathan. You're good."

I, the writer, share the same goal as a clown: to make others smile, even if it's only for a moment, and even if it can't erase the pain that awaits the reader when the story is over.

N.D. Coley (MA, English, University of Pittsburgh) is currently a college English composition instructor. His work has recently appeared in *Shotgun Honey, Coffin Bell Journal Close 2 the Bone, Indiana Voice Journal, Corner Bar Magazine, Grotesque Quarterly, Jakob's Horror Box, Massacre Magazine, Crack the Spine*, and *Funny in Five-Hundred*. In his spare time, he laments the human condition, reads depressing literature, plays with his son and daughter, and irritates his wife.

I, CHERYL RUSH COWPERTHWAIT

I think perhaps I was always a writer. Not that I always wrote, no, that came after learning my alphabets and attending school, but I believe it started even as I was a little one. I was the youngest of five children and often left behind as they had more grown-up playmates. I spent a great deal of time imagining.

I still can see that little girl with fly-away blonde hair hunkered down on the side of the house. I broke stems to make small cottages and made roofs of yellow dandelion blooms and was content on imagining what took place in that house. I also carried around an imaginary cat, as we were told we couldn't have a real one. Now, my mother was a beautician with her beauty shop attached to our house. I would 'entertain' her customers by shoving my invisible cat into their faces and laps. It wasn't until much later I learned the customers favorite saying to my mom was, "Kid, aren't you worried about her?" If only they knew it would get much worse...I would become a writer!

The true nudge came in my freshman year of high school. I had recently moved from Oklahoma to California and was ahead of the curriculum. Terribly bored, I tended to chat away in my English class. Mr. Wood was an attentive teacher. I always had my work done before chatting and so he would inspire me to do more. Every day he brought in a picture, a painting or something for me to look at and imagine. Then, he would tell me to write a story or poem inspired by it. That influence has stayed with me through the years.

The best way to explain what a large impact that one thing had, is to tell you how I decided to write my first novel. It was a grand fluke. I was playing with a photo app on my mobile phone and made a cute picture that had me with a dragon. Well, I posted it on Facebook with a short little paragraph that I only learned later was a book blurb, or a hook put on the back cover of a book.

Much to my shock, my friends wanted more! There was no

more. It was simply something to say about the picture. They didn't relent so I decided I would add a bit more of the story every day for one month.

Fear gnawed inside my belly. I wasn't used to sharing my writing with the public and had only recently forced myself to join a writing group so I would write consistently every month. The oddest sensation happened. Like magic, words flew from my fingers when I sat down to create more of the non-existent story for that picture. I could hardly sleep, for one of the main characters, a wise old dragon, would sweep into my dreams and tell me all about the story. I started the book on the last day of March 2017 and completed it in July. The first edition was published December the same year. It has gone on to be a four-book series. It's amazing what a little picture can do.

Before writing novels, Cheryl Rush Cowperthwait wrote poetry. She had two poems published in an anthology around 1988. As an author of fantasy fiction, she wants her readers to have an escape, to go to places only found through their imagination. To that extent, Cheryl Rush Cowperthwait currently has eight high fantasy novels published, one illustrated book for children and two more books, one is a poetry book and the other a Christmas book in the Hallmark fashion, scheduled for release by the end of 2020.

I, GARY CRAWFORD

My enjoyment of reading led me to want to write like the people who wrote the books I read. I was encouraged by my mother as well as my teachers. They seemed to think I had the ability to do it.

I wanted to see my name on the cover of a book someday. Or as a byline over an article in the paper or a magazine. I wrote on any subject I could think of. I had a few hobby interests and wrote on them. I loved doing the research and writing my version of the story.

I contributed articles to the school paper and received compliments on my work. I wrote short stories about most anything that struck me. Looking at them today, they were a little (a lot?) rough, but I can see my progress looking over my "archives."

I was blogging long before I knew what that was, much less anything computer related. I just liked to get my thoughts down on paper, in longhand.

Mom made us kids take typing in high school. I'm sure glad we did, not knowing then how important typing skills would be in the future.

We had an old Remington typewriter. It almost made you get a running start to press a key. How someone could hammer away on that old relic all day is beyond me. Secretaries must've had arms like weight lifters back then. Electric typewriters had to be cause for celebration.

I worked at a job where I was holding down a chair most of the time. I was a movie projectionist and had lots of free time. So I wrote a novel, in longhand, in a wire-bound notebook. 80 pages, both sides. Each day my writer's cramp got a little worse, but I was on a quest. My right hand was practically crippled by the time I finished the story. I gave in and went to the doctor.

The diagnosis was bursitis, similar to carpal tunnel syndrome, just a different place in the wrist. I had to wear a removable cast for two weeks to keep my hand in one position so it could heal. And I couldn't write during those weeks while held in that vice. I noticed that my printing used to be so neat my Dad said it looked like I typed it but was now growing sloppier.

My mother came to the rescue with an electric typewriter that was also a word processor, surplus since an early computer came to her home. Now I was on a roll!

Not long after, I acquired a small early laptop. Just a word processor and a few games and programs, not able to connect to the Internet, as basic as it could be. But it was the gateway I needed to write in earnest. Flying fingers in action!

Not long after, a desktop came into my home. Big fancy color screen, the premium machine of the day. With a fan-shaped ergonomic keyboard that was as comfortable as it could be.

Now able to enter the realm of the Interweb, I discovered a chatroom. Not the usual aimless posts, this room had writers. We didn't write one-line posts, we wrote short stories. I found it a great educational workout. Many ideas about things to write came to mind. And write I did.

Another portable laptop followed. Creative juices flew!

I didn't publish much at first, until my mother asked why I was hiding my stories. Time to submit!

I co-authored a local history book in 2002, my first published work. It came from my love of local history. The Arcadia books are incredible. (And they pay royalties!) I made my bones, as they say, having my name on the cover of a book for the first time.

My first fictional novel was published in 2010, followed by another in 2014. Several short stories were published in anthologies and contests.

Over a year I wrote my 160,000-word Great American Novel, and that beget a sequel, and then a trilogy and a prequel from the original. With tangents from the original story, if I expand what might be just a few lines of a new direction, there would be 17 books in the series! I doubt they will all be written, but you never know. The first in the series was published in 2017.

I wrote a 50-year history of a steam railroad museum I had been involved with, and it appears on their website. I wrote news releases and articles and newsletters for nonprofits I worked with. I wrote a local history and trivia Monday column for a large newspaper, as well as local weekly papers. A few magazine articles followed, mainly on historical subjects. My love of all things historic kept me writing.

Having an equal interest in the occult and things that go bump in the night, my three fictional novels all touched on dark subjects such as witchcraft and the paranormal. I loved these things since I watched the old Hollywood monsters on TV long ago. Obviously, Halloween (Samhain) is my entire family's favorite holiday. Horror movies, even the cheesy 1950s offerings, inspired my love of the genre and forced me to write out my versions of things-to-keep-you-awake-at-night.

I started a blog a few years ago that is mostly a George Carlin-esque look at everyday annoyances. Lots to inspire me there! No shortage of things to grumble about. My mother inspired the blogsite title, "Creative Bellyaching," her saying all I ever did as a kid was bellyache.

I find inspiration in everything. My grandkids are a never-ending source. When I drove a taxi, I kept a journal of all the unique people I had in my cab. Same with driving a school bus. No shortage of inspiration.

As long as my eyes and ears work, I will be inspired by the world around me.

Gary S. Crawford is an award-winning author and historian. His published works include horror novels, local history non-fiction, numerous articles, short stories, and a blog, and is active in several writing groups. He's involved with the American Legion and places almost 800 flags on veterans' graves for Memorial Day as well as volunteering with other nonprofit groups. Gary is a lifelong resident of the Jersey Shore, as were his parents and grandparents. He lives with his wife, grown daughter, and four grandchildren, and is trying to be retired.

I, JAY CROWLEY

My Youth

My mother was not happy about being pregnant, as she had a musical career to pursue, and her husband was gone a lot. Because of this, she stayed with her folks in Sacramento until the baby was born. Eight months later, she gave birth to a little girl. I was born in June, a happy baby girl.

Edith wanted to pursue her career, so she left me with my grandparents. My grandfather taught me how to fish and hunt, and my grandma taught me how to sew, cook, and can. But they were getting old, and it's hard to raise a child, but I'm thankful they did.

As I was growing up, I hardly ever heard from my Mom. At sixteen, my grandpa taught me how to drive. I was a quiet child with a bad stutter, especially when I got nervous. Because of this, I read a lot and started writing. I had a short story sold to Reader's Digest, felt so proud. I worked on the high school newspaper but basically stayed to myself. After High School, I went to college.

Whenever I visited my Mom, it was always at a bar where she was playing. Everyone would tell me how lucky I was to have her as my mother, and do you have any of your mother's talent? And so on. I would almost barf.

As stated, I was raised by my grandparents, not my mother, my mother may have given birth to me, but that was it. After years of counseling, I learned that my mother being an entertainer and a spoiled child, was self-centered, and no one else mattered. Which must be true as she was married nine times.

As I grew older, I tried to understand her and have compassion, but it just didn't come. What I did learn is I would never treat my children that way.

Now and then, I will play her theme song, "Pennies from Heaven" – "*So when you hear it thunder. Don't run under a tree. There'll be pennies from Heaven. For you and me.*" I would listen to her sing this song and hoped it would stir up pleasant memories. Sadly, even now, years later, no tears ever came or come.

My Current Life

In my professional life as a Human Resource Director, I wrote many manuals. Then retired and worked on the Virginia Truckee Railroad Foundation, writing grants and a newsletter. Over the years, I overcame my stuttering, and now you can't shut me up.

However, I had this concept that maybe I could write a book. It can't be that tough, what the heck, I had written newsletters and some manuals. Being brave, I decided to try writing a children's book.

I joined Facebook writing clubs. I saw I had a lot to learn; also, everyone has their hand out for money to teach you how to write. I took some writing classes, bound and determined not to waver.

First, I wrote flash fiction, where you're shown a picture, and you must write 500 words or less in a short period. I entered the contests, didn't win, but had fun.

Well, one day, a gentleman from South Dakota sent me a request to be a Facebook friend saying he was an editor and liked my writing. Well, how many editors come from South Dakota? But I thought what the heck, I can always de-friend him.

That decision was the best I ever made. I never met the man personally, but over the years, Alan Seeger and I became friends. He was my mentor, my tormentor, and my confidant. Alan challenged me to grow and try new categories, some I didn't like, like Sci-Fi, but I did it. May not be my best work, but the reviews were favorable.

He encouraged many a struggling writer with confidence issues—me for one. Many times I was ready to give up. But in his quiet manner, he would talk you back into being excited about writing without even realizing it. With Alan's help, I wrote three novels, a children's book, and a novella.

Alan was an unassuming man who lived most of his life in a

wheelchair, whose life was his family, friends, Rock and Roll, writing Sci-Fi, and his computer. A couple of years ago, he received his Bachelor's Degree, an immensely satisfying occasion for him.

Three times a week, he went to dialysis for his kidney, waiting for a transplant that never came... over ten years he waited. He likewise had diabetes, but he never complained even when they cut off his big toe...

In January 2018, we lost this remarkable man. I can't say enough kind words about Alan. All I can say is I am blessed to have had him as a friend and mentor.

I have written four novels and a novella since Alan's passing. I am now the Whistler's Mother of the writing world.

Jay Crowley lives in Jack's Valley near the base of beautiful Lake Tahoe, Nevada. All of Jay's stories originate in Nevada, which offers an exciting background for story opportunities. "A little history of Nevada with a mystery." Jay has won several writing awards. This year, Jay was selected to be in *Who's Who of Emerging Writers 2020*. Jay is a storyteller, making the writing crisp, fresh, and a fast read.

I, ANDREW C. DAKALIRA

"Of all the things you can do, why write? You are destined for so much more than that."

"While we loved your story, we regret to inform you that it's not what we're looking for at this time."

"You are putting so much energy in something that will probably never pan out. You're educated. Stick to an office job like everyone else."

"Sorry, but we can't publish your story. It still needs work."

Sound familiar?

Ever since I embraced the writing life, there have been a lot of such statements. Be it from friends, family, or editors, there are bound to be words that question whether it is all worth it. I wondered whether I wasn't just wasting my time like most people said. There are, in almost every writer's life, moments when you just feel like giving up.

In my case, writing was a passion of mine as a kid. In my early teens, it was fun to create my own little stories, be immersed in my own worlds and have fun doing it. No one else saw what I wrote, and I suppose that was fine at the time. As time passed and college came calling, I stopped writing. Those worlds were replaced by an entirely new one, involving studying, partying and occasional girlfriend. It was only after college that I started writing again. This time around, I stuck with it.

Writing for yourself is one thing; you write, read it to yourself, maybe show your work to a few friends. That's it. It's a wonderful world. Then you decide that writing is more than a hobby. You want it to be a profession. You start submitting your stories to magazines and contests, and you realize just how bad things can get.

I do not care how many times you get rejections; you never get used to them. Granted, you expect to get them from time to time, especially as you grow in the profession, but it still stabs at your essence of creativity knowing that someone thought you weren't good enough. I remember at some point in March, 2020, I received six different rejection emails within the space of five hours. I was devastated. I drank heavily for the rest of that week. Worse still, I couldn't talk to anyone about it. Everyone else went on with their lives. The writer's path can be a lonely one.

The pressure that engulfs a writer can be intense. Not only are you worried about whether your story or manuscript is going to be published, but you also have to deal with personal things. How you're going to pay the bills, or why you're not getting a job and settling down like the rest of your peers. It would seem, in the eyes of most people, that the time spent writing or reading to perfect your craft is 'wasted energy.' There are some moments, when it gets too much, that you start to believe them.

In spite of the gloomy picture I have painted, writing does have some of its great moments. The satisfaction I get after finishing a story is incomparable. Even better is when your story is actually accepted in a magazine, anthology or gets a prize in a contest. Hell, even being recognized by someone as 'that writer' is a great boost. Quite ostentatious, I know, but I don't care. These are good moments. However, that is not why I keep writing.

I write because, despite the moments of depression and discouragement, it is something I love. I write because nothing is as therapeutic as creating something beautiful from your mind and watching it transform onto paper. I pick up the pen because sharing my stories with some people on this planet is fulfilling. And when after I'm gone, someone picks up a story of mine, reads it and says 'hey, this story is not bad at all,' my tormented soul will be smiling wherever it shall be. For it will have been worth it.

Andrew C. Dakalira's stories have been published in several international anthologies as well as online platforms such as *BrittlePaper* and *The Kalahari Review*. His debut novella, *VIII*, appears in *AfroSFv2*, a collection of five science fiction novellas by

African authors. Andrew won the 2014 Dede Kamkondo Short Story Contest and third prize in the 2018 Africa Book Club Short Story Competition. His story, "The (Un)lucky Ones," was shortlisted for the 2017 Writivism Prize for Short Fiction. He lives in Malawi's capital city, Lilongwe.

I, P.C. DARKCLIFF

I believe you need to be slightly nuts to be a fiction writer. At least, I suspect that is my case.

My imagination has always been almost disturbingly vivid. I managed to convince all my kindergarten friends that I was the grandson of a tribal shamaness, and I made up so many stories about Grandma's magical feats and jungle tribe that I believed it as well.

When I learned my letters, bullshitting my friends no longer seemed adequate—so I started to write.

I remember sitting at the kitchen table and handwriting a story about a talking dog. Whenever I made a mistake, I didn't scratch it over and continued like a normal kid would do; I tore the page out of the notebook and started writing from the beginning. Needless to say, I never finished the story.

Next came a novelette about four boys abducted by aliens. I think I wrote that one on my grandpa's ancient typewriter. Typing became my nerdy passion, and when I had no story ideas, I at least copied my favorite books while my friends played soccer in front of our apartment building.

As puberty crept up on me, I used to write lyrics for an imaginary metal band, and poetry for the girl I madly and eternally loved on a particular week. I never really formed a band, though, and I soon gave up on poems. They seldom worked, anyway.

In my late teens, friendships, relationships, and *beerships* took over my life, and I don't remember writing anything worthwhile during that blurry period. Oh, those wasted years. Oh, those years wasted...

Luckily, my wits and liver recovered in my early twenties. I spent the following decade writing a historical fantasy novel, which I knew would become an international bestseller. Please remember me whenever you go to the bathroom: the manuscript might have been recycled into your toilet paper.

I don't see working on that unpublished novel as fruitless, though. It sharpened my writing skills, and I learned a valuable lesson: plot your novels carefully or you'll ramble like an idiot and never get anywhere. Besides, I'm using some ideas of that novel for my current series.

I self-published the first book of the series, just like my two novels. Years ago, I spent some time sucking up to literary agents, but they all rejected me. I thought they were drooling imbeciles, too dumb to appreciate my poetic, flowery style. Now I don't blame them. I used to read a lot of nineteenth-century classics back then, and I unconsciously tried to adopt their prose. The result: I sounded like a pompous prick.

It took me over a decade to find my voice and be happy with it. I'm also happy being an indie writer, although promotion and networking take too much of my time. I haven't tried to get an agent for years, but my stories have been accepted for various publications, so at least I can say that my writing is now publishable.

Apart from that alien-abduction novelette and a few horror stories, I've always written fantasy. To me, fantasy is an escape. You can read about real lives in newspaper or magazine features, but I prefer books that transport me into different epochs and dimensions. Saying that, I don't read or write epic fantasy as it usually deals with different worlds exclusively. I like reading and writing novels where magic slithers into ordinary lives. It feels more material.

I've been fortunate enough to live in six countries and on three continents, and my semi-nomadic life has had a huge influence on my writing. My first novel takes place in the Czech Republic, Portugal, Bulgaria, and Spain. My second novel is set in Turkey, while the first installment of my series will take you back to the Czech Republic.

My love for history and the occult, and for classic horror novels (Poe, Lovecraft, Machen...) has also influenced me. All my books and most of my stories feature malevolent entities that make people fight for their lives, souls, and minds.

Sometimes, at the end of a long day of writing and promoting, I feel that self-publishing is also a monster that might soon make me go insane. Despite that, I'm not giving up yet.

P.C. has released two novels, *Deception of the Damned* and *The Priest of Orpagus*, and co-edited a fantasy anthology called *Dragon Bone Soup*. His short stories have appeared in various publications. In October 2020, P.C. launched *Celts and the Mad Goddess*, the first installment of *The Deathless Chronicle*. P.C. has recently settled with his wife in Southern Spain, where he teaches English in a private language school. He goes swimming and cycling whenever he isn't too busy writing.

I, CURTIS A. DEETER

It's cliché, but writing saved my life. Twice.

The first time was while I was growing up. Before eighteen, I lived in four states (Missouri, Wisconsin, Illinois, and Ohio) and thirteen houses. At the same time, I made and lost countless friends, faced more bullies than I care to recall and have the scars to tell the tale, and struggled to find anything solid to keep under my feet. Besides video games and mischief, all I had was reading and writing.

Since I wasn't satisfied with reality, I used pen and pencil, keyboard and mouse, to create new versions. The possibilities were endless and, more importantly, I was in control. One StarCraft fanfic at a time, I took back what I could and found my little niche in the world (which, of course, as a preteen was a world of one). Eventually, I embarked on my first world-building journey for a series I have on the back burner. Life was good, my restless mind was stable, and I had a solid albeit shaky stool to stand.

As I got older, and decided I was Too Cool for School (wallet chain, black graphic tees, and afro to prove it), I no longer needed literary distraction. I was too busy chasing girls and pretending to be Someone.

The second time was also while I was growing up. I was an adult then, who had more to learn and less to prove than when I was a kid. I met a young woman at work and thought I was in love. She was who people might call my second love: The Hard Love. I was going to spend the rest of my life with her no matter the cost. I lost myself to her version of me. I graduated college, bounced around from low-paying job to low-paying job, and paid more and more of my soul to her (Charon comes to mind, except I'm the only one on the ferry). I would, in the end, be left alone in a house full of cats, drained of self-confidence, and in the deepest depression of my young life.

It could have ended there and almost did on several occasions.

Between heavy drinking, poor decision-making, and serious contemplation as to whether life was worth living, I somehow made it through. Writing, in part, served the dual purpose of life jacket and searchlight in turbid waters.

On a side note, this is one of the most important things I learned growing up: you don't need to "learn to look on the bright side" or to "think about other people for once." Sometimes, that's not enough. Sometimes, you just can't. I beg you, cling to every little thing. Everyone needs purpose. Do you have a song you listen to on repeat? Sing it at the top of your lungs. A furry (or scaly) buddy that needs feeding every morning? Be there for Buddy. A particularly pleasing patch of flowers on your walk to work? Stop and smell them until people look at you funny, then smell them some more. Seriously, if living is simply not a good enough reason to keep on living, cling, cling, cling. This too will pass but only when you're ready. And never forget, you are important. There is something only you bring to this world. You are a band's greatest fan, a pet's entire universe, and a purveyor of the fine art that is a flower garden. You matter, even when it doesn't seem like it.

Anyway, my Hard Love left me mere weeks before our wedding, taking with her a child I grew to consider my own and everything I'd dedicated my early twenties to. I was devastated. I was lost. I didn't have any motivation left. Nothing seemed to matter.

Then, I found writing again. Or rather it found me. It happened my first semester of grad school. Somehow, I had managed to sneak one last English class into my Geography and Planning curriculum. For the first time since my undergrad, I read some seriously good books and wrote some half-decent responses to some of them. A lightbulb flashed and I, The Walking Dead became I, The Writer.

I dabbled with old, abandoned projects. I rewrote, revised, discarded, rewrote, banged my head on the desk, drank a lot, and cursed ever having picked up a pen (I still practice this ritual from time to time). I can't say exactly when it happened, but in 2015 it dawned on me: I wasn't the same person anymore. I was a copy of a copy of a fading shadow. Something like the telephone game we used to play in study hall. As such, I wasn't the same writer anymore either.

But I was alive and, for the first time in what felt like forever, I was thriving.

In 2018, I made the decision to pursue writing as a career. I'm not quite there, but I have made great strides in a short period of time. I married my beautiful wife, Danielle (my third and Forever Love), held her hand while she gave birth to my son, Theodore, and wrote every chance I got. I still write fantasy, but I write it less to escape reality and more to discover potentiality. And I'm starting to write it well which never would have happened had I experienced Coming of Age differently.

Yes, it's cliché, but writing saved my life. And, no matter what else happens, I'll cling to it forever.

Curtis A. Deeter is an author of fantasy, science fiction, and horror. He has a dozen short stories published, and his debut novel, Morning Blood in Mio, is set to release fall 2020. When he isn't writing, he enjoys spending time with his family, discovering new music, and taste-testing craft beer at the local brewery.

I ADITYA DESHMUKE

What is the one defining quality of a writer? Is it the devotion to ideas and words? Is it the incomprehensible love we feel towards pens and notebooks, keyboards, and vintage typewriters? Is it the desire to destroy the world?

Okay, maybe I turned into one of the antagonists of my dark sci-fi stuff there for a moment. Well, yes, there are many things that can define a writer. Now that you are reading this book, you'll realize that we writers are so similar—it's as if we are one hive network. Ooh, that gives me shivers. It's a general belief that minds are limitless. But if that isn't true, a writer hive mind will surely be infinite. Writers are gods of their worlds. We also work in all kinds of fields, because writing usually doesn't make people rich (so do buy our books instead of outdated classics XD). This united brain force can instantly raise a utopia or obliterate everything, depending on our mood.

Do you know what can cripple this awesome Writer Force though? You will need to disable only one part of the writer brain: imagination.

Imagination is both a blessing and a curse. Ever since I was a child, I knew I was different. I didn't know whether it was good different or bad different, but no one really cared. So I didn't think about it for a long time. Eventually, I could feel normal, at least on the surface. Or that's what I used to think.

In retrospect, I have always been different. It's not good different or bad different. It's *writer* different.

I don't know what a shrink would say about this, but if there is any reason why I'm a writer, if I wasn't already born this way, I think the process started with the loss of one of my good childhood friends. I don't really remember anything. It's as if my brain dug up a hole to bury everything related to this incident. Brain is infinite in its small tricks to keep unpleasant things hidden. It's a hole so deep, I haven't reached it yet. And perhaps for my own good.

The blow must have hit me hard, as I always struggled with making friends. I didn't even have imaginary friends. But imagination then became my one true friend. When other kids would play, I'd talk to leaves. I'd gaze up in the sky and fly through the clouds. At nights I'd wonder about the stars and dream of becoming an astronaut.

Childhood went in a flash. Something changed in me when I entered high school. I think it was the first time my inner writer truly woke up. My grades improved significantly. I also started making friends. And I started writing, not on paper at first, but in my head. These new imaginations made much more sense. They were more solid. Soon, I was a walker between realities. It's fun, but there is a very real danger in this grand tour between the worlds: escapism. One can now never be satisfied with this world. One can also never quite escape it. Writing is one of the ways to cope with this.

My very first poem was called "Night." I showed it to my English teacher, Shruti Gaikwad. I don't remember her exact words. But I remember the surprise, joy and pride on her face. I thank her all the time for giving me that little push I needed at that critical time.

Strangely, I didn't write much in the following school years. In India, people are insane about education and grades and all that bullshit. I wanted to see my parents happy, so I snuffed my inner writer for quite a while.

Of course, that's impossible. We writers like to think we are gods of our worlds, but in fact we are slaves. We are nothing but vessels with a vintage typewriter fetish possessed by an invasive alien species called stories.

At that time, like most science students of my age, I was preparing for the IITs, India's most prestigious engineering colleges. I tried my best to appease my parents and my inner alien story lord. I'd study during the day and wake up at the witching hour to write. I suck at discipline, and even if I didn't, this plan was going to fail. IIT is not a joke. Many might disagree, but writing can be even harder. I couldn't do both. I had to choose one over the other. And the consequences were grave.

I never made the decision. I'm a scaredy cat. I run from uncomfortable decisions and let the universe do its thing. I continued trying my best to balance both. It wasn't just my parents' wish that I do well in the exams. I have a romantic idea of what it means to be an engineer, and I wanted to be one. So I continued doing both: studies and writing.

I was unsuccessful at *both*.

My writing SUCKED. I hadn't spent any time reading books on writing. The 150,000-word manuscript I wrote in these two years was full of all sorts of mistakes. My exams also didn't go very well; as always, the competition was insane.

I'm always sincere in whatever I do (except for stupid college assignments). So when nothing worked out despite doing all I could, I was kind of broken. Fortunately, I did get admission in another decent uni. But I can't help but wonder how life would have been if I were in IIT. If I had a second chance, would I abandon writing completely?

Writing can be painful. It can break your mind and spirit. But there's nothing I'd rather do.

Back then, I just had a vague notion that I have come to realize much later. The question "What defines a writer" can be answered in several ways. But what defines me, Aditya Deshmukh?

You guessed it right.

Yes, I'm a weirdo! I mean, a writer. :)

Aditya Deshmukh is an engineering student from India who likes exploring the mechanics of writing as much as he likes tinkering with machines. His ultimate dream is to help erase environment problems (and perhaps also the people responsible for them) and become a cyborg (it's either that and fight or be some robot freak's pet). He writes dark fiction and is obsessed with space opera. His upcoming big work is *Allworld*, an Indian space opera story spanning three trilogies and several novellas.

I, DAVID M. DONACHIE

There are many reasons for wanting to write. You may have a story to tell, you may write for yourself, you may want to get rich, or perhaps to become famous. None of these reasons is wrong.

For ten-year-old me, however, there was only one reason — to have my name on (or in) a book.

Exactly why my childhood self was convinced that having your name on a book (a physical book of course, since digital books didn't exist when I was ten), was the be-all and end-all of writing, I no longer know, but that's how it was.

To achieve this dream, I latched onto the cunning plan of making my own books. There was a stationery shop a short walk from my parent's home which had an off-cut paper box by the door. On one visit I was able to obtain a massive stack of colored construction paper, approximately A4 in size, and all different colors. This paper enabled my publishing dreams.

Lacking any actual knowledge on how to make books (this was the 1980's, pre-internet), I approximated by cutting the sheets in half and sellotaping them together in bundles to make books (later I would hit upon the superior plan of stapling folded sheets into booklets, but somehow this didn't occur to me at first). Once the pages were assembled, I would start to write.

As well as having a generous stationer close-by, my parent's house also had a well-stocked shelf of 60s and 70s science fiction anthologies. I devoured these books as soon as I was old enough to read them, so naturally I filled my makeshift books with science fiction short stories. When filling every page with words became too laborious, I added poems, drawings, even the rules for board games, anything less dense than actual fiction. One of the books, at least, had an illustrated title page before every story. Then, to round them out, I added a contents page (contents always came last, I never knew what was going in the book till it was full), a cover (drawn in felt tip pen), and even blurb on the back cover — which usually stated how wonderful the stories contained inside actually were.

The final stage was to create a publisher for my books, a company that I called Spirits & Serpents, of which I was merely the chief (or only?) star. It even had a logo, though I fear that I no longer own anything that contains it. With a shelf of Spirits & Serpents books with my names on the cover, what more could I need?

Two decades later (give or take) it finally happened for real. I had a story included in an anthology, and my name was finally on an actual book (if not on the cover). You would think that this would be the realization of my dreams, but it wasn't.

You see, during most of that intervening time I'd given up on writing. I concentrated on art, game design, and programming, pretty much every creative activity *other* than writing. The opportunity to have a story in that book, when it came along, was actually connected to the ARG (Alternate Reality Game) *Perplexcity*, which was putting together a fan-made story collection. They happily accepted any story that came along, and I mean any — my story was bad. Possibly terrible. The idea was good, but the execution wasn't, and I knew it.

I realized that it wasn't enough just to have my name on a book, or my words inside — those words also had to be *good*, good enough that someone would choose to read them, good enough that they would choose them over someone else's writing. All of a sudden that childhood dream took a different tack.

I am a firm believer that to write well you must read, as widely as possible, and I've always been a voracious reader. I assumed that reading was enough, but that's not true. Writing is like any other skill, it needs to be practiced. I'd spent decades practicing drawing, painting, and design, but like many new writers, I kind of assumed that my writing didn't need to be practiced. I was wrong.

So I started writing. I re-wrote things I'd done as a child, making new versions of them. I wrote tiny, stupid stories, just to learn economy of words. I practiced dialogue, improvising conversations in my head and then wrote them down. I sat down in 2011 and started work on a novel, trying to hone the craft of it, not just the story.

The novel wasn't bad (in fact, I found a publisher for it just this year, after a very long wait), but I couldn't find an agent interested in it, so I doubled down. I conceived of a short story anthology with twenty-six stories and wrote over fifty, throwing out half of my own work to pick the best ones until I finally had a book that didn't just have my name on the cover, I could also be proud of seeing it there.

And, it didn't end there. After the anthology was published, I began to submit fiction to competitions, calls for submissions, anthologies, and the like. Early acceptances into free venues turned into paid ones. Now, my name is on many books; it's even on the *cover* of many books, and the journey is just beginning. I can always get better, and I'll keep trying to get better.

Maybe, one day, I'll even find a space to fill a book full of fiction, drawings, maps, games and puzzles, just like I did when I was ten.

David M. Donachie is a writer, artist, programmer, and games designer, who lives in a draughty Scottish garret with two cats, a frog, and a large number of reptiles. He is the creator of the Solipsist roleplaying game. His short story collection *The Night Alphabet* came out in 2018, and his first novel, *The Drowning Land*, will be published by CAAB in January 2021

I, JULIE EGER

My family wasn't interested in literature. Bless their hearts, they didn't read anything more than the labels on feedbags or monthly bills. By the grace of some desperate saleslady, wearing a purple dress and cat-eye glasses who passed through our town in the mid-60s, we acquired a set of encyclopedias. I was introduced to the world of words. I read those books from cover to cover.

I loved to read but never thought about becoming a writer. I loved to draw but we didn't have a lot of paper at our house so I wrote and drew on everything I could find. Cardboard boxes. Grocery bags. Receipts. My mother encouraged my creative mind, although she didn't always understand it. We didn't know until I was out of high school that I was dyslexic, but my creative mind somehow pulled me through and I never stopped trying to understand things.

When I was eight, I convinced my parents to get me *Trixie Belden* mystery books for my birthday. It was a lot to ask for when they needed the money to pay bills, but somehow those books showed up next to my homemade birthday cake. I'd crawl under the hay wagon with a paper sack full of apples and a book and read as much as I could on my break from chores.

In middle school I tried my hand at poetry and won a contest with a poem I drafted on the back of a soup can label. In high school I argued with my sophomore English teacher about what made a good story—she in her tight straight skirt—I in t-shirts and patched blue jeans. She would become frustrated and punish me. I spent a lot of time sitting next to her desk, staring at walls. That's when I started scratching out stories and what I called *doodles* on my jeans with black and red ink. I didn't know it then, but those doodles were my way of remembering things, through pictures.

As a teenager, before falling asleep, I'd scribble out poems and pictures on my pillow case. I drove my mother crazy. Sometimes I wrote on rocks. Or in the sand. Part of our yard resembled a crop circle, as I scratched out words in the grass.

Then I received a Smith-Corona Coronamatic electric portable typewriter, Coronet Super 12 with a snap-in ribbon, for my sixteenth birthday. My ability to string words together grew. I memorized the placement of all the letters on the keys and the words began to fly onto the pages. I no longer had to worry about fitting the circles and lines together to make letters of the alphabet.

After that I discovered an abandoned shed in the woods. The shed was tipped on its side and covered with grapevines. I took a knife and cut those vines. It was only the beginning of cutting things open. I tipped that shed upright and hauled my typewriter down there along with an old extension cord. I began banging away at the keys; poems, stories, songs—amongst the chipmunks and red squirrels.

At a young age I married a man who tried to control me. When it came to things I'd written, while he was in the house, I was like a squirrel trying to hide nuts where no one could find them. I didn't want to him to know my thoughts and ideas. There was never a private place to write. I wrote at the edge of the kitchen counter, next to the rolled-out pie crusts, or pattern pieces on my sewing desk. Next to the pin cushion or the baby powder on the changing table after my kids were born. In the car or in the bleachers at T-ball games.

Then, when I was forty-four, after I was divorced, I inherited my dad's roll-top desk. I put it in the corner of my home business office, with my new husband's fishing and hunting shows blaring on the TV in the background. It was at this point I felt driven to write. One of the catalysts for that urge to write was the unsolved murder that took place in my neighborhood when I was nine. To date, that murder has never been solved. The other factor was alcoholism and mental illness in my family. Trying to make sense of things. My family was good at breaking rules so it was interesting to see how their choices worked out for them. I could never resist taking notes. It was then I typed out a 300-page draft of a novel. Something I never knew I could do, string that many words out in a row to make a story that big.

I showed my rough draft to Barbara Fitz-Vroman, co-author of *Tomorrow is a River,* a popular historical novel written back in the 70s. She liked my draft, said it had potential. Barbara had been writing for a long time. She had connections. She began introducing me to her writing friends. I was terrified. I had no formal education when it came to writing. I was dyslexic and suffered from dyscalculia, a problem with numbers. What did I know?

She took me to The Clearing, a folk school in Door County, Wisconsin. Introduced me to **Norbert Blei**. "This kid's got potential," he said. They helped me with my novel, but they both died within a year of each other from different types of cancer. I missed them terribly. Norbert's biggest fear for me was no one would be able to read my work because I was hesitant to submit my stories and poems. I never thought they were good enough. I didn't write again, seriously, for the next four years. But in 2016 I decided to try self-publishing my novel and other little books I'd written. I had some success. It gave me confidence.

In 2018 I started submitting to online journals, garnering acceptances of my work I never dreamed possible. I've been writing ever since.

Julie Eger was born in a town known for its wild roses in central Wisconsin, USA. She also writes under the names Copper Rose and A.J. Lawdring. Copper provides the meat for the sandwich, A.J. is the unexpected condiment and Julie is the marbled rye that holds it all together. She raised two sons and now lives with her husband and a black Golden Doodle. Julie has been accused of playing well with others. Credits include nine anthologies at **Clarendon House Publications** and numerous online journals and other anthologies.

I, DJ ELTON

When I was younger my mother always seemed to think I should become a journalist because I was curious and wrote things. We came to Australia on the boat for 'ten-pound poms' as they were called, stopping off in Ceylon as it was then known. Our family of three roamed the streets taking in the sights. I was eight. A beggar woman with her child approached my parents and asked to sell them her baby for two shillings and sixpence. When we arrived in Australia, I wrote a story about this awe-inspiring experience and it was published in the Sunday newspaper children's Possums Pages as they were called, maybe after Dame Edna? I received a prize and acknowledgment. When I was around nine, I wrote my first 'book' – a story set on the border of England and Scotland called *Trouble in Little Border.* I seem to recall it being a crime mystery that only a nine-year-old could conceive. My mother and aunty were both avid readers. Mum got me reading all the classics and I especially liked Hans Christian Andersen, as well as *Alice in Wonderland, Narnia,* and a few books about tiny people, called *The Borrowers*. (Homily, Pod and Arietty. Ring any bells?)

In primary school I was good at English and a poem I wrote called "The Lump" about a sculptor modeling clay went into the school magazine. I don't recall thinking about what life career I would take when growing up, and I didn't have the aim to go to university as I was more interested in living out in the world. It was 1969 and the Woodstock era. At that time music had a bigger impact on me then than writing. I left school early which I did regret for some years, but I've made up for it now with further education. I also worked as a community mental health nurse for quite some years before getting serious about writing for publication.

I have always written poetry although I never considered getting any of it published. I was pretty committed to my mental health nursing career and also being a meditation student, on parallel lines balancing each other out. My writing lay dormant until about 2015 when I decided to write a book which was a fantastic truth called *The Merlin Girl* set in medieval times and the present. This novella was 15,000 words and took me *three years* to write. I found out so much since then about writing, publishing, and the literary world in general. I have learned a huge amount about getting published in anthologies particularly. Currently, I'm not itching to write a novel as I'm quite happy creating micro-fiction, short stories, and poetry.

The big influence on the direction of my writing was getting a 100-word micro-fiction piece called "Crow" accepted by a small indie press in Melbourne. I was totally rapt; unstoppable after that. Since May 2019 I have had short and longer stories published. Keeping up with the works in progress as well as keeping myself balanced and disciplined is important to me. I retired from work two months ago and can now follow my writing pursuits, so I'm getting busier by the day. I'm studying postgraduate Writing and Literature with Deakin University online which gives good stimulus to my speculative musings. It also makes me consider the history of literature and how it is revisionist. Mostly I write sci-fi and fantasy stories and write occasional horror but I like it to be humorous and not intense. I need beauty and sensibility in my work, and try to keep to that as a standard for myself.

I write at 5:00 am and often spend an hour pouring out 500 words at least. My head is clearest at that time. I can write anywhere, although before lockdown I preferred going to a library for quietness and anonymity. I would finish drafts and edits easily and quickly. Now in Melbourne, the libraries are shut down, so I write from various places at home; my favorite being in the office which is an unruly, cluttered space so I can tend to get distracted.

I'm slowly developing my blog and recently interviewed three horror writers as to why they chose to write in that genre. Like all writers seeking publication I've had to tolerate rejection, and I also love the intoxication of getting an acceptance. Earlier this week I had news of my first accepted poem which was *so exciting*. I felt such a sense of achievement because I have been writing poetry for years but never intending for it to be published. Most of those poems were about love, relationships, and life's challenges whereas my current work is more speculative around those themes. I love writing poetry and am working on an epic one about a lion-rider. A lot of my old poems are getting gradually re-invented.

My family hasn't quite understood that I am a writer. They don't seem to get it. I guess it's because I have worn a few hats in the past, (health professional, meditation teacher…), and they are slowly getting used to this idea. My cousin arranged to have her young daughter read a speculative *Alice in Wonderland* story I wrote to my mother and two aunties which was pretty innovative of her. My close friends are always interested to hear my stories, and I've "trained" a couple to give feedback, however the greatest camaraderie is with my online writing groups and independent publishing houses. That's where the *real* writing connections are. It's a great space to be in – the literary world – so much to learn and act on. I'm pleased to have this opportunity to write and reflect on my writing, so a big thanks to Steve Carr, Priti J, and others who help at Sweetycat Press.

DJ Elton is an author from Melbourne, Australia who writes speculative fiction short stories, poetry and micro-fiction. She's had work published in several anthologies; with Black Hare Press, Insignia Stories, Little Quail Press, and others, as well as a self-published novella, *The Merlin Girl*. Currently, she's working on a long poem about a girl who rides lions and has several other works in progress. When not pushing a pen, she getting social, reading crime novels, and visualizing the end of lockdown. She believes her strengths comes from many years of meditation practice.

I, XIMENA ESCOBAR

El pudor…It's one of those feelings I cannot translate satisfactorily, yet one I am overcome by as I finally sit down to write these words. It burns in the face like embarrassment and modesty; but it's both and neither at the same time. It's ironic, that after a lifetime of calling myself a writer, even if I wrote very little—hardly anything—in comparison to my fairly public aspirations, I should now feel less of a writer than ever; now that I've been actively and regularly doing it, and publishing, for nearly three years.

But I also know I want to be a part of this book and share some of my journey. Not only because, true to the writer in me, I want this journey to exist in words, but because I want it to have its place amongst those of my author friends, without whom I'm sure I'd have given up before I even started. So, I thank them now—as if anyone is going to read this it's going to be them—for their ongoing company and support. And I persist with this reflection, somewhat saddened that this moment has caught me on a low. Even if 'the low' is an honest and relevant shape of—I'm sure—any writer's journey.

What did I think being a writer would feel like?

In one word: fulfillment, I guess. But not only for the duration of a paragraph or the day's word count; a fulfillment beyond that of the writing experience, pertaining to the outer world's perception of me. A validation.

From very early on I felt misunderstood. Writing, my art in general (I used to paint, I love photography, I sing and play a little) was always an avenue to *try* to connect with others. So often they barked at me—when I hadn't had a chance to say anything—I didn't think—I *intuited*—that perhaps if they let me say something, if I got to "finish speaking" before they judged me, maybe then, they would love me.

They—I'm not talking about my parents. I'm talking about all those circles in the playground. I'm talking about the mediocre grades when everyone at home assured me I was so smart and talented. I'm talking about primary school, when everybody knew me as "horse face." I'm talking about having to lie about missing my grandad, when really, I was sad at everyone's unkindness.

I remember my vivid awareness of the past even then, the comfort being able to travel back to a particular, intimate moment in time gave me; capture it, stretch it all the way until *the now*, that I could be *the then* and *the now* all at once. *Be* who I was, or who I knew I was, despite the distorted mirrors. I didn't write the words down, back then, of course. I didn't have them. But I walked through life with that sensation, permanently daydreaming. My self-awareness, like writing without writing.

When I finally started putting those words down as a young adult, that was always the experience I wanted to bring to life. All the while from the pang of nostalgia for my earliest memories, for the warmth of the love of the beginning—the time when I was happiest and complete. Writing was always, therefore, personal and close. Poetry the most fitting way of, weaved into prose, getting my unique—because the substance is intertwined with the form—elusive emotions and revelations across, seeking always to satisfy my eye for beauty.

But none of this ever meant being understood. Nor, in other words, that my writing was any good. I put it aside because failing was unbearable. Perhaps there was nothing, no one, to love between those lines; no words to throw light on another's unnamed corner; no mirror of another's darkness, *in my writing*.

Then, at long last, I was mature. Ready to forget the fear and screw it if anyone got it or not—I don't need anyone to be someone. But the anti-climax hurts. I'm so self-absorbed creating and discovering, enamored of, if not entirely my craft, of crafting. What happens at the other side though, where the words are read, or worse, *aren't*? Nothing. No fruit of the fruit sprouts. Nothing worth the guilt of not contributing financially to the family, despite the investment of time and space. Of not doing anything worthy of admiration. I don't even have the kudos of sacrificing my lifestyle for this hobby of mine, because money isn't really an issue—not thanks to me. Who am I helping, with my self-indulgent ladies-who-lunch pastime? It's far too late to be Henry Miller. Too late, or too early, to deserve this selfish introversion. (Knowing, also, it's too late to impress anyone. Too late to impress any of *them* now we're all adults—including and especially myself.) How do I make the world better with my words?

Yes, books are precious. But I want my writing to mean something. I want it to be dignified. I want that communion with the reader yet, it's like I'm still pretending to be a singer, playing my songs behind my closed bedroom door. There is no reach to my words—aimless scattered arrows lifting fleeting breezes, faint little echoes, because I'm at the foot of the slope—and I can feel how very steep it is from here... You know you've got so much to learn and that's truly what it's all about; it's where the "high" of my journey has been. The wonderful learning. The endless possibilities.

But I, the student, want to give something. And I wonder if I'll get there.

Ximena is writing short stories and poetry. Originally from Chile, she lives in Nottingham with her family.

I, MARÍA J. ESTRADA

This writing journey began with absolute boredom and racism. See, I grew up in the desert, between Yuma and Somerton, Arizona. On the U.S.-Mexico border, being brown in the 1970's meant racism. It still does to a great degree. I learned about racism the hard way in the first grade, where I had a nervous breakdown due to hateful practices—brown kids punished for speaking their language. At the same time, I became an avid reader of Spanish comic books or *novelas*. My favorite was *Bolillo*, and it taught me that stories could be about the poorest of the poor.

I was a sickly child. I missed a lot of school, and mix that with not feeling welcome in the American public school system, and I flunked first grade. One of the most traumatic moments a child can experience isn't being in bed for weeks due to a nervous breakdown or the cruelty of teachers. No. It's the raging anger from a drunken father so disappointed in his child. I had no idea what flunking meant, but I knew it was something awful.

You'd better believe after that tantrum of broken pictures and vases that I absorbed English. I devoured everything in both languages. That's when a love of writing really blossomed. What happened to the boredom? You bet I spent hours world-building. There was not much to do in our dilapidated house in the middle of the orange groves, but that was a blessing. All of it was a blessing. To this day, these experiences are fused in my writing: poetry, fiction, essay, articles.

After that initial failure, I wrote stories in *mis lenguas*. I read everything from Susan Cooper to C.S. Lewis to Stephen King, all while absorbing all the Spanish books I could get my hands on, most of them not age appropriate. Ironically, the first time I won a writing contest was a Father's Day poem for my dad, a poem pointing out all the reasons I loved him, despite his flaws. He cherished it.

The summer after first grade, we moved to the desert, and that zip code led to a school in Yuma. The teachers there were amazing. I can name almost every single one, and I loved everything English: grammar, reading, and *writing.*

That passion ran deep. I knew from an early age I wanted to be a writer. In my teens, I thought I wanted to be a comic book writer. Turns out I was pretty good at poetry and fiction.

All my teachers through high school encouraged writing and reading. I became an A+ student and the biggest Latina nerd in the *barrio.* I was into science fiction and horror, comics, movies, T.V. shows. McKinley, Asimov, Heinlein, Vonnegut, Le Guin, King were my daily bread. I wrote all the time. I entered contests. Wrote school plays. As a teen, along with a clan of boy-nerds I founded the Pen & Quill Club in high school.

My neighbor, Julio, would get so fucking annoyed with me. He would pester me to stop writing and go play basketball or baseball in 100+ degree weather. Staring at my notebook with disdain, he would ask me, "Why are you writing all the time?" He was a "math person" and never read a book in his life.

When I write stories, often, I write for him, the reader who has never read a book.

I carried all of these experiences with me to college. I earned a B.A., M.A., and Ph.D. in English, and I took every creative writing class, sometimes twice. Other English professors encouraged me. As an undergrad, Victor Villanueva—my mentor and narrative writer, who from the first day he met me, holding a crumpled story in my sweaty palms—told me **I was a writer**. The way he said it hit a chord. Barbara Anderson, award-winning poet, encouraged me to find my voice. Later, in my doctoral program, Alex Kuo would discourage me from getting into an M.F.A. program because I was already a writer. They all were right, but when you grow up with internalized racism, you don't believe it.

I was in my forties when I finally started seeing myself a writer. I mean I had the volumes of stories and novel revisions, bad scripts, but I didn't believe it. Not really. I was still looking for a Great

White Editor to tell me I could write. I felt *menosprecio*, self-deprecation, the idea that brown and woman are never good enough.

What changed? Teaching English at a community college. Teaching organic intellectuals with the same internalized racism, really helped me uproot my own. After all, you can't try to point to the strengths and beauty of writing for people of color without seeing your own, right? Today, I teach Creative Writing, Literature, and Composition at Harold Washington College. I love it. I live for midwifing students into believing in their writing abilities.

During this terrible pandemic, in response to racism, I launched a charity press—Barrio Blues Press. That took *courage*. Believe it, and the quality of contributing writers, both emerging and more established, is amazing. The press is fused with my love of words, and the dream of supporting others along their journeys.

Now, I write for my own excellence, an idea that was birthed by Matt Sedillo. I don't care what others think about my work or if it doesn't meet their standards. I am developing and honing my voice on *my* terms. Yeah, it's the voice of a first-generation American, a Chicana from class struggle. It's strong and often loud. That's fine because it is what it is supposed to be. I write for others—the Julios of the world. I write for readers who need that special story. It doesn't mean I'm arrogant or narcissistic.

It means these beliefs have taken my writing to a whole new level, and I can't wait to see what comes next.

María J. Estrada is an English college professor of Composition, Literature, and her favorite, Creative Writing. She grew up in the desert outside of Yuma, Arizona in the real Barrio de Los Locos, a barrio comprised of new Mexican immigrants and first-generation Chicanos. Drawing from this setting and experiences, she writes like a *loca* every minute she can—all while magically balancing her work and union and family obligations. She lives in Chicago's south side with her wonderfully supportive husband, two remarkable children, and two mischievous cats—one of whom has killed at least one laptop.

I, J.W. GARRETT

Writing for me is a journey, one I've been ensnared in a love hate relationship with for as long as I can remember. How many times have I written pages of words, then frustrated, trashed them again in one go? Often. Too many times to count. But that's now with some years of experience and cynicism behind me.

When I was younger, I wrote to get thoughts down on paper. Somehow, they felt safer there than inside. I didn't dare to dream that one day I'd write words people would *want* to read. Poems led to short stories and fantasies of writing longer works. Thoughts of a novel brewed in my head, but I could never do that. Could I? I left those scribbled sentences where they belonged—shoved in a drawer and closed off from everyone.

I'd never spoken seriously about "writing" with anyone. Seemed like a ridiculous topic to bring up and a moot point as well. Success lay elsewhere for me. Some place more concrete...real.

My journey took an unexpected turn when my father wrote a poem for me—a gathering of his emotions all in one place, a way to say what he couldn't out loud during an intense time of my young adulthood. I didn't know he wrote; he'd never talked about it or shared it with me or my siblings, but the evidence lay right in front of me, tied up in his poignant words.

The realization that we shared that common bond sparked life into my dream again, and I spoke with him about my desire to write. Neither for nor against my efforts, he'd nodded, understanding the need, but also much more about this particular struggle than he shared with me at the time.

Life happened and I hung on for the ride, burying the desire to write, but not quite putting out the flame entirely. From time to time I'd jot down thoughts that wouldn't go away, and I accumulated them, saving them for later—tucked away for when I had time.

Time, like a freight train raced on by, not caring that I had plans, big ones, for when that calm would hit and everything would fall into perfect alignment waiting just for me. Needless to say, that never happened. The day that I assembled together those scraps of paper I'd been hoarding wasn't special, not to anyone but me. I'd committed that day to just begin, and trudge ahead, holding myself accountable to a goal, because I wanted to find out if that dream I'd shoved in a drawer so long ago could be more.

Days of work, family, life...flowed into nights of writing, and once that beast was unleashed it wanted to be fed. When I ignored my work in process the characters would rant and rave during the night anyway, so writing seemed like the better option I'd reasoned, even though long days stretching into endless nights left me drained on an ongoing basis. Still, content on a different level, I continued because now, I couldn't stop.

Those scraps of paper eventually became the basis for my first novel and the first book in my sci-fi fantasy series, Realms of Chaos. Three books in my series are published; the fourth is in draft form at present, and I have many smaller works published as well. I'm grateful that train let me tag along for the ride after all.

I write for those words that are so hard to choose, ones that fight to exist on the page, and as I wield my pen, balancing, weighing them against my mind and heart, I'll determine if they stay or are erased in the cold brutal light of day.

J.W. Garrett has been writing in one form or another since she was a teenager. She writes speculative fiction from the sunny beaches of Florida, but loves the mountains of Virginia where she was born. Her writings include novels as well as short stories and poetry. Since completing *Remeon's Crusade*, the third book in her sci-fi fantasy series, *Realms of Chaos*, she has been hard at work on the next installment, scheduled to release in 2021. When she's not hanging out with her characters, her favorite activities are reading, running and spending time with family.

I, KELLI J GAVIN

I love being a writer, but haven't always done much of it. I wrote short stories as a kid, often with the help of my dad. As a teen, I wrote a lot about new experiences. Space Camp, summer camp, trips to Colorado and Chicago, relationships, heartache, family turmoil. I guess I stopped writing anything other than poetry at the end of my senior year of high school. Poetry flowed out of me so fast and ferociously, that it actually scared me a bit. Raw emotion found its way onto the page before I had a chance to realize what I was writing about. But school, youth group, high school musicals, singing, relationships, and then the busyness of college made all that writing take a back burner.

I married young, worked as a Banker for years and then as a Bank Consultant and a Professional Organizer. I love being an Organizer and working in a different person's home every day. I enjoy approaching each new task and finding a solution to the organizational woes of the American home. But I have only been actively writing for four years. Why? Why is it that something I love doing is something that I walked away from? Why is it that I let the busyness of life overtake me and that I let it steal what brought me joy?

Being overly confident has been my downfall. Yet, I found myself struggling with jealousy. I had two friends who were writers and saw book after book published. One of my friends made an attempt at a career change and booked 16 public speaking gigs in the first 6 months. Another friend quit her job of 21 years so that she could pursue her artistic passion and sold piece after piece. When I poured out my heart to a dear friend about how I was feeling, watching everyone succeed around me, she said something that shocked me. She said I wasn't a failure because I haven't yet done something amazing.- I never saw myself as a failure until she said that. I was fully aware that she was trying to comfort and redirect me, but the self-doubt set in. Was I a failure? What have I done to make a name for myself or did I even want my name to be known? Have I failed because I don't live up to everyone else's level of success?

I found myself stuck in a state of discontentment, analyzing and overthinking. I cried one evening talking with my husband. He hugged me and asked when it was that I started letting others set the bar for me. He asked me why I was concerned about what others thought of me. He also was very good at pointing out what I had accomplished. He told me how proud he was of me as a wife, mother and small business owner. He also complimented my efforts at helping others and my desire to meet the physical tangible needs of the underserved local community. He told me he loved me, supported me and would help me do and accomplish anything that I set my mind to. And then, Josh Gavin, God love him said, "Stop comparing yourself to others. Stop viewing yourself as a failure because others have succeeded differently than you."

That was it. There isn't a specific tool that could be used to measure success. Success is determined by the person who has set a goal or has decided to pursue a passion. My success and the path that I chose to take would be left up to me. No one would be grading me. No one would say, you shouldn't pursue your passion anymore, it is too late. Your time has passed—my age wasn't going to be a factor anymore. I have had a life well lived so far with experiences and wisdom and so many stories to share. If writing had been so important to me once, I needed to pursue it again.

My mother passed away 7+ years ago. I wanted to honor her and write down my memories, but I couldn't even pick up a pen. I am a note taker. Each time I thought of something that would make for an interesting story, I would write it down. Sometimes a single word, a sentence, a paragraph or random words all thrown together that only made sense to me. Basement. Flowers. Wood ticks. His smile. Ability to make friends. Christmas tree. I was able to see stories taking shape, and rather than being stuck on the loss, or pain of a memory, I was excited and the stories started to write themselves. Some of the stories were like a weight being lifted from my shoulders.

I started writing for the local newspaper and entering poetry contests. I won a couple of prizes for entries I had made and loved it. People stopped me at the library or at Target to tell me they enjoyed reading my newspaper articles. I began to write more. I realized I was creating a habit by writing frequently. I had to write. I was boring friends and family with long stories of days gone by, and they always said, write it down.

I now enjoy blogging, writing for newspapers, poetry and short story journals and magazines. I have 17 anthology books published and 2 of my own. My idea of success was never to become famous. My idea of success was to inspire others through telling stories that matter.

It took me 40+ years to find what I should be doing. Writing enables me to share stories, it fills my soul, inspires me and brings me joy. Mostly, it means I didn't fail. I need to remember that daily, even when I am discouraged. The realization that it took me a long time, but I am doing what I love, is of the utmost importance to me.

Kelli J Gavin of Carver, Minnesota is a Writer, Editor, Blogger and Professional Organizer. Her work can be found with Clarendon House Publishing, The Ugly Writers, Sweatpants & Coffee, Zombie Pirates Publishing, Setu, Sweetycat Press, Passionate Chic, Otherwise Engaged, Flora Fiction, Love What Matters, Printed Words and Southwest Media among others. Kelli's first two books were released in 2019 (I Regret Nothing- A Collection of Poetry and Prose and My Name is Zach- A Teenage Perspective on Autism). She has also co-authored 17 anthology books. Her 3rd and 4th books will be published in 2020 and 2021.

I, SHARON FRAME GAY

I was six years old when I first noticed my connection with the sky. My legs barely straddled an old mule's back as I followed the adults in a snaking line through a gully in Arizona. It was midnight. We were riding from one ranch to another, the ranch hands leading the way. My mother and brother rode in front of me, their laughter echoing across the desert.

The moon and stars were our only light. The moon was full that night, painting the Arizona landscape with its milky brush, showing us the way home. Since then, I have been trying to find my own way back home, and the sky has been a constant companion.

As a child of the highway, I relied on the sky to be the same, no matter where I lived. Whether it was the rolling hills of the Ozarks, the tundra of North Dakota, the wind-washed foothills of Montana or crowded city streets, I always looked up to find my compass.

We never stayed in one place very long. My brother and I went to a different school each year. Our family hurtled down highways that were far more familiar than the houses we passed in the night. Walking along city sidewalks, I latched on to the light from other people's windows and fed on the teat of normalcy, if only for a while. I imagined they led lives better than my own. Maybe they didn't go home to abuse or uncertainty. I concocted stories about the families who lived behind the windows as I walked by.

I dreamed of living somewhere long enough to find my way around the house in the dark. And wished that my life didn't consist of cardboard boxes, frayed and over-used, packed in a hurry and wedged inside a U-Haul truck.

***

When I was seven, I asked my grandmother if I could use her typewriter. I wrote a story about a horse. It never made it into those cardboard cartons, but I remember it. An anxious child with stomach issues, I missed almost half the school year wherever we lived. I'd lay in bed and draw pictures of horses and make up countless tales.

The stories were comforting. My imagination took me to places that allowed me to cope. As a kid I wrote letters to the Universe and tossed them in the fireplace, in hopes someone read the smoke signals from the chimney and might answer. I wrote songs and poems, a soundtrack of my growing years.

Tucked away in a small trunk, along with yearbooks of schools I never attended for long, my writings slept in the attic for decades. I never dreamed of sharing them with anyone.

On the night of my husband's death, I stepped outside into a sharp February night and looked to the sky. There was the moon, full and fecund, peering down at me. I was just another little person in this vast world, trying to keep my foothold on this planet. Sometimes it spun so fast over the years that my balance is forever impaired.

"*It's the same moon*," I thought, looking skyward. The same cold sphere, whether I cry beneath its light in sorrow, or howl in outrage at life's unfairness. It hung in the sky when I danced under its spell in the throes of love. Or flung away the promise of tomorrow with the abandon that only comes with youth. It never changes, even though my own life has taken many turns.

I wrote an essay for my husband that February night. I was reluctant to read it at the memorial, so the minister read it for me. After hearing my essay, a friend suggested I take a creative writing class at a local college and meet other writers.

It was lonely after Ben died. The moon hid behind a north wind that rained down upon me night after night. I thought of the papers in the attic, the poems and songs, sealed against the stars and left to slumber beneath the rafters.

That spring, I signed up for the writing class. In doing so, I found my tribe. I met people who touched my heart. People who treasured creativity. My stories sounded safe in their mouths. Sharing my writing with others wove those words into a map where at last I found my way around the house in the dark.

Newfound friends encouraged me to publish my work. I submitted the very first non-fiction essay in 2015. The editor published it, and nominated the essay for the Pushcart Prize. Beginner's luck!

Since then, I have been internationally published in many anthologies and literary magazines. I've been fortunate to win several awards and nominations. I now have a collection of short stories in a book, "Song of the Highway".

When I write, I never forget that little girl in the desert on the back of an old mule. I insert the moon, stars, and sky in almost every story I write. If you look closely, you will find them.

Just last night, the moon glowed through the bedroom window, my companion through life. I may be just a little person in this vast world, but I think the Universe read my smoke signals from the chimney so many years ago. It set me on a course that allows me to share with others, and perhaps help someone look to the sky and know they aren't alone.

Sharon Frame Gay grew up a child of the highway, playing by the side of the road. She has been internationally published in anthologies and literary magazines, including Chicken Soup For The Soul, Typehouse, Fiction on the Web, Lowestoft Chronicle, Thrice Fiction, Crannog, Saddlebag Dispatches and others. Her work has won prizes at Women on Writing, Rope and Wire Magazine, and The Writing District. She has been nominated twice for the Pushcart Prize. Sharon's collection of short stories, "Song of the Highway," is available on Amazon.

I, NICK GERRARD

I never wanted to be a writer. I wanted to be a punk rock musician. So, during night shifts behind the bales of jute in the run-down, corrugated iron factory, where I worked at sixteen, I wrote punk rock lyrics. We had never really been pushed to read at my school. Only one year we had a good teacher who introduced us to Orwell and Barry Hines and Alan Sillitoe. These guys I liked; all the other classic literary writers bored me senseless. But these guys wrote about things like my life. They wrote kitchen sink working-class stories, things I could relate to. I couldn't relate to Virginia Wolfe or E. M. Forster or the Brontes. What World did these people live in? Certainly not mine. I later discovered that the US had all these cool writers like Kerouac and Bukowski and Steinbeck. And I loved these guys. So through meeting weird people during my punk days, hipsters I suppose we would call them now, through the underground alternative community, I discovered writing and writers I liked and could relate to.

In the meantime, my own writing trip had begun. I was writing reviews of gigs. Pamphlets on politics to give out at gigs. And the more political I got involved the more political articles I wrote. We started an Unemployed union and we produced a little 6-page magazine; hand-designed with clips and glue and articles and hand-printed on an old off-set printer we cranked by hand (Jesus how old am I? Sounds like something from the Paris commune!) After being politically active for some years, I got a bit disillusioned and decided to up sticks and go off travelling. Well, travelling and going to live in various countries. Paris, Barcelona, Brazil never got me writing but got me drinking and meeting characters and having adventures I later used a lot in my short stories. I started writing travel bits. I tried to write for the guide books, but reviewing was never really my thing. Then I wrote some auto-fiction travel pieces about my adventures in Africa and there I found a style I liked. Returning to the UK I decided to do some creative writing courses…one with the Workers education association. This was great, a 2-hour class a week but with a published author who got us writing all sorts of stuff. I started to turn my auto-fiction into more just fiction based on experiences and stories I had accumulated over the years; about the characters and places I had met during my travels and looking back to the punk lifestyle and the lives of the working-class people I knew.

I then did a more serious course with the Open College of Arts; a correspondence course. This really taught me a lot about style, and plot building etc. I had my first auto-story published funnily enough by the US underground magazine *Thieves Jargon*, about twenty years ago. It was one of the first new online mags around. The story was about my experience in a Czech drink tank and mental hospital. I then did some more work for them, my second story about a Czech gypsy girl and how she fought for a better life; a subject I write about a lot. I sent more stuff off to other mags and people really liked my style which I would say is dirty realism. I write about the underbelly of society and the experiences of ordinary working-class people.

I shoved together a load of essays and opinion pieces with some stories into a kind of travel book. It got published but the publisher was crap so I self-published and it sold well. I got involved with online writers' groups and had a lot of contacts with magazine editors and other writers. Having this online presence helped me with sales of my books. And myself and some other writers set up Jotters united writers' group after the original writers' group Jottify got shut down. We started as a Facebook group (And still are) where we share news, opportunities and push each other's work. We then went to a monthly online magazine called *Jotters United*. We produced about 30 issues and over 130 writers over a number of years. I enjoyed being an editor and designer, but it got to be very time consuming so we have let it lie for a while, while we get down to writing our own stuff; but I may go back to producing it, at some point.

I then did a poetry book, just to get it out of my system I think...I had all these lyrics lying around and thought, shit turn them into poetry and put a book out. The last ten years I have concentrated on my short stories, which I enjoy writing and complements my style I think...short and sharp. I have one collection out which was well received and I ventured into the writing of a Novella called *Punk Novelette*. The length of the book again suited my style. I have no great desire to write a novel, I am happy with short fiction. My first short story collection was about the underclass, lowlife world of drug addicts and freaks. The one I am editing now I wanted to be more positive, so it is still about ordinary people but about their struggles and lives and all political to some extent; but in a positive way. The Working-class win for a change! Not sure what I will do next. I'm thinking; maybe crime. I like to read crime stories for relaxation and I've read a lot of it. So, maybe I can run my hand to that, we will see. I never push the writing process; I wait for the inspiration to find me.

Nick's short stories, flash, poetry and essays have appeared in various magazines and books in print and online including *Breaking rules, Rye whiskey review, Spillwords, Pikers press, The Siren, The Platform, Ramingoblog, literati-magazine, Minor Literature* and *Bluehour magazine*. Nick has three books published available on Amazon. His latest short novel, Punk Novelette is all about a group of friends growing up with punk in the 70s in the UK and the effect the movement had on their lives.

I, R.A. GOLI

I always said I was going to be a writer; I talked about it often. I don't remember when I first fell in love with books or storytelling, but I do remember writing stories in high school classes; maths, geography, any class I could get away with it and have the teacher think I was taking notes. It's no surprise I'm terrible at both maths and geography now.

Once in English class we had a guest children's author, Isobelle Carmody, who read a story from each student. She told me mine was very good. I eavesdropped to see if she told everybody the same; and was pleased to hear she didn't. I'm sad to say I no longer have the story and barely remember what it was about, other than there was a barbarian, elf, dwarf, and sorceress foursome going on a quest. I have bouts of decluttering where I throw everything away, and sadly this includes all of the stories I had written as a teenager.

At twelve I was deciding on my career options for the future. I wanted to be a veterinary nurse or a writer. Veterinary nursing seemed the more sensible option so that's what I have done for most of my working career. Writing took a back seat for many years. Occasionally I would do a short creative writing course which I would hate because I was never allowed to write genre fiction. Not being able to write a fantasy or horror was beyond frustrating; I might as well have done maths calculations.

Most of my family and friends are supportive; some have bought copies of my books, though it has taken a while for others to take me seriously as a writer. Probably because I don't make a huge income. Though many have commented on the quality of my writing, and seem pleasantly surprised. I hate the phrase "Everyone has a book in them." Sayings like that show how many people have no idea how much work is involved in just a single story. How many hours, how many read-throughs, how many tweaks and changes.

I can tell you who didn't support me; my year seven English

teacher. She felt I had a bad attitude, and perhaps I did with her as she seemed to be constantly on my case. I didn't have the same volatile relationship with any other teachers and would have been considered a good student before her influence. I was looking forward to telling her how I had a novella and a collection of stories published, at a high school reunion, but unfortunately, she wasn't there, so I didn't get to live out my revenge-fantasy of shoving my book in her face.

Much later, when I decided to go to university, I completed a science degree thinking it would offer me better opportunities for employment. It didn't. In hindsight I should have just done an arts degree and learnt a little more about the craft. It doesn't really matter. Every story is a new chance to learn and improve and I believe I grow as a writer all the time.

I remember the feeling of my first acceptance. It never gets old; that feeling. Even if you submit to a publication where you're confident your story will be accepted, you still give a little "yay," when that acceptance email comes through. There is certainly a feeling of validation to having a publisher enjoy your writing. It actually took a while before I believed I was a good writer and it wasn't just 'a fluke'. Writers often have impostor syndrome. You can go from feeling like a creative genius one day, to a complete fraud the next. Rejections are easier to take the more you get. If it's not a good fit, you still have a (hopefully) great story to submit elsewhere.

I'm not sure I can pinpoint what life influences have affected my writing. Every heartbreak or death, moments of joy and everything in between seeps into a writer's work. One major life curveball would be my diagnosis of a rare type of cutaneous skin lymphoma called Sezary Syndrome. It's a strange disease, the biggest disruption to my health being a constant itching of my skin and the subsequent disturbance to my sleep. The fact that it took about four years to get the diagnosis means I haven't sleep well for a very long time. Writing is well known to be cathartic, and there have definitely been a few stories I've written recently where the protagonist has a strange itch or requires a bone marrow transplant, much like my lucky self.

I can't say whether cancer will make me a better or worse writer, or person. I've always had an appreciation for life, but I have a lot less empathy than I used too. People complaining about minor things compared to cancer can be frustrating, and when I hear of someone in their eighties dying, now I think "Lucky bastard, I hope I make it to my eighties."

There is a possibility I could reject the bone marrow transplant, get a serious infection or a number of other complications and die. Potential side-effects of bone marrow transplants are numerous and terrifying, but this procedure is my only option. Having cancer sucks, but it's not going to stop me from writing. At least my stories will be my legacy to the world.

But not yet. What would my dog think? It's time to put on my fighting pants. Full recovery can take up to two years; that's a lot of writing time. So, I'll use this disease to drive me to write; to learn; to grow. I'll find motivation from fellow writers, and the support of my family and friends and I'll kick its arse. Because I have many more stories to tell. Watch this space. I might be different, but I'll be here.

I, Writer.

I, Survivor.

R.A. Goli is an Australian writer of horror, fantasy, and speculative short stories. She is currently fighting an epic battle against the villainous, Sezary Syndrome, a rare type of cancer. Interests include reading, gaming, the occasional cemetery walk, and annoying her chihuahua, two cats, and husband. It is rumored she has two imaginary werewolf cubs living under her bed.

I, CHITRA GOPALAKRISHNAN

Think of a game like this. You draw rows of dots, separated by a generous half-inch, in a grid of ten by ten columns. Each player takes a turn connecting one dot to another, horizontally or vertically, one move at a time. After a while, the board begins to fill with a series of horizontal and vertical lines, some connected, some not.

As a fifty-eight-year-old Indian woman, now living in New Delhi, my life has been about connecting the game dots quite like this, or not, sometimes looking back and then ahead.

After an undergrad and masters in literature in the city I live in, preceded by a school life in the south of India, that etched many writers into my consciousness leading to an excitable, mnemonic mind, and followed by a packed, full-time career in reporting, then in social development communications for non-government organizations, which took up 25 years of my working life, with their many frequencies of equal intensities, I veered off in my forties into a different game of dots. A board game where I played solo for the first time in my life.

This is a game where many of the dots do not connect, are not meant to connect. It goes by the name of freelance writing. This gig takes you to an amorphous space that makes it easy to wander into many open, unconnected stretches and loiter in them at will. It is an enterprise that allows you to feel the raw, throbbing kinetic energy of these unconfined expanses.

Yet, on hindsight, the spaces I chose in this side-hustle were familiar, or at least somewhat familiar. They were tame and natural corollaries to my earlier pursuits intended to draw in money. At this stage, I was far too fragile to bring myself to risk spaces that were out of my comfort, to enter areas where my center of gravity tottered. My fear of facing realities with unsteady rhythms or futures whose certainties did not stand was too deep.

When the stable spaces I sought began shrinking, over the years, with cash crunches becoming real, with social media overtaking traditional reports, with age making me not-so-useful and with-it anymore and with my family's move into the city's outlying part which forced isolation upon me, I had to learn the art of playing the game differently.

Whether the mindfulness I came to in this game of dots, where miraculously the dots seemed to connect at the tapering end of my career, happened by the slow dawning of consciousness or through a series of spontaneous mental sparks, I cannot say with certainty.

All I can say is that when my dormant imagination became ignited, I saw the face in the flickering flames, what people call the "big picture," the past side of yesterday and the yet-to-come side of tomorrow.

I knew had to keep writing. But writing differently. Writing for me. Not putting out other's truths or messages but mine. I had to make my isolation, my imagination work for me.

This was where a lifetime of cerebral acrobatics was leading to me. To fiction.

To a disposition that allowed me to challenge beliefs. To be open to new ideas. To make unreasoning a reality. To make anomalies the norm. To build on ideas and turn them into something entirely different. And, more, to accept that sometimes, oftentimes, there are no solutions and that to live with uncertainty is all there is to life.

In the two years that I have been writing fiction, I may be still joining sentences and stringing ideas together as I have done all through my studying and working life. But this experience is radically different. Like a leap across the chasm. Because here I trade beyond experience and am able to produce something that never existed before by putting together a range of disconnected pieces together in a manner never attempted before.

It may be of small consequence to many but it is my soul journey. One that is satisfying in its aloneness, in the soul-rich interiorities it takes me into and in the buoyed up life force it infuses

110

within me. In the same measure, this journey of mine with words is intensely frightening…when it drags me into inchoate spaces where meaning, reason, logic and time lose their shape.

To say that fiction has turned my worldview, my sense of smell, touch, feel and taste for life upside down is an understatement. I live now with ears beneath my feet, with fragrant secrets in my eyes and with the courage to refuse to conform to expectations. I have developed the courage to sit in the corner meant for fools. I am happy to just write even when the financial returns are poor. Or none. The dunce cap makes me happy even though I know many of my well-earning friends scorn and pity me by turn.

Two years, hence, I have no means to tell you where creativity comes from in fiction or how it works. Why words flow with felicity on days but curdle up on others. Or why now my life will henceforth always be about this process, about this restless, insane effort where my mind is never at rest. Or why this space is and will remain the only one where my brain and the universe meet.

Chitra Gopalakrishnan uses her ardor for writing, wing to wing, to break firewalls between nonfiction and fiction, narratology and psychoanalysis, marginalia and manuscript. As a New Delhi-based journalist and a social development communicator for 30 years, she enjoys this career of trying to figure out issues of social development and its impact – or the lack of it – on people. Her fiction has appeared in the *Celestial Echo Press, Black Hare Press, Me First Magazine, Terror House Magazine, Literary Yard, Truancy, Spillwords, Fleas on the Dog, Twist and Twain, Sky Island Journal, Scarlet Leaf Review, Breaking Rules Publishing* and *Runcible Spoon.*

I, DAVID GREEN

I've finished. At last. This new piece, my magnum opus, has taken weeks to write; hours of typing and planning. I've scratched my scalp long into the darkness of every night for the last month as I mold it into a state people can read.

My beta-readers like it. Some love it and want more. Isn't that great? The highest compliment a writer could ask for. It made them *feel*. I've gone through it one more time; read it out loud in my slowest, clearest voice. Tried an unfamiliar accent, too, just to hear how it sounds from someone else. Not like that ever works.

That word; that pesky, passive "was." Struck from the record. Adverbs, too. I used to hear famous authors pour scorn on them, saying they made your writing weak.

"What's so bad about them?" I'd say, sprinkling "ly's" around my sentences like confetti.

Not anymore, a few rejection letters saw to that. I try to learn from each one, as I take rejection to heart, despite knowing it comes with the territory.

So it's done. The email's typed out, ready to send. My bio, the thing I loathe to write, stares back at me. Black font on a white screen, boasting of my perceived prowess. I struggle with it, I'm not that interesting.

"It's going to get rejected, you know. Magnum opus. Who are you kidding?"

That voice in my head. Pondering my bio has let it in.

Doubt.

It plagues me, and I often give in to it. My old, familiar friend.

"I know," I reply with a heavy sigh. The optimism I feel for any finished work fades soon after completing it.

I move the cursor, hover it over the send button, but don't click it. Instead, I stare through it, thinking of the days and weeks I'll spend waiting for the reply. Convincing myself that a "sorry, not this time" will wing its way back to me.

"Why do you even bother?" Doubt asks, its whisper filled with gloating. "You're a hack. No-one cares about what you write."

"I enjoy it," I mutter, trying to silence the part of my brain it comes from.

"Do you?" Doubt replies with a cruel laugh. "Tell me the truth."

My eyes flick beyond the computer screen and fasten on the baby monitor sitting to its side. It shows my son, fast-asleep, dreaming of who knows what. I ask him every morning. He always says "Mummy."

We've spent the entire day together, like we do most days. At one point, he told me to call him Max, and he responded by barking as he attempted to lick my arm. He's three just before Christmas and told me he wants a scooter from Santa so he can play with the girls outside. We read stories today. Tales about bears in caves and pirates searching for riches.

I watch him, and I smile as he mumbles something in his sleep, his little hands raised into the air before the fall above his head on the pillow.

"I write," I tell my doubt, "because one day, I want him to pick up a book with my words in it, and I want him to feel proud of his Dad."

Doubt evaporates, as if it never sank its claws in my mind. I click send and decide to take the rest of the night off.

David Green is a writer from Manchester, UK and now lives in Galway, Ireland. Beginning his writing journey in 2020, David has appeared in fifteen anthologies spanning genres such as fantasy, horror and science-fiction and will release his debut novelette in November 2020, as well as his debut novel in March 2021.

I, E.A. GREEN / THE GREENMAN

To those who don't know me personally, I am Author E.A. Green and I go by The Greenman. Those that do know me either call me Ed or Eddie amongst close friends and family. Currently, my publisher at Breaking Rules—"due to my writing style"—refers to me as The Really Extremely Dark and Fucked Up One.

Something we both like to laugh about.

That Dark Morbidity was planted early in my life thanks to my dad Denis Lancaster and his love of horror movies.

This is where I give my age.

In 1974 "at the age of five" we watched *The Texas Chainsaw Massacre* at our drive-in theater. In 1976 it was *Carrie*, in 1977 it was the *Incredible Melting Man*, and in 1979 it was *Dawn of the Dead*.

Now this is where the true depth of my dad's depravity really shows. In 1980 "at the age of thirteen and just two weeks before going to summer camp," he took us to see *Friday the 13th*. And wouldn't you know it; the camp was not only in a very large forest nestled on a big lake, but our campsite was the very last one at the end of a very long trail set in the darkest part of the forest.

RIGHT WHERE THE KILLER ALWAYS STARTS!

My love for reading is due to my wonderful grandmother who began teaching me years before I was old enough to start school. By the time first grade ended I was already reading at a third-grade level. By third grade it was a sixth-grade level, and then there wasn't anything that could hold me back and keep me from reading whatever my hands could get ahold of.

That first book to grasp my attention was *For the Love of Benji*.

I read that book over eight times.

Then came *Where the Red Fern Grows*, *A Wrinkle in Time*, followed by my first really big book, *Watership Down*.

It wasn't until my senior year in high school—Go Pirates!—that

114

I attempted my hand at writing. The library had a poetry contest and, against all odds, I won First Place.

And with that, the writing bug began to scratch just beneath the surface of possibilities.

That's when, in 1993, I tried again, and my poem "Mother Earth" was picked by The International Poets Society, and I was invited as one of the 300 finalists to compete for a $10,000 writing contract in Washington D.C.

Sadly, I didn't win but thankfully I was paying attention and understood its valuable lesson.

They were not looking for or interested in a writer with a cause or a cross to bear. They were looking for the storyteller.

The exact same thing all readers are searching for too.

A great story.

And that's when my handwritten notes for M.A.D. started. Now most would think that this would end up being my first published book, but it wasn't. M.A.D. Malphas, Angelo, Dumas ended up being my ninth book and it's still not finished.

My first published book ended up being *Year Of The Cicada*, and that book took sixteen years before it came to fruition. That time frame was due to the fact that it was only the title, "not the story," that popped into my head in 2004. The story wasn't born until 2012 while sitting on my front porch listening to the windchimes as a supercell began to blow into Oklahoma City.

As a professional writer one of the best pieces of advice that I can give to a newbie is to never lose an idea or discount it as nothing more than a brain fart. Some of the best stories to date have come to an author through their dreams or a dumb idea.

So Always take that random thought serious.

Thankfully, I seem to be one of those rare individuals who can not only pull a story out of thin air sometimes, but I also have the ability to remember most of my dreams.

I'm the guy who wakes up screaming because of how vivid they can be at times.

I'm also the guy who will knock the shit out of you if you are not careful about how you approach me while sleeping.

A few of my friends and family can attest to that due to their busted lip or bent glasses.

"Oops. LOL."

By now a few of you have noticed my unusual writing style. I like to use capitalization in the middle of a sentence when I'm trying to stress an opinion or fact.

Just like I do with all characters in my books.

If a character is upset and trying to get their point across, I will stress that by Capitalizing the 1st letter of Every Word. If they are Extremely Upset, I will CAPITALIZE The Entire Word.

Seems that kind of writing can be off putting because most writers don't do that.

But I'm not most writers.

I don't just wish for you to read that the character is upset, I Want You To FEEL IT Too.

Seems that another famous Author used to write that same way and I am More Than Honored to have my writing compared to his.

Vonnegut.

Kurt Vonnegut.

WHAT AN HONOR.

That honor of being compared to another author now includes Steven King with my book *Year Of The Cicada*. Just recently my latest book *Real Skin* has been compared to Thomas Harris the Author of *Hannibal*.

My goal is for my fans to eventually have no one that can be related to me due to my uniqueness.

My hope is to eventually be defined as One Of A Kind.

So, if your itching to read something that actually makes you feel what the character is feeling as they start to scream or fight for their lives, The Greenman has just the story for you.

Author E.A. Green/The Greenman's books can be purchased at

Breaking Rules Publishing and through Amazon and most online book retailers. To date there are 10 published books by this Author. Four novels, *Year Of The Cicada, Father May I, Flesheaters* and *Real Skin*, three children's books, two short stories, "Just Jellies" and "M.A.D." And an anthology containing one short story and two of my children's series *Don't Let The Bedbugs Bite, Bedbugs 4* and *Delta Dawn.* Future release dates are pending.

I, HÁKON GUNNARSSON

I've been told that once I started talking, I started to tell stories. They all began: "I know a man…" and then I would go on for an hour or two. All from that beginning. Apparently, I was very open as a child, but then for some reason I started to withdraw into my shell, and I took my stories with me. They kept on coming though. I can't remember a time when there wasn't a story playing in my head. I could go on with the same one for days, weeks, and occasionally, months at a time.

When I finally learned how to read, my love for other people's stories began, but I didn't like school very much. What I was into, wasn't to be found in school books. When I finished the Icelandic equivalent of the American high school, I was just scraping the bottom. I could tell you that I just liked reading different stuff than they wanted me to read in school, and that wouldn't actually be a lie, but it wouldn't be the full story either. You see, by the time I was in my teens I'd found another way to express myself. When I should have been working on the school stuff, I was much more likely to have a camera clued to my face, or be in the darkroom developing films, or printing photos.

So when I'd made my way through the educational system, the principal of my school told my dad that I wasn't cut out for studying, and he had a point. I got a job, as a laborer in a dairy, slicing cheese, boxing cheese, turning cheese around, working machinery that made cheese, and basically doing all sorts of cheese making things. My work life was cheese, but with a lot of reading and camera work in my spare time.

My favorite photographic subject was landscape, and for while I thought about making a career out of that. I started a postcard company, and sold a bit of my photography through that, mostly colorful picture postcardy landscapes of tourist destinations. My heart was much more into B&W photography though. That was

118

where I could express myself the best. This postcard company never really took off. I don't think I ever gave it enough time to develop.

A few years doing this, and I came to a fork in the road. Did I want to continue to be a dairy worker? Or did I want to do something else with my life? Turns out, I didn't want to continue to make cheese for a living, so I applied for university, which probably sounds like the most ridiculous thing that someone that didn't like school could do, but that's what I did anyway. Maybe to prove my principal wrong, who knows?

Anyway, it worked. Probably because I found the correct way through it. No, I didn't go there to study photography. In fact, when I started university, I gave up on my photography. I went to university to read books in the comparative literature department. I'd always loved to read, even though the school system wasn't very good at choosing the right literature for my taste, so it seemed like a good idea. Five years, stacks of books, and surprisingly many films later I finished university with a good enough MA degree to go for a Ph.D., but I'd had enough of studying so I didn't go further down that road.

I wanted to write. I began writing a book on cinema. One thing about my time in comparative literature. I wrote a lot about films during that time, my BA essay was about Disney, and my MA essay about James Bond, so I figured I'd continue to write about films. But the book I wanted to write, never really came together. Out of the frustration about not being able to get it off the ground, I started to write stories instead.

That felt like coming home. It was like that was what I was supposed to be doing. So instead of telling stories like I used to do as a kid, or having stories that just played in my head as a teenager, I was now writing them down. There was never any shortage of material to write, time was more of an issue. Years pass, and one of my dog dies. He'd insinuated himself into my writing routine, and when he died I couldn't make myself sit down to write stories anymore. The reason may have had something to do with the odd fact that the last story I wrote before he died was about losing a dog, even though I had no idea I was just about to lose him. Days, weeks, months passed and I couldn't sit down to write. Finally, I got myself a camera, and started to photograph again, and a strange thing happened. I could write again. It came easy.

That's when I realized that in my head there is this an ongoing struggle between those two things, the photographic and the narrative. When I look at a photo of people, I hear a story. When I read a book, I see a photo. That's why so many of my short stories begin their life with me looking at photos. Mostly other people's photos, because my own photography tends to be more conceptual than narrative. Landscapes, flowers, animals, compositions, but very few people. My stories on the other hand can sometimes take on a photographic form. For example, there is a short story I wrote about a photographer working, taking B&W photos, and there are references to black, white, and shades of gray, but there are no colors at all in the story. So this short story is in B&W, like the photos the photographer in the story is taking. That's how these two elements seem to live in my head, and turn into stories.

Hákon Gunnarsson is an Icelandic writer, who has an MA in comparative literature, and has written fiction, and nonfiction. Even though he did at one point want to become a novelist, he fell for the short story, and sticks mostly to that form these days. His work has appeared in literary journals, and anthologies in Icelandic, and English. His only solo project so far is called *Swimming in Space: A Collection of Sci-Fi-ish Flash Fiction.*

I, MARLON HAYES

When I was a boy growing up in the urban landscape of Chicago, my mother provided me a window of escape by teaching me to love books and reading, and I viewed them as magical carpets that could whisk me away to different worlds and different eras. My grandmother would read me the poetry of renowned Black poets and I fell in love not only with the cadence of their prose, but also with how they conveyed a feeling or a story in so few words. I felt the magic of their work, and I wrote my first poem when I was five years-old.

As time passed by, my love affair with written words intensified. I wrote poems which I displayed to my mother, and then, in sixth grade, other people found out about my so-called talent as a writer. I wrote a short story based on a prompt, and not only did I receive an 'A' on the paper, the story was passed on to others, and I was placed in the Gifted Writing Program of the Chicago Public Schools. One day a week, I had to attend another school, where I and fourteen other children learned how to write.

I guess the world of writing opened up for me then. Over the next three years, I learned iambic pentameter, haiku, story arcs, and the difference between wanting to write and needing to write. There are people who have learned all of the skills needed to be a good writer, and they yearn to write something fresh and entertaining, but it's hard for them. They want to write, and then there's the people like me, who sometimes hate writing, but our souls aren't at peace unless we're scribbling or typing away. I was challenged by my writing teachers to find something to write about every day, whether an essay, a poem, or a story. They taught me to never sit down to write a story with preset boundaries, but to let it flow into whatever it was meant to be. I carry that lesson with me still, and even though I may sit down with the intention of writing a short story, it may blossom into a novella, a novel, or even a series. No limits and no boundaries became my mantra as a writer, and it has served me well.

In high school, I kind of got lost in the shuffle, because I wanted to blend in socially more than stand out academically. I hid my writing from the world, except for the women I attempted to woo with my poetry. I think that part of it worked out nicely, but I abandoned my dream of being a professional writer because it seemed too hard and not financially beneficial. I buried my talent in the closet, only bringing it out on occasion to write poems for obituaries or stories which I didn't show anyone. I felt as if no one would care or be inspired by the writings of a guy who didn't even finish college.

I became an "Over-the-road" (OTR) truck driver in 1998, and I found myself filling up spiral notebooks with poetry and stories inspired by the places I saw in America. The need to write had returned, and I indulged myself whenever I could. I started transcribing my written work onto my computer, with the result being our computer slowed down. My wife insisted that I "find something to do with all of this." I read an article about how to self-publish a book, and I only read enough to clear up space on the home computer. I put together a book 'The Colors of My Mind' with poems and short stories and I wept when I received it in the mail.

Looking back, I can only shake my head because I didn't know enough then to successfully publish a book, and there was no one in my world to help me. I knew I had a lot to learn, and I set out to become a better writer. Meanwhile, I was earning money as a Spoken Word poet, having one-man shows, writing and performing at weddings, graduation celebrations, and even bachelorette parties, where the "customers" requested ribald limericks and erotic poems. For a while, I earned decent money reciting my own poetry. It wasn't enough.

I joined writing groups on Facebook, and I listened to the advice being given by what I assumed were seasoned writers. A few of them were, but the majority were at my level, and while they might know what worked for Neil Gaiman or Stephen King, they couldn't quite figure out what would help them with their writing. I went back to my lessons from the Gifted Writing Program, with the motto of "no limits and no boundaries." I began to write in multiple genres, just to see if I could do it. Romance, suspense, erotica, Westerns, and even Sci-fi. No fear.

I did receive some valuable pieces of advice from a couple of writers, and I'll share them here, because they might help someone else on this path. The first piece of advice was from a writer named Kari Holloway who told me to "quit treating writing as a hobby, and treat it like a job." The second piece of advice was from another writer, who told me "if you get stuck in your writing, exhale, close the file, and start something new." Those two pieces of advice keep me writing daily, and juggling multiple projects, adding a new project when I finish something.

I received my first publishing contract in 2016 for a short story "Daddy's Boy" and it made me hunger for more. I'm an eager student, and I've learned a lesson with each success or failure. Since that first contract, I've signed dozens more, and it hasn't made me arrogant or given me a swelled head. It's made me thankful for the people and lessons that have helped me along this path…

Marlon S. Hayes is an author from Chicago, Illinois, who loves cooking, sports, and traveling. He's self-published six books, and his stories and essays have appeared in multiple anthologies and magazines. In the fourth quarter of 2020, his debut novel 'Eleven Fifty Nine' will be released by Oghma Creative Media. A short story collection 'In the Pale Moonlight' will be released by Voices from the Bleachers Publications.

I, RICK HAYNES

I was born in South London, England, not long after the end of the Second World War. My family was poor, but I never knew because my childhood was fun.

I was lucky enough to be offered a place at a local grammar school, but any desire to read was lost in a world of sport and watching those strange and beautiful creatures - girls. Even though I had to study English Literature, general reading didn't interest me.

Little changed until my 30th year. I read the *Lord of the Rings* and was captivated. I began to devour books. Anne McCaffery with her dragons, Isaac Asimov with his robots, Brian Herbert with his giant sand worms, I was truly hooked, but time moved on and my interest in reading ebbed away once more.

In my 50's, I read a book about a hero, Druss, a giant with a code of honour, and my love of David Gemmell's work exploded.

Like a kid I fell under the spell of pure imagination, yet I still had no desire to write. But time waits for no one and my body started the downward spiral into decay. I was diagnosed with cervical spondylitis in the neck in 2006 and was forced to give up my job that I loved, due to the pain, but I wasn't finished at the hospital, not by a long way. I went so many times that they nearly gave me my own parking space. As if ? But as a substitute they did give me a lollipop for being a good boy - true.

In all, I had five knee ops, two shoulder ops, several injections in my neck and was diagnosed asthmatic.

Why is it they give you a nice shiny metal knee and forget the oil can? My knee squeaks louder than a horde of mice at times.

After so many months of housebound imprisonment, I was sitting in the lounge, feeling sorry for myself. I asked my beloved where I should go, to release me from my incarceration.

"Try the kitchen," she said.

"Come on love, what should I do?" I asked seriously.

"Try the washing up," she said. That didn't go down too well either.

But then my wife suggested I write my feelings down. It was that light bulb moment. I was up the stairs just faster than a snail, and I started typing. Only I couldn't type but I'm a tenacious sod and I refused to give in.

I eventually wrote a diary of getting old. I had no idea what to do next but a local writing group had started and I joined. I showed them my work. Euphoria lasted 5 minutes as I saw their faces. They were trying to be kind but my writing was crap. I did the only thing that I could. I listened, learnt and spread my wings. My teacher was inspirational and her style of teaching suited my fledgling career perfectly.

I started writing Drabbles, those little 100 word gems, and won an international Drabble competition with:

SPECTRAL MORNING by Rick Haynes

As the dew gently caressed the leaves in the wood, a soft light slowly grew in luminance. The coalescing sparkles began to take the shape of a young girl. A pure white gown swished and swirled around her as she moved towards the graveyard, her slender feet leaving no tracks in the soft soil.

The fresh grave had been hastily re-filled but all her attention was focused on the sobbing cries of a terrified infant.

Holding out her hands to the cold earth, she spoke soothingly.

"Come forth you beautiful child, for I will take you to your true home."

I got my first break soon after. Four authors had decided to write an adult story for Halloween, Drabble style, but one pulled out and I was invited. It's a naughty, sexy, adult tale. It was fun and my confidence grew. Along came a novella for all the family, short story collections and eventually three novels.

Writing my first novel, *Evil Never Dies*, scared me to death. I remember talking to myself. "How do I start? Where do I start?" I had the shakes. In the end the answer was simple. I found the right cover and drew a map of my imaginary world, and then I was up and running like a three-legged donkey. The imagination flowed, I became a recluse, and divorce papers were issued. Ha! Ha! As if?

Evil Never Dies was professionally edited, published, and we took a holiday as my wonderful wife needed a break more than I did. I love her dearly for her support is amazing.

I am pleased to say that so far it has received 15 reviews all 4 or 5 star. And it made my day when 2 top reviewers likened by book to those of the great David Gemmell.

After a good break, I started the follow up but had no idea where it was going. *Heroes Never Fade* is the 2ndin the Maxilla trilogy but is a standalone book. Once more a reader compared my work to that of David Gemmell, but this time it was an Amazon top 500 reviewer. They loved *Heroes Never Fade* and my head was in the clouds but with much humility.

I'll continue to write until my time is up, for the power of my imagination is beyond measure and I love to see my tales on paper. Like tiny seeds they gradually grow and blossom into one magnificent tree.

I always say this to my wife. 'This time next year love, we'll be millionaires.' I'll leave you with this thought.

If you don't have dreams, how can they ever come true?

Rick Haynes is passionate about writing. His fantasy novels, *Evil Never Dies, Heroes Never Fade, Outcast* and his collections of short stories, have received excellent reviews. Here are two of them. '*Game of Thrones* fans must read *Heroes Never Fade*. "Chocolate Chunks from Crazy Crete" landed on my Kindle this morning and I haven't stopped laughing.' Want to know more? Take a peek on Amazon. With humour running through his veins and his eyes sparkling with the thought of another funny story bubbling away inside his head. Rick warmly welcomes you to the world of his vivid imagination.

I, NANCY LOU HENDERSON

Where do I start telling you about my journey to become a writer? It was never my intention to be a published writer/author, but that all changed for me at age sixty-five. Sitting on my patio, hot and sweaty from yard work, and having been a widow for eighteen years, I said a prayer to God for a renewal of purpose in my life. That night I had a dream, which led me to an old cedar chest sitting in a shed in my backyard. This cedar chest contained letters written to me by my husband, Frank, while he was in Vietnam in 1971. The prayer, dream, and letters put me on a course of writing a memoir and becoming a writer/storyteller/author.

God has always been the most significant influence in my life, and I have felt his love surround me since a small child. Another influencer in my life was my grandmother. She was a go-getter with a bigger than life personality, and she taught me that you could achieve anything that you set your mind to do. My parents were high school teachers who showed us all so much love and introduced me to the love of learning and giving my best in all I did. At eighteen years old, I found my soulmate, Frank, we married, and then he and I set off together to see new places. Frank taught me self-confidence and belief in myself. He did this by loving me profoundly and unconditionally for who I am, encouraging me to love myself.

Growing up as a child in the 1950s was so different than now. Since my family lived in the Panhandle of Texas, we spent most of our time outdoors using our imaginations to make many inventions out of scraps of wood, tin cans, string, rope, and bent nails. The Little Rascals had nothing on us.

While playing outside, we spent lots of time tunneling in the sand, digging holes for forts, playing dirtball on a makeshift dirt baseball field, riding on boards with old metal skates nailed on them for wheels, throwing balls over the house playing Annie Over. After dark, we rang doorbells then would run and hide or play the old sling the statue game. These things all taught me about the beauty of a carefree childhood and the appreciation of costless treasures of fun. Being the only girl and number two in the pecking order with four brothers helped me to understand a lot about the male species in general. Much to my surprise, my brothers though all different in personalities and emotions, were only different from me physically. I think growing up with them gave me more in-depth insight beyond the preconceived notion that men have to be fearless and tough. Marrying Frank while he was in the Army, then moving to Massachusetts, Okinawa, and then back to Texas, opened my eyes to so many new cultures and different ideas. Having been born and raised in Texas up until that time, I found that even northerners seem like actual foreigners. Living around other races and cultures solidified in my heart that I could never be a racist and that racism has no place in this world. All of the above experiences have affected the way I write and what I write.

Tragic experiences in life either break or strengthen us, but they always give us an inside perspective of how they affect us and how we handled them. When Frank served his last tour of duty in Vietnam in 1971, I learned how the genuine fear of losing a soulmate love feels. After trying to have a child for six years, being told that tests showed Frank and I would not ever have a child, on October 15, 1973, our only child, a son, was born. I knew God had given us a real miracle strengthening my trust in Him in all things. In 1997 after 29 years of marriage, Frank suddenly became ill. After five days in a coma in the Neuro ICU, after a blood flow test showed no blood flow to his brain, I made the lone decision to turn off the machines that were keeping him alive. Setting by his bed, holding his hand and praying he would breathe on his own, but knowing he would not, I watched him die, and he took half of my heart and soul with him. I know a broken heart and profound grief. When I allowed myself to breakdown and cry, Frank touched me, and his spiritual being has remained by my side ever since, reinforcing my belief in life eternal, giving me no fear of death.

Having always been an outline person, I did not have a problem in deciding how to set up my Memoir, but while writing and having the tunneling experiences of being in the room like an invisible third party watching and hearing Frank and me, came as quite a surprise. Computer knowledge for me was a real bummer of no experience, so at age sixty-eight, I learned how to set up a website. Since considering my Memoir to be a God-given project, towards the end of its completion, I branched out into seeing if I could write fiction, wondering if I was a real writer. Since I believe that inanimate objects pickup and store energy from emotions of life around them, I began to write perspective stories and poems with the object telling the story. As I watched my great-grandchildren play, poetry filled my mind, so I wrote them each a poem.

Rejection and criticism, as a writer, makes me want to do better, but not change my style. Although I am learning in writing that a denial of publication of a story or poem on one site can mean acceptance on another. Confusing, but a choice of style. I have also learned to trust my gut instinct. If I am enjoying what I am writing, then usually others do too.

Nancy was born and raised in Texas, where she met and married her soulmate in 1968. Frank was in the Army, so they lived in Massachusetts then Okinawa together before Frank went to Vietnam in 1971. When he returned home, they returned to Texas. In January of 1997, Nancy became a forever widow and is still devoted to her soulmate. After a prayer and a dream in 2015, she discovered a box of letters. God's inspiration led her to write and publish a four-book Memoir, including all letters. Nancy has branched out into writing Flash Fiction, Short Stories, and Poetry.

I, SHEILA HENRY

It was July 11, 1972 when I got my first job working for a major insurance company. I was excited because I got the clerk typist position I wanted. I had recently taken a beginner's typing course, and I looked forward to using those skills. To me the typing position was much more prestigious than the clerical position where the functions were to post figures and filed cases. So in applying for the job, everything banked on my ability to pass the required typing test. I was barely efficient at typing. I typed about 50-60 words a minute, if that much. But fortunately, it was sufficient for me to meet the requirements to get the sought-after position.

Once in, I worked hard, did my job well and made sure my supervisors knew I was a star performer. I was quite the ambitious young woman always on the lookout for advancement opportunities in the company. Throughout the years, I applied for several positions that suited me, and quickly worked my way up in the company.

One such opportunity was a higher-level position, Technical Claims Supervisor, that increased my job functions vastly. It included written correspondences to insureds and/or their representatives to explain the company's position—why a medical procedure was deemed not necessary and therefore not covered for benefits under their plan. My prior positions did not require much writing. I remember for a few months I agonized about how to improve my writing. I knew I had a big problem. I did not write well. In fact, my writing was horrible, and definitely not okay to represent me or the company. My sentences were too long, they went on forever without proper punctuation.

However, I found a means to get around my lack of skills. I parroted from filed letters previously written by the department's senior, and altered them to fit my particular case. Is that plagiarism? After a while, this got old. It was not my idea of writing and it was not something I wanted to do for the rest of my life, poach on someone else's ideas. It got me thinking that I needed to learn the craft. And that's the point when my writing journey began.

The first reference source I used was a book on how to write a proper sentence and how to use punctuation. I don't remember its name. It was a skinny book with about 80 pages. The contents of which improved my writing skills considerably. It was only the first of many teaching sources I used throughout the years to develop my craft. I can still hear Natalie Goldberg's voice like the sound of a drone in my ear. I listened to a few of her books on tapes—*Writing Down the Bones, Thunder and Lightning: Cracking Open the Writer's Craft, The True Secret of Writing* and there were others. I didn't have to sit in a classroom to learn the skills I got from Ms. Goldberg's teachings; "Show vs. Tell", I think was one of the most valuable tools I've learned from her. "Don't just say it's a flower, what color is it." As a matter of fact, "Imagery" is what I love most about reading Hemingway's work. Yes, I also learned to write by reading the works of writers whose work I enjoyed. Danielle Steele was another of those writers.

I had previously set my writing goals to write memoirs. I've got many notebooks filled with nonsense written about my life to prove it. Not that the experiences were nonsense, but putting them down on paper was nonsensical.

One day, while at work, I was sitting at my desk with nothing to do, and out of boredom, I wrote a poem. I asked myself the universal question, "Who am I?" The following is a quote from that poem. I wrote

> I am the breath of life;
> Vacillating from day to day;
> Wondering what's right from what's wrong;
> Wishing I was more than I am;
> Forever wanting more;
> Giving, loving, caring, forgiving;
> Breaking the rules and repenting as I go along;

Enjoying the ride as I aspire to achieve;
I am... who I am.

I've written a lot more since then. I feel at ease writing poetry more than any other genre. It's less of an effort, and I have a great working relationship with my muse who is way smarter than me. I've only submitted my work to one press so far. But you won't believe the trauma I put myself through when I release my work for public viewing.

I think my writing journey exemplifies what one can achieve by saying "Yes, I can do it." And that goes for anything we dream of doing!

On Trinidad, the larger island of The Republic of Trinidad and Tobago is where Sheila Henry was born. After a rewarding childhood, she migrated to the United States in the summer of 1969. Soon thereafter she became a Naturalized Citizen. Though she never took a Poetry class, her passion for poetry compelled her to a prolific self-scholarship. Perhaps it is the reason her writing style can best be categorized as Visual Poetry, blending emotion and vision into a poem of color. Sheila resides in New Jersey where she spends her time enjoying her grandchildren and preparing her collection of poetry for publication. Her poems are featured at *Spillwords* publications.

I, STEPHEN HERCZEG

"You are the perfect example of an only child."

In *The Young Ones*, Vyvyan's comment to Rik could be seen as a cutting demolition of the eighties (represented by Rik) by the seventies (represented by Vyvyan), or to someone like me, an actual only child living at that time with my single mother, it was something different altogether. I remember hearing the comment back in the eighties and it made me wonder, at the time, whether I was a perfect example of an only child.

I'm still unsure, but I do know I spent a lot of time alone.

At one stage we lived on the opposite side of the city to my school. So, building and maintaining friendships was a little difficult, plus living with one of Mum's boyfriends with, whom I shared a mutual lack of respect, brought its own level of withdrawal from the world.

I think it was having no siblings that tended to find me alone a lot of the time and drove me deeper into my own mind, there to create new worlds and characters in a way to entertain my young self.

My memories of my early life are a cavalcade of creation. There was always drawing and doodling, as a way of redirecting the fidgets that any young child develops. There was also Lego. Yes, even in the days when dinosaurs ran wild outside, we had those little colored blocks. They didn't come in as many neatly designed prefabricated models as they do today, just big bags and boxes of different shaped blocks. You had to use that thing called imagination to bring the bricks to life.

In my isolated world, I'd recreate episodes of *The Thunderbirds, Batman* and other shows. My train set also came in for the odd adventure and eventual rescue as well.

Still alone in my teens, I moved on to more drawings. My room was home to a hand drawn and colored map of Middle Earth, plus an entire wall dedicated to a hand copied interwoven mural of album covers from bands like Black Sabbath, Pink Floyd, Led Zeppelin, Iron Maiden, etc. I can state for a fact that my mum's boyfriend was not impressed by that.

Then came the writing.

My first big productions were a pair of comic books. Hand drawn and lettered via a typewriter. I was really into the *Alien* movie and wrote *Life of Alien* and *Alien Wars*. Basically, rip offs of *Life of Brian* and *Star Wars*, but with the alien xenomorph as the central character. I even wrote, in long hand, the start of a novel called *The Alien of the Rings*. You can guess what that's about. Strangely enough, I still have all of them. Possibly the most ancient artifacts of my life that I still possess.

Sometimes I do wonder. Did my life as an only child bring out the creative streak in me, or was it always there? Or was it more the fact that I leaned on my innate creative abilities as a way of coping with the solitude?

To seek out an answer, I checked up on some other notable only children in the literary world. They are few and far between, but include such writers as Hans Christian Anderson, Danielle Steel, E. M. Forster and Jean-Paul Sartre, plus some notable others like John Lennon and Robin Williams.

Disappointingly that didn't answer the question. All it did was to tell me that you can be an extremely creative person with or without siblings, but from a personal perspective, I feel that only children probably lean on their creative bents a lot more than those with siblings as a way of coping with the feelings of loneliness.

In researching the above, I did come across a book that I will definitely have to investigate, called *Only Child: Writers on the Singular Joys and Solitary Sorrows of Growing Up Solo*. The book is filled with essays from writers talking about their lives as only children. According to some of the reviews, most were basically lonely, and turned to reading and writing as an outlet. So, I can sort of relate, and it backs up my opinion. As an observation, I have a massive library of books and movies and have always been a voracious reader.

Those creative juices have never left me. Well into my adult hood I began to write once again in earnest. First it was prose, with a couple of attempts at novels, then screenplays, and finally back to prose.

The attraction to writing may be a remembrance of days long gone, or perhaps it is a way of being drawn back into that solitude. A return to a time when I was alone with my thoughts. A time that although isolated, brought untold joy through my shear creative endeavors.

Now, as I've grown older and have a wife, family and pets, I seek out time and places that possess that same solitude in which to write, but life has a way of getting in the way of such pursuits, so I have also developed a way of isolating myself from the world wherever I am, so that I can switch back into the writing mood when I need to. It can be a little disconcerting to those around me and can frankly be a pain when I'm drawn away from that world, as the return can take a lot of effort.

But, it is a productive place and one I seek out continuously.

Admittedly, at the time of writing this essay, I couldn't crave more for a return to that place of solitude, my son has returned home from school, come into the rumpus room which serves as my writing space and is playing *Fortnite* right next to me.

Plus, the batteries in my headphones just ran out.

Stephen Herczeg is an IT Geek based in Canberra, Australia. He has been writing for over twenty years and has completed a couple of dodgy novels, sixteen feature length screenplays and numerous short stories and scripts. He has had over fifty short stories and seventy micro-fiction drabbles published through *Hunter Anthologies*; *Things In the Well; Blood Song Books; Dragon Soul Press; Oscillate Wildly Press; Black Hare Press; Monnath Books; Battle Goddess*

Productions; Fantasia Divinity; The Great Void Books and *DeadSet Press*. He has also had numerous Sherlock Holmes stories published through *Belanger Books* and *MX Publishing*.

I, JESSE HIGHSMITH

Fiction is a steaming bowl of soup on an otherwise frigid table of ice. It's a melting pot of ideas that swirl around your brain cavity and fill your heart with warmth when all around you is desolate negativity and the illusion of purpose. We all crave entertainment. We all crave substance. We all crave escapism. "Why is that?" you might ask. Well, the truth is usually hard to swallow.

We're all chasing something. Usually, it's money, security, love, or good ole fashioned accomplishment. As for the latter, it can sometimes feel more important than all the rest. That is because we live in a great big world full of wonder and mystique, and daunting is the task of chipping our own mark within it. Difficult as it may be, the possibility of creation is there for the taking, and it *calls* to us.

We have created a societal structure based solely on numbers- births, deaths, sales, losses, etc. When it comes down to it, that's what we are. Statistics. Anyways, we're all competing for our own slice of heaven in a metaphorical diner that's been filled much more than any reasonable fire marshal would allow. I remember a time when another writer assaulted me with the question "what makes you think you're so special?" Now, I was heated, but I calmly thought on it, and my response was plain and simply "I'm not." In a world of nearly *8 billion people*, it's hard to think of oneself as special or above average in any way.

However, through stories, we can live in fantastical worlds of our own making, led by casts of colorful personalities that make us cherish the best sides of humankind. Therein lies the greatness. From my own rambling perspective, it is our *connections* with each other that make us special. That, and our ability to create. Our bonds, our shared passions, and our experiences shape who we are, and give us all purpose. Why do I want to be a writer? To tap into the very things that make us human, and to dig out the madness that resides in my head.

My writing journey started out small. Like most teenagers, I had a lot of pent up emotions I needed to release. As the son of a struggling single mother, I was not immune to the woes of poverty, abandonment issues, and that oh-so-difficult task of figuring out who I was. Poetry evolved into song lyrics, and music became my creative release over the years. Three of those years were also spent at a local college. My favorite courses were Ethics, Sociology, and Psychology, and ironically enough, I dreaded the 20-page English Composition report one professor threw my way. Unable to further fund my education, though, I did what many small-town youths had done. I dropped out to get a real job.

Last year, this pest control technician with a brilliant fiancée, a (then) seven-year-old son, a mortgage, and a cover band, decided he wanted more. I poured over one of my many stacks of notes and papers, and stumbled upon an old list of story ideas that had collected copious amounts of dust. It was time to brush them off and take a crack at it.

Very quickly, I learned that most of the ideas from yesteryear weren't as great as I had remembered. I scrapped many of them and decided to start fresh. I joined a few writer groups on Facebook, which gave tremendous insight into the industry. From there, I worked up the courage to challenge myself with flash fiction. The intimidation of story construction fell to the wayside when all I had to do was set up such simple scenes and make them modestly interesting. As for my blue-collar job in the service industry, it had opened my eyes to many ways of life, along with real-life characters that would inspire the people in my stories. After all, this is Florida...no one is immune to our *unique* wildlife.

The ideas didn't just trickle in, though. They poured. I filled many notebooks of basic story structures complete with twists, mysteries, and kooky characters. Most of which were fleshed out from back-to-front, because, as the infamous Mort Rainey said in *Secret Window, Secret Garden*, the ending is the most important part. I stand behind that statement, and use it as a basis for all of my works.

Of course, I'm partially inspired by King. I'm also inspired by George R.R. Martin's world building and effortless ability to let go of his best characters, seemingly without mercy or remorse. For some authors, that's a hard thing to do, and their stories suffer for it. I hope to avoid that pitfall as well. Another aspect of Martin's work that I absolutely live for is the flawless monologues and one-liners that he gives to Tyrion Lannister. Ideas such as using your flaws as armor? Brilliant! J.K. Rowling also achieved this with Albus Dumbledore. I guess the takeaway from this is that old adage: great things come in small packages. Flash fiction is a prime example.

At this very early point in my writing journey, I now have several drabbles published, along with one poem. It doesn't sound like much, but it is enough to have me hooked. The inevitable rejections to follow are frightful, but as my grandmother once said about her lotto tickets - "you can't win if you don't play." So play I will. I am currently knee deep in a pile of short stories for a collection, along with the several chapters of my first novel, and I have even begun a pair of children's stories that may just see the light of day. All of this resides on finding me time, of course. Speaking of time, I think I've rambled enough, for now. Take a sip of adventure, and don't burn your lips on someone else's imagination.

Jesse Highsmith is an aspiring wordsmith, musician, podcast enthusiast, and internet jokester from Central Florida, U.S. His specialty is short form flash fiction written within the confines of a large pesticide truck. However, he is currently writing the first of two novels, along with a collection of short stories. Much of his work centers around realistically flawed characters and a skewed perception of the world around them. He and his partner Sami live in a rural countryside with his son Logan, dog Snowy, and a shadow-chasing cat dubbed Sir Liam Frederick, Duke of Cuteness.

I, HEATHER HOOD

Why would anyone ever write about the worst moment in their life? There is only one reason: to help other people. In the time it takes to breathe, your life can change. When it does, you face a choice. Either you hide everything away where no one will ever see your feelings, or you use that incident as a springboard for change.

I became a writer to overcome pain. I worked as a psychiatric intake worker and later a palliative care home nurse when I returned from Mexico at the age of twenty-three. Those are intense, painful occupations, but it was Mexico that broke me. It was Mexico that made me start writing.

Picture a sunny beach where you are safe with a trusted friend, only to find that friend wasn't trustworthy. In the next instant, you are surrounded by twelve men who haul you to a house where you are held captive for the next three days. This is the stuff of nightmares. All you can think of is "What on earth have I done to deserve this?"

Don't waste your energy thinking that way, it won't help you. I had done nothing. This was supposed to be an honor killing – something I had never heard of, as a Canadian in the 1980's. My Mexican husband and I had lost our twins a week before. He was an alcoholic. In his mind he somehow twisted the information the doctor gave him into believing their early arrival meant I had been unfaithful to him. This was his way of getting back. I was not supposed to get out of that situation; I am small and slender and was recuperating from a cesarian delivery at the time.

Your brain does funny things to protect you in times of extreme stress. I have almost no memories of those three days, aside from flashbacks in episodes of PTSD: smells that trigger short scenes, flashes of light off glass where I remember being tied up in a courtyard made from mint-green, decorative cement blocks, the pain of coconut rope fibers that bit into my sunburned skin. And thirst.

Raging thirst – there was never enough water. I know what was done physically to me because I bear the surgical scars of later operations. But I can't remember the details, and I don't want to. I know I had to make choices if I wanted to get out of there alive.

Here it is. We all have a toolbox. It consists of everything we've learned in our life: those Tai Kwan Do lessons your parents bought for you, the Social Studies classes you hated in school where you learned about sociology and how sociopaths manipulate people. Maybe you learned how to act in a high school play. That's enough to save your life. Use those things to your advantage, play one person against the other. That bully that picked on you, he/she was an expert at that. Read their body language. Do whatever you have to, to get yourself out of the situation, hate yourself later. This isn't the movies, there is no hero coming to rescue you. Tell yourself you are strong. You are brave. You are resilient. Repeat it in your head like a mantra.

On the third night I managed to convince one of them to take me outside alone and I got away. I was blind by then, but it didn't matter, I was free. That was the scariest night of my life. The Yucatan jungle has tarantulas, scorpions, snakes that can kill you in five steps and so many different spiders, if I thought about them, I would still be there in a little heap beneath a tree. You put one foot in front of the other and pray, that's all. Someone found me and took me to my doctor.

It's taken a long time to tell this story. Many books and stories have gone before this one, so why now? I write everything with a purpose; to empower that one reader who may be suffering from something they can't talk about. This was my one thing. Somewhere out there is someone hurting because they think they are broken. They may have been told the things that have happened to them are just too awful to be true, that they've made the story up. That they are just looking for attention. They are suffering in silence thinking they are not worthy of love.

None of this is true.

You are worthy of a life full of happiness.

Your past is a stepping-stone, not a rickety bridge that makes your world collapse. Anyone who tells you otherwise, well, do you need that negativity in your life?

I'll just leave that thought with you.

Things take time to process and everyone's brain is different. Children are good at throwing things off faster than adults, so don't beat yourself up if you can't defeat trauma in one day. It's taken me forty years to get this far. I will never be able to take the final step and talk about forgiveness with my husband. He died in an earthquake. I must live with that layer of pain as well. No one ever said being human was easy.

Everything happens for a reason; this is something you must believe. When we go through intense emotional pain, we become sympathetic to those suffering around us. I find I write better characters because I understand what they are going through. I may not touch everyone with my words, and that's ok. For the person suffering, I may be the only one who can understand what they are feeling. If I help them, then my job is done. My words are sufficient. and isn't that what the job of a writer is all about?

There is nothing so terrible that we can't get through it together. When you read my books, I hope you take that message away with you.

Heather was a Psychiatric Nurse for 25 years (which explains her irreverence and sense of humour). She is also a Certified Herbalist on a small homestead in the Rockies of British Columbia Canada. She freelances for healthcare and gardening magazines, and blogs about writing and homesteading. She champions mental health and human rights.

I, PRITI J

For as long as I can remember, I have been good friends with words, and the ones who made me feel obliged to perform a swinging act between moments of quiet intensity, and a penchant to revel in the ridiculous. Over a quagmire - never forget the quagmire of embarrassment. Written ones, spoken ones, unspoken ones and unmentionable ones – I've had a lifelong affair with them all. Oh, so many ones. With all of them. Oh, I've been around with all of them! Ones you love for life, ones you wouldn't want mother to hear too...

Then, in a world where I could be anything - I chose to be a bank auditor. Then I started to complain about it, and even the bankers found me boring (with due respect to the color gray) "Get a major in finance," they said. "Join the exciting world of finance, they said!" Well, I'm looking for them now and they're hiding. If you see them, call me. There'll be a reward! I've traveled a bit, looking for them, and now can curse in nine languages. Yes, I have put sailors to shame. So I quit, and right on time as my daughter chose to present herself then, and earned her moniker "Jungle Girl." It's been a long five years. Are bank audits exciting yet? As you know by now, I also need to be told to stop talking. Never used a word where I could use four (read paragraph one) "Better sense prevails," they said. "But nonsense persuades," I retorted. Now I'm hiding and they're looking for me. Don't tell them - there'll be a reward. I also got a major in education while working - which thankfully nobody said I should.

Over time and circumstances, facing vagaries and trying to skip the vicissitudes (big words too) I found myself in the midst of some excellent company (my husband Jay's friends initially - the writing community he was part of) who became my dear ones eventually, rallied around me, helped me up, and set me down on firm feet. I found more comfort in the kindness and compassion I was shown

144

than ever. I'd always known writers to be a kind and sensitive tribe, and this reaffirmed my knowledge. I got a job as a teacher, teaching the 5th grade, and Covid struck.

Well, I can be a mule, and the ghost of creativity which lurks inside and lay dormant inside me ever since I quit the college debate team years ago began to take over my soul. It whispered "Priti, how would you like to write?" I was too weak to fight it. It had me dig into the maybe thousands books I must've read, and I wrote, I showed my work to some stellar writer friends, and was told it was good. That I should submit. I did, and publications started to accept:

ICW Magazine - my first publication, *CafeLit, Writers Club, Twine & Twain, Academy of the Heart and Mind, UNITY* anthology, *The Personal Bests Journal* edited by *David Gardiner* and many more accepted my writing and the word was I was with the words. Again!!! – I've always loved poetry and humor so I began with these genres. Everyone always said I'm a funny girl – I don't know what they meant by it, but I'll take it.

I started to write more, and I found the sensitive variety too... speaks to me. So now I write all three. The creative ghost wasn't satisfied with the writing I fed it - it had designs upon my mind. So I designed. I was encouraged to do more, write more, design more, and put it out there, by my friend, my benefactor and mentor, whom I owe all my success and happiness - Steve Carr. I put it out, and the community once again responded with alacrity. PritiJ Designs was added to Author PritiJ, and here we are, marketing manager for the excellent Sweetycat Press too!!!

I want to write; I want to make sense to someone who needs it on that particular day. It is for that day, that hour, that very mindset prevalent at that very minute - that I write. That moment when a sentence alleviates hopelessness and provides a sense of relief. That moment. I've been there, so I know!

I warned you earlier. I need to be told to zip it. But will I listen? That's another essay altogether!!!

Priti J has lived a life across cultures. She is an outspoken representative of her gender; still unsure whether she represents liberation, or equity. Priti currently lives in Mumbai, India. She writes short fiction, satirical pieces, and poetry. She also has designs upon people, and when she's not writing, she pounces upon the unsuspecting to imprint them with her digital imagery. Armed with majors in finance, economics, and education, Priti finds inspiration for her stories, poetry, designs, and her reading glasses in odd places.

I, ESTHER JACOBY

My name is Esther Jacoby, and I am a writer. Neither of which is exactly true. I am Esther, and I write. What's in a name? I was born Esther Jacoby in a small town in about the middle of the west of Germany, but my mother changed my name when she married a second time and preferred people to think that we were one happy family. I grew up with another name and hated it, because it stood for abuse, neglect, and isolation. In the small village where we lived, I was not allowed to play with the other kids because of what my stepfather was. We moved a lot. Later, I was adopted by my mother's third husband. That is the name that is in most of my passports now and goes as my maiden name, but whenever I married, I took my husband's name. At one stage, I carried ID documents of two countries, plus a green card and all in different names, causing the guys at customs to give me odd looks.

I have a career and am known in my field. I have a global reputation in a man's world. This is why I said above that I am not really a writer. I am a professional of some standing. I stand my man - I would have stood by my man, but he was a pig and tried to kill me, and that was the end of that!

I was saved as a baby by my grandparents, and now I am giving back, looking after my Grandmother, who is almost 100 years old, losing her not to death but to the slow onset of dementia. Once she is gone, there truly will be nobody left who would claim me as theirs.

I was sick, I overcame cancer. I was pregnant twice, lost them both times. I moved over sixty times, across countries and continents. The world is mine, I have no roots and I belong to no-one. I am myself—I am Esther.

I came to the written word the long way. I started in school, but could not read. The strange lines on the page made no sense, till I got this little book from my teacher about a young African girl and a baby lion. After that, there was no book I would not at least try to

147

read, and through the years, I read a lot. But I have the character of a terrier: once I get my teeth into something, I find it hard to disengage them and let go. So reading soon was not enough, and I started to write at age eight.

What with my career as a kind of engineer, and Grandma and reading, there is not much time for writing. I have no time for research, in more ways than one, but with all that I have experienced, I simply can write about what I know and it is a good enough story. I write fast, I can type blind so that I read what I write and do not have to focus on the keyboard. I write in English, because the words roll much better and after having spent so long in the English-speaking world, I feel more at home than with my native German. I do not like to think in categories, so I claim to be a teller of stories, of life; there is generally a little bit about love, love lost, about violence and hard times, about joy and laughter. There is not so much about genre. That is hard to sell, but then, I do have a job apart from writing. Writing for me is an outlet for everything that is tough and hard to digest, and a means to come to terms with all I experienced.

Words for me are important, they need to taste good and feel nice in my mouth. I read aloud all my writing, till the words fit like a glove. I have been outside mainstream society for so long due to the way I was brought up and later through my own travels, that often I am a watcher rather than a partaker in life. Grandma almost accuses me of collecting weird people: I have friends amongst addicts, gangs, criminals, mentally and physically challenged. I can talk to most and have little barriers. I do not care about people accepting me. But I wish that my writing would find more takers, so that my pain would have been worth it.

Esther is an international woman. By day a manager, she spends her spare time writing novels, short stories and now poems. Originally from Germany, she has spent most of her life in the English-speaking world, and writes in English in the first instance. *New Life Cottage*

148

was released in 2015. In 2016, *The Boy in the Wardrobe* followed, in 2017 *Came the Wait*. After the suicide of her cousin, 2018 saw the release of *Musings on Death and Dying* – a collection of short stories. 2019 has seen the release of *Musings* and *The Cottage* in German.

I, KERRI JESMER

Growing up, my family struggled financially. My dad was in the Army for twenty-three years and my mom worked as a nurse, mostly at Army bases that we lived near or on in base housing. We moved often and this influenced all of my siblings and me. New places, new people, lost friendships were all part of the cycle. What was always a constant in our home was books. And for me, reading was a great escape. One of my sisters was nine years older and she read to my younger sister and me all the time. Every time we read a book, I stepped into the world presented and traveled along with those characters. I dreamed of having a dog like the one from, *Harry, the Dirty Dog*, or having my very own, *Secret Garden* to play in. Or to save, *Black Beauty* from the abuse he endured. I wanted to write just like those stories, filled with adventure and characters I could love, mourn, want to know, and remember.

I started out telling silly little stories to my siblings and parents. And as soon as I could write, I began to put them on paper. But the true turning point for me was in high school when I studied creative writing. My teacher was Mr. Eli Dragoiu and my junior year in his class was the last one he taught, retiring after. We called him Mr. D because his last name was often mangled by students and faculty alike. We were assigned to write a short story and when I got my work back, he told me it was excellent, that I was a good writer and should continue doing so. That was the day I knew what I wanted to do with my life.

Funny how things turn out, though. I worked, even during junior and senior high school, and just kept working for more years than I realized without giving too much thought about writing. I would write a short story here or there, had a few false starts on novels I wanted to explore, but it was put on the back burner while I pursued other goals. I was ambitious back then and had a single focus on climbing the corporate ladder at my jobs. I only wrote to relax my nerves from a busy career life.

After becoming a mother and reading to my child daily, seeing that same magic light up in her eyes with every book, being begged to read, "one more chapter", as we earnestly poured through the Harry Potter books as soon as they came out, the fire to write lit up inside me like a volcano. I *needed* to write. So I chose the genre my almost grown child had come to love from our weekly trips to the library. I leaned toward fantasy.

I joined a few writing Facebook groups to learn how to write to publish. And finally, I found two things that culminated in reaching my long-desired outcome. One was meeting, via a writer's group, my mentor. His name is Steve Carr and he is a prolific author of short stories and a novel, which I highly recommend. The novel is titled, *Redbird, a Paranormal Horror Story*, and it is well worth the read. You can purchase it on Amazon.com. Steve Carr encouraged me to write more, suggested where I send my first story to be published and wrote an extremely informative book titled, *Getting Your Short Stories Published, A Guidebook*, that explained exactly what I needed to do to submit a story someplace.

Well, that short story was published in *Dastaan World Magazine,* an online ezine. I credit the gentlemen who ran it at the time with helping me gain my title of author, which I would not add to my name until I was published.

The second connection was joining a Facebook writers' group named, Inner Circle Writers' Group, started and run by Mr. Grant Hudson of Clarendon House Publishing. There are other groups and specific people who helped me along the way. Many groups have positives and provide support and learning for new writers.

Writing is hard sometimes. You pour your heart and soul into your writing. You cry, laugh, edit, rewrite, and sometimes even walk away for a bit. Not every story will pour out of you every time you want it to. Not every story will be any good. But every story will have the potential to be good. The novel I'm writing now has been in the works for far too many years to name. At 57,000 words, it could be complete. But I'm still writing it, improving, putting it to the side to meet deadlines for short stories.

I feel lucky that for a long time, I only had a couple of rejections. But as time goes on and I continue to write and submit, those rejections come more often. Sometimes it's about the genre. If I've written in a new genre I am not experienced in, I may not do well. But that does not mean I will not give it a try, anyway, learning and stretching my knowledge base and boundaries. That, and reading the genre, is the best way to learn and perfect. I'm also not good at meeting the request for specifics in a story. My mind goes where it will when I begin to put those words down. My characters may not want to go down the path I intend. And sometimes, what I've written just isn't good. There are ways to fix that, though. Editors and beta readers are treasures. Choose people you can trust to be honest. People who won't beat you down, but will tell you the truth, regardless of how you may feel afterward.

Want to write? Do it with joy, and intention. Live your dream. I waited 57 years to live mine, but I'm having the time of my life.

Born in Germany, Kerri was raised on the Eastern plains of Colorado and currently lives in Utah with her husband and adult daughter, two dogs, and three cats, one of which is a fur grandbaby. She is an author, mentor, and part-time editor. She has been published in *Dastaan World Magazine, Fifty-word Stories, Spillwords.com, Inner Circle Writers' Magazine, Dark X-mas Holiday Drabbles Anthology,* and *Portal, the Inner Circle Writers' Group Children's Anthology,* among others. She spent several years mentoring her daughter's middle and high school writing groups. She currently has two blogs, the newest on writing, and has been blogging since 2004.

I, ARCHIT JOSHI

If I could title this essay differently than required, I'd title it "Chasing Paradoxes." To think that I, an anxiety-fueled, "needs to be in total control" fellow, could find pure bliss in something so awry, so petulant, is baffling. If you asked me which some of my most peaceful, cheerful moments were, I'd say they were those which I spent sketching out stories of loss and darkness and sometimes death. I was at my best when fictional people in my head were at their worst...trying to claw their way out of the many trenches I threw them in.

My days are spent trying everything in my power to control the variables, ensuring I look behind every under curtain and under every rock to catch any unpleasant surprises before they hit me on the head with a baseball bat. And then I spend my nights (most of them anyway) surrendering the reigns and letting my capricious mind wander. It leads me to places I find tricky and threatening, to thoughts I can't fully reconcile. You spend so much of your time falling in love with the peaks and troughs of your life, only to find unadulterated delight in escaping it all and diving into a blank page. Doesn't make much sense to me. Will I stop writing then? Couldn't if I tried.

Writing is my superpower. And like any worthy one, it has an origin story. One that I'm afraid will be told and retold because it has shaped a lot of what I've become. It all began back when I'd first fallen in love with reading. I was your typical bookworm, and preferred the company of stories to most people.

Like several budding readers out there, I started with Enid Blyton. Not finding enough time to read (who in the world does?) I would skip the Table of Contents, the dedication page, the preface, to jump to Page 1. After the end of the story, I would shove it in my cupboard and pick out another one.

One day though, after I'd finished one of the books from the

Famous Five series, I took the time to turn past the last page to the author description. And there it was, "Enid Blyton, 1897 – 1968." My innocent mind hadn't yet grasped the concept of death, but it was around 2003 and 1968 seemed way, way back in the past. Somehow, I understood Enid Blyton wouldn't be found in the world right then. But didn't I already know her as a close friend? If I were to meet her, wouldn't my heart explode with an "Ah, she's exactly as I imagined she would be" moment? Here I was, holding a sliver of someone long gone. Isn't Enid still alive because I can hold in my hand something physical and concrete that she created? Doesn't she continue to exist through the pages that hold a part of her heart, her mind, and her emotional inventory? When you are in a room full of books, you're surrounded by dead-immortal souls. Another paradox? I decided then I would do something similar that could outlive me, though not in so many eloquent words.

Words. Lovely little creatures, aren't they? The things you can do with them! You can send a cold chill down someone's back on a warm summer day, or bring tears to someone's eyes when there should've been a smile playing on their lips. That I could control how wildly your heart beats from thousands of kilometers away or — again — even after I've turned to ashes, is nothing short of sorcery. Getting a little better at using words every day, that's my continual labor of love.

You can't fall out of love with words, that's rule *numero uno*. But where to find them? Over the many months I have taken to writing with serious intent, I've realized they hide under the cloak of "ordinary." I find words and stories peaking from everyday activities. On my frequent long walks, I will come across a girl at a bus stop, staring into an irresolute distance. My mind will throw at me two words: "disturbed" and "excited." Is she waiting for a bus that will take her back home or away from it? Is she "excited" to return home after a harrowing day? Or is she "disturbed" because she doesn't have a safe environment at home and desperately needs to hop on this bus and get away from it all?

That's how a story will start turning its gears in my freakishly imaginative brain. I will glance around the girl and try to guess from her belongings which scenario might be most fitting. Uh oh. She has a work briefcase with her. She's definitely heading home. But you know what? A million people are eager to head home after a boring day at work. That's not interesting to me. The other scenario's much more intriguing, don't you think? A hundred different possibilities. The logical part of my brain screams, "You idiot, it's obviously not so dramatic as that!" The creative part of my brain then subdues it by bribing it with a fresh dose of serotonin. And that's how the adventure begins.

One thing that helps me refine the experience of this adventure is allowing myself to be changed by it. Writing reaches for the parts of me I've kept locked under secure vaults. The words I type inform me of my own beliefs. What is my outlook of the world? What does it say about me when I greedily seek escapism through the stories of other authors or my own? That's something I investigate in the intimate space between me and the blank page.

My only regret, perhaps, is not writing enough. There are stories haunting the cobwebbed corners of my mind, but I feel they will take me to strange places I'm not yet ready to explore. Writing them will be agonizing. Not writing them is also agonizing. Just one more paradox I have to chase.

Archit Joshi is a published author who loves writing character-driven stories. He also works as a content writer, and is eager to add more and more writing styles to his arsenal. His fiction has found a home in many reputable anthologies and online magazines, with works ranging from short stories to drabbles (100-word stories) to 10-word micro-fiction. Until now, he has over 30 short fiction pieces published traditionally. Archit had zero regard for coloring between the lines as a kid.

I, CHRISTINE KARPER-SMITH

I, Christine Karper-Smith, am a writer. It took me a long time to say that, even though I have had things published as far back as high school. That was back in the eighties, for anyone who's counting. Although, I began writing poems in the late seventies. We were given an assignment to write one for class. My teacher loved it, and I learned new words by looking for possible rhymes in the dictionary. New words are always good for a writer.

I got a taste of being published when one of my poems was accepted into the school paper. The poem was formatted how I had written it, but it was still exciting seeing something I had written in print. Soon, a few more appeared in the school paper and literary magazine. My dream was to go into broadcasting, so writing poetry was just something I did on the side.

By the mid-90s, I had achieved my top three goals in life – I had gotten into radio, gotten married, and had four children. Finding time to write was nearly impossible, even though I had given up broadcasting to raise my family; my children were four, three, two, and newborn. To complicate things even more, my youngest had health problems. He was hospitalized two separate times, for the total of a month and a half, and was on tube feeds for a year. And because nothing comes easy, my husband was injured at work and was home in bed for two weeks during our son's first hospitalization. But when you enjoy writing, it finds a way to creep into your life.

I had become a fan of a country music singer and had gotten to know him. I traveled the mid-Atlantic region of the US going to his shows. He'd see me in the crowd and dedicate my favorite song to me. I would go backstage afterwards, while he was doing a meet and greet. Someone would ask him when he'd be playing closer to where they lived and he'd look at me, "Chris, when will I be in (town)?" I would tell him and then he'd tell his fan. During this time, I, also, got to know his fan club president. His newsletter came out four times a year. She asked me to write an article for it. I then wrote for the next five issues. Technically, I was paid. I got free membership into his fan club for the next few years.

As much as I loved writing poetry, I never progressed past using the ABCB, AABB, or some other similar rhyme scheme. Writing for the newsletter showed me how much I enjoyed telling a story, using the written word. My articles were always more narrative than news story. I liked when a person was excited to learn what happened next – and still do. Writing poetry had shifted to wanting to write a novel.

So, I sat down to write a book. This was before home computers, so I was writing longhand. However, I never finished it. After a few months, I got a legal pad and started writing another book. I didn't finish it. When my kids were all school age, and now having a desktop computer, I started another book. And guess what? Yeah, I didn't finish that one either. My desire to write a novel never wavered. My ability to not finish writing it, unfortunately, never failed either.

Early in the new millennium, my husband retired. The six of us relocated to a tiny town in the southwest, a few months before our oldest started high school. We all experienced culture shock moving from a major east coast city to a southwestern town with as many people as the kids' previous school. But the need to write stuck with me. I just couldn't finish what I started. I had a strong beginning and an okay middle. But I never had an ending.

One afternoon, I was telling a friend about the time I met a celebrity while working at the radio station. They say to write what you know. As I thought about it more and more, I knew I had the perfect story for my novel. I took meeting the celebrity, the times backstage with the country singer, and things I like about my favorite rock singer and made them into a book. I wrote at night, after my kids had gone to bed. Three months later, for the first time ever, I wrote, "The End." I shared it with a few friends, edited it, shared again until it was perfect. Then came the tough part. The rejection letters poured in. A few requests for a chapter or two propelled me forward.

Deep down I knew I needed to learn more than I knew about writing. I enrolled in college. The same college my children attended. I learned what I was missing. I learned what I did well. I learned different styles. I learned how to write poetry in other ways. I graduated in 2015 with a BA in English with a creative writing emphasis.

I took the leap and self-published, but I didn't give up on writing something that a traditional publisher would want. I wrote another book. Even though it was well-written, it was a bad story. It happens. It's the writer's version of a burned entree. I went back into the kitchen and whipped up a poem. I submitted it and it was accepted into an anthology. My first traditional published writing was a poem after all.

Since then, my writing has been in two other anthologies, both being flash fiction. They're not the novel I still aspire to write and get published, but it's another steppingstone on my way there. When it comes to writing, it's the endgame that counts. Through all of this - thinking about writing, actually writing, finishing something others want to read - I learned and achieved my greatest desire – my children saying, "I'm proud of you."

Christine Karper-Smith lives in Las Cruces, New Mexico. Her flash fiction and poetry are in three different anthologies. She has also self-published two novels. Christine graduated with a BA in English from New Mexico State University in 2015.

I, NERISHA KEMRAJ

To write is to make your dreams come alive...

Be it on a keyboard or pen to paper, the words fight to escape the depths of your mind, screaming for freedom. And those who dare to release them, are called Writers.

I am a Writer.

My love for writing stemmed from a love for reading, which began in Primary school, brought on by a newly-built library quite close to where I lived. My mum and sisters and I spent entire afternoons reading there, and then still taking books home afterwards.

Years later, when I moved away, my reading hobby was fueled with books, borrowed from a dear friend.

This love for words continued into high school which is when I began to write poetry. I preferred rhyming poetry because that's what I thought poetry was – although, I have now learned to write different forms of poetry. Sadly, I eventually outgrew the reading and poetry phase, and they were forgotten during my love-sick teenage years.

Fast forward to 2016 where an emotive dream pushed me into writing short stories. I must have had that dream about five times before I stifled its recurrence by writing it out, as vivid an emotional as it was. (Some say that when you dream, your soul leaves your body, entering a place within your dream world, and sometimes you can get trapped inside the dream. I don't know how true that is, but the emotions you feel in those dreams, creep out into the real world when you're lucky enough to wake.) That dream stayed with me until I set it free from my mind. Fear, loss, love, and heartache, all poured onto the page, and with a few embellishments I turned it into a short story, which was later published. I've been on a Writing Roller Coaster, ever since. And a roller coaster it is!

Yes, there are days where my muse escapes me, but then I only need to look at world-experience to harness material from. Heartbreak and pain make good writing material, and everyone has been through it at some point in their lives. It's about channeling all those experiences and emotions into my writing and sharing it with my readers. It is a writer's wish that their readers are able to identify with their stories, to feel what the writer feels, to imagine that world as their own, that they are a part of it. I wish to master that wish as I continue on my writing journey.

On some days when I'm unable to muster up ideas from the depths of my mind, I turn to my greatest supporters for help: my five and seven-year-old daughters who are ever so eager to throw in story and poetry ideas.

However, I write stories that fall under a dark genre, so my encouragement of darkness does not sit well with my husband (who disapproves of my disturbing, horror stories), especially since their drawings are sometimes morbid and creepy. I have since attempted to discourage their assistance.

My family have been great at supporting my writing, and my sisters often read my stories. It's a great ego boost when doubt tends to cast its ugly face, leading me to question my worth as a writer. During the self-doubt phases, creativity is stifled and it takes a while to get back into the zone. I was once on a "no-writing" period for so long that I said to my husband that I should just give up writing, I was shocked at his response because he said it was a good idea because he thought writing depressed me but truthfully, I expected more, instead of discouragement. But that response definitely kicked me out of my writer's block and I was all the more determined to continue writing. He gave me the push I needed, not necessarily the one I wanted.

Writing is in my bones. Depression looms over me when I am unable to write. Yes, there are times when it has to take a back seat, but it is something that brings me joy. Especially when those finished stories and poems find homes to be published. And those pieces that are rejected, only increase my drive as a writer. While rejections dampen my spirit, they push me further into improving my writing. There's always room for improvement because we never stop learning.

It is an absolute pleasure to know that my work is out there, being read by someone, strangers even. Positive reviews and compliments from fans are heart-warming. That's enough to make me continue on my bad days.

Writing is an art which allows for an escape into different worlds, for writers and readers alike.

I am a Writer. And I love it.

Nerisha Kemraj resides in Durban, South Africa with her husband and two mischievous daughters. While poetry has been a love since high school, she began writing short stories in 2017. A lover of dark fiction, she has over 100 short stories and poems published in various publications, both print and online. She has also received an Honourable Mention Award for her tanka in the Fujisan Taisho 2019 Tanka Contest. Nerisha holds a Bachelor's degree in Communication Science, and a Post Graduate Certificate in Education from University of South Africa.

I, LUCIA KENNEDY

I grew up in a small row home in South Philadelphia during the seventies. The hustle and bustle of the big city overwhelmed me. When not in school, I read in my room or sat on the front steps, making up stories about my neighbors or random people walking to their errands. Most people walk everywhere when you live in the city. Myself included. Often, I'd arrive at my destination with no idea how I got there because my imagination ran wild with stories of the people I encountered. My parents were my biggest supporters. I thought I didn't have the talent to do much of anything. My mom was a talented poet and artist. My Dad was intelligent and kind and could give you directions to any remote place without looking at a map. As a young child, my baby brother wrote detective stories and could draw. My middle brother and I were storytellers as youngsters but never thought to jot them down.

Through elementary school, I was introverted and anxiety-ridden, fearful of the nuns and new people. Back then, anxiety wasn't a diagnosis. The nuns told my parents I was immature and backward. The insinuation devastated my mother, and my father was furious at what the nun claimed. Reminiscing, I now know that I suffered from anxiety, and it affected my childhood and my learning capabilities. I shut down, and my grades were terrible because fear prevented me from participating. Lost in my head as the nun would lecture, praying that she didn't call my name to answer a question. My stomach was in knots, and my brain repeated, "please don't see me, don't call on me." In my first year of high school, I drafted an essay, and the teacher requested that I stay a minute after class. She handed me my paper and said that she, "laughed hysterically." that writing was a talent I should pursue. I was funny, but only when I felt safe with someone. At that moment, she made me feel safe. In my third year, I was in an English class with seniors. There I was, this tiny Junior and overwhelmed with the upperclassmen. The nun came into the classroom that first day and passed out a syllabus. Included was a paragraph that we must read ten books by the end of May and draft an essay about the books we read. Piece of cake! I finished by Christmas break. In January, she made a big fuss that the only Junior had completed the required reading and earned perfect scores on the essays. She called me by name, and I almost died on the spot, overwhelmed with panic. The memory is so vivid. After class, I heard her call me as I packed my books. She wanted to discuss a new release about a woman with a split personality. The title of the book was "Sybil," and she was eager to read it. I brought it to her the next day. She then asked if I planned on college. Back in the mid-seventies, not everyone went on to further education. I wasn't sure, and she insisted I seek a school for Journalism. The following day, several seniors who had part times jobs begged me to help them with their essays. They accepted me, and it felt beautiful. They saw me as a peer.

After high school, my self-esteem improved, and I had more confidence. A bank hired me at seventeen. I loved my job, and the manager promoted me in six months. I stayed for two years and moved onto a career in the government. I loved numbers and eventually became a budget analyst. I wrote procedural manuals, and many managers asked for my help with writing projects. My love for words overpowered my passion for numbers. When I lost my position because of Military base closure, I became a stay at home mom. I'd write small paragraphs or stories between raising my children. My mother, consistently supportive, begged me to use my talent. She'd remembered all the stories I told during summer nights in our place at the Jersey shore.

I'd say, with joy, that I began writing sixteen years ago. My fear still impedes submitting, yet I write. Many people have inspired me to write, my husband, my oldest friend. I feel my upbringing brings honesty and understanding to my writing.

Many people don't believe in communicating with the deceased. I do. After I'd written my first novel, the old anxiety, fear, and self-

163

doubt resurfaced. Alone in my house, I spoke out loud to pictures of my parents, asking them to send me a sign that writing was what I should do. The bathroom light turned on, and their photographs moved a complete turn simultaneously. I laughed and said loud and clear, "Message received, Mom and Dad."

I haven't submitted since last year after reaching out to fifteen Literary Agents and two publishers. All rejected. I cried, I freaked out, utterly devastated. I called friends. I had a pity party, a long pity party. I resolved at that point that I am not a quitter, and I was going to continue with my passion, writing. Master Class has allowed me to learn to become a better writer and to listen to the knowledge and experiences the renowned authors shared.

Losing my younger brother last September threw me in a tailspin, and I couldn't focus. Then in February, I lost my job of twenty-two years, leaving me scattered and without purpose. Grieving the loss of my brother and my career. Now I am fully focused and have completed almost nineteen manuscripts.

Lucia is a writer, a wife, the mother of three boys, and owner of two rescue pugs. She lives in Washington Township, New Jersey, and splits her time between there and her future retirement home near the beach in Delaware. She wrote poetry and lyrics before attempting a much dreamed about a career as a novel writer. When not writing, she volunteers for a Pug Rescue in Southern New Jersey.

I, SHAWN M. KLIMEK

…am a writer. Why not an artist? The comparison is not as random as it may first appear.

As the middle child of seven siblings, I had reason to trust that being singled out for my artistic skills even before kindergarten was more than mere parental flattery. "Look at his attention to detail. He's even drawn fingernail on his stick figures," my mother once bragged to a visitor. When my kindergarten teacher singled out two crayon drawings as worth displaying on the bulletin board—mine being one, I remember being jealous of having to share the glory with a classmate. Art was my territory, the identity which, from that early age, I had already attached to my ego. I studied my rival's drawing for what she had done effectively, so that I could imitate it, to add her techniques to my toolkit. She had outlined her shapes in bold colors before coloring in them in with smooth, steady lines. Her crayon yellow sun was tightly encircled with red crayon. The smoothness. The clean lines. The bright contrasts. Noted and assimilated.

By second grade, I was attempting human portraits, although flawed. The pencil drawing of my best friend made his jawline appear too long, making him look older, as though he'd already gained his adult teeth. I was twelve when I committed to mastering perspective, reflections and shadow. These proved simple mathematical deductions and were added to my repertoire within the year. I received my first formal art classes during my senior year of high school. A drawing of mine won a merit award and my hastily compiled portfolio earned a modest fine arts scholarship.

Do I seem to have strayed from the topic of being a writer? And for of all things, to boast about art? My purpose is to illustrate how deeply rooted my ego and ambitions were to something else, to better explain what a momentous personal decision it was for me to choose to become a writer.

My initial excitement at taking my first formal art classes dimmed when I realized how primitive the lessons would be. Despite my advanced skills, I was disallowed from taking Art-4 because I had never finished Art 1. To cut me down to size, my art teacher frequently mentioned another gifted art student of hers, one at least as talented yet far more dedicated. In contrast to me, who spent my evenings rehearsing comic sketches and weekends attending interscholastic thespian competitions, this rival I would never meet delighted in drawing constantly, embracing every assignment with enthusiasm and even volunteering to draw posters for various clubs. By contrast, being tasked to draw what other people wanted me to draw sucked the joy out of it for me. The effort was a tedious bore.

In college, I learned the truth about how ordinary my talent was; how truly small the pond was in which I'd been measured a big fish. I might even have been the most talented freshman art major, but I was soon no longer even the best artist I knew. By this point, I could do a "perfect" portrait within about a half-hour, but my teachers could do the same thing in five minutes. My fine arts counselor saw that I was spending all my free time acting in theater productions while falling behind in my art classes. My professor asked whether I was sure I wanted to be an artist.

I did some soul-searching and visualized the future. I estimated that I could, with sufficient dedication, become a competitive professional artist. I had the advantages of a better-than-average head start, plenty of imagination, and original vision. But to what end? To regain the right to boast? Art had always been fun and ego-boosting, but it's lonesome work, and any skill sufficiently advanced can also be alienating. With few exceptions, I wasn't drawn to other artists. They were often fussy and mousy or self-absorbed and pointedly eccentric people.

If it were true that with sufficient discipline and dedication, I could master visual arts, didn't it follow that by applying similar time and effort I could master something else? Now that I realized I was not God's gift to art (nor had ever been), who was I, really? If I

166

could choose to be whoever I wanted, (assuming I was willing to do the requisite work), who would I choose to be?

Aiming to be "the best" at something, I also realized, is folly. Artists aren't valued most for their comparative skills (although that still matters), but for their originality—for their style and personality.

After one year of college as a fine arts major, I formally chose to become a writer. To begin my discipline, I joined the U.S. Army to become a journalist, writing what other people wanted me to write. Learning how to not only enjoy the task but achieve a result enjoyable to readers was one of many valuable lessons.

Deep down, I'd always been a writer. I was nine when I wrote the first of many poems my Dad thought was worth typing up and duplicating on the Xerox in his office. A comic sketch I wrote during the summer before college for my classmates to use in those interscholastic competitions, was used to win the tournament in which it debuted. Teams from rival schools adopted the script, three of whom eventually qualified for the state tournament. I never stopped writing flash fiction and poetry, and even wrote a few plays. After leaving the Army, I finished a bachelor's degree in creative arts with an emphasis on creative writing.

Apart from journalism, I've never made enough money to live on as a writer, and perhaps never will. But no matter what else I've done to pay rent, I've taken that identity with me since I made the decision long ago.

I, Shawn M. Klimek, am a writer.

Shawn M. Klimek is the author of the illustrated, poetic-fantasy book, *Hungry Thing*, and more than 180 published poems and short stories. He specializes in speculative fiction with a touch of humor. He lives in Illinois with his military-nurse wife and their Maltese.

I, GREG KROJAC

2012 was, as Her Majesty Queen Elizabeth II referred to 1992, an *annus horribilis* for me. I was defrauded out of a substantial amount of money by someone with whom I had a close personal relationship and trusted, and my father died back home in England (I've lived in northeast Brazil since 2007). Due to the battering that my finances took, I was unable to visit him before he passed away. I'm pretty sure I suffered a nervous breakdown – certainly some of my actions that year were irrational, to say the least. Not having the finances to seek professional help, I was forced to muddle through alone and wondered if writing about the experience might be therapeutic and help me deal with the trauma.

It didn't and I abandoned that idea.

I did, however, discover that I enjoyed the process of writing. Having abandoned the personal memoir of the events of 2012, I wrote a contemporary thriller titled *Virtual Messiah*. I never published it, but I do consider that novel a great learning experience, often referring to it affectionately as having been written with training wheels, interspersing writing the story with reading about the art of writing. *Virtual Messiah* hasn't disappeared completely – I plundered the story of its psychopathic villain, John Henry Foster, made a few tweaks to his role and now he has resurfaced as a serial killer in my most recent work, *The Janus Project*.

The writing bug had sunk its teeth into me and was in no mind to let go. I had no choice but to continue writing. Under no illusion that writing would make me rich and famous (although I'm certainly not going to complain if it does), I suddenly found my brain awash with ideas – ideas that demanded to be allowed to escape my mind and taste freedom in the outside world.

I was fortunate that I spent six years of English tutelage under the care of an extraordinary old-school English teacher, Mr. Stanley, a man both frightening and awe-inspiring in equal doses. His passion for his subject and his unfailing desire to impart his knowledge to a motley class of thirty teenage boys – a class that included the now best-selling author Nick Hornby – is something I'll be eternally grateful for.

So, I had the tools to write at my disposal but what should I write about? I've always had a passion for science fiction, ever since my childhood days of watching William Hartnell as Doctor Who and consuming the constant diet of children's sci-fi offered by Gerry Anderson's Supermarionation Studios – "Fireball XL5," "Supercar," Thunderbirds," "Captain Scarlet" et al. It was an easy choice.

Now, eight years later, I've penned ten novels, two novellas, and one short story.

Living in Brazil brings with it certain unanticipated problems for a British writer. Unlike those who live in my home country of the UK, or who live in the USA, Australia, or other English-speaking countries, I'm surrounded by non-English speakers. This means that I don't have a domestic market to sell to – so there's no point in attending conventions. I'm thousands of miles away from the nearest English-speaking market and the sheer cost of attending a convention in the USA or the UK would be prohibitive. This situation is compounded by those Brazilians who do speak (and read) English not having a culture of reading fiction. I've asked numerous Brazilians if they like to read books, received the answer "yes," only to be told that the books they read are about their jobs. Their relationship with books is completely different from that which I experienced as a child – my weekly visits to the library to borrow books by Anthony Buckeridge, Richmal Crompton, Gerald Durrell and others, were my favorite trips with my mother.

Two personal writing philosophies have emerged from my writing experience. Firstly, I am a pantser. While I admire those who plan out their stories well in advance and work to that framework, that just isn't for me. I like to be as surprised as my reader by developments that occur during my stories. New characters enter the tales uninvited and act in ways that I could never have imagined beforehand, often taking the plot in a completely unexpected direction. This keeps me both on my toes and entertained. To plan ahead – in my opinion – would stunt my creative juices. My second philosophy is that a story should be as long or as short as it needs to be. I refuse to pad my stories out just to reach an arbitrary word count. For my part, to do so would be dishonest and disrespectful to me, the story, and – above all – the reader.

This latter philosophy has led to an exciting new project with a fellow author, Adam Stump. I have no idea how long my stories will be when I start writing and recently realized that all my works are what can be considered short reads (short stories, novellas, or short novels). They're not short reads by design but this shorter story length seems to be something I gravitate to naturally. Now, Adam and I have created a podcast, "Short Is The New Long," whose audience consists of writers and readers of short reads.

Life in Brazil hasn't been easy – and still isn't – but I often wonder if I would have taken up writing fiction if I had stayed in England. Unless someone invents a time machine and lets me borrow it, I'll never know. But my instincts tell me that I probably wouldn't have. The ill wind that was my year of 2012 appears to have blown some good after all.

Greg Krojac is a British expat, who grew up in the town of Maidenhead, England, and now lives in northeast Brazil with Eliene and their three pets - Tabitha and Jess (the cats) and Sophie (the dog). He teaches English as a foreign language at a local school. He writes science fiction and has written ten short novels, two novellas, and a short story. He also co-hosts a podcast aimed at writers and readers of short reads, titled "Short Is The New Long."

I, JahART KUSHITE

I, JahArt Kushite embarked on this journey the day I was conceived. I realized the gift bestowed in me when I was a young boy in my early teen-age years. I had two best friends that I knew growing up, thus a paper and pen, with whom I would express my thoughts and feelings when down emotionally or high with enthusiasm. Locking myself in my room most of the times I would scribe down anything that would at the moment flow in my mind. I should mention that whilst in my youthful days I didn't know much about poetry let alone little of its existence. I grew up in a poor family though I was blessed to be raised by a father who was a primary school principal back in the 80s from a small poor country of Southern Africa in Malawi. He contributed more to my knowledge of English as a second language. It was until I was at High School late 90s when I opened up clearly to knowing Poetry and I developed more love as I found myself in it. Poetry was my only part of writing that expressed me as a being in all situations that surrounded me. I should confess that before Poetry there was in me love for music. I loved Reggae music and I remember when I was about seven years mimicking the lyrics of the legendary reggae icon Bob Marley as my brother owned some cassettes, LP's, and 45s. And then I developed my writing skills from the way music inspired me. Music had so much influence on me developing my love for writing as I regarded it as a tool that carried our emotions from the mental plane to the outside world and then subsequently, I used the same ideology to put my writings into poetry. Having the opportunity of attending high school I made sure I did my best in English and Literature. I only did English and Literature as a constituent subject of six subjects that enable you to qualify for a senior certificate. I excelled in the subject that even my English teacher was at times amazed at my marks and being a national examination board examiner, he motivated and encouraged me a lot and would give me extra assignments in private to write and submit to him for marking and corrections.

I am a very deep emotional soul. I feel things deeply beyond the depth of an average soul. I was born with no silver spoon in my mouth and had a great deal of upheavals and winds of turbulence growing up. Circumstances I went through propelled and were a driving force behind me writing now and again. I couldn't further my college studies in Electrical and Electronics Engineering because of lack of funds for my tuition fees. I dropped out and looked for a job to get going. I left the country when I was in my early 20s (twenty-three) and came to live with my Uncle in South Africa. I had had intermissions of writing in between the years of working.

I've been in relationships that moved my soul. And when I love, I truly love from my bone marrow but contrary to what they say that love is blind, I personally say love is unfair. I feel deeply so having that said chances are I love deeply and that's a burden I carry. I get hurt easily and it hurts so bad. And when it's hurts so bad emotions flow and that's where the other side of me jumps in as a writer. I fell in true love more than twice. But there was one relationship break up that completely expelled me from a cocoon of dormancy. My world tumbled down and lost myself from the normal realm. Hurt, the pangs of pain I succumbed to launched me sky high into poetry where I found refuge to soothe my heartache. Since then I discovered who really I am and my purpose in life.

Not only love kindles the fire to write, disappointments of all sorts does. I don't write to fancy the ideas of a common man. I write what I feel. From poverty, hunger and nakedness to atrocities that's our world leaders put us through and the eyes of judgment of fellow mankind. Death has also played a big role in catapulting me into seas of poetry. Loss of life brings so much trauma and messes your life around into total chaos. The grip of poverty has also printed its mark on my writings. Seeing the youths who are energetic and intelligent but lack support to uplift themselves from the grassroots level and backward communities where they hail from makes me feel their pain and myself too has been the victim of the system. Pain is the window from where you see things from a different perception and

172

when treading through such twinges, I flow like water with inspiration to write.

It was in 2019 when I made my first attempt to submit a piece to an online literary magazine. In anticipation for good news I unfortunately received the bad news of my submitted piece denied for publication. I felt low and down because it was such a great beautiful poem that had received a huge wonderful reception on Facebook. I was perplexed and vexed but in the end, I allowed myself an opportunity of perfecting my write-ups. I gradually improved and since then I have witnessed my works accepted for publication and featured in anthologies. I love reading ancient poetry. It has a great effect on my life as a writer. I never studied Creative Writing and hold no degree in literary studies. So no level of studies that the next man holds intimidates me as a writer. I am a natural writer. I am gifted. I realized my potential and my God-free given talent. My best friend has played a big role in encouraging me to write and a number of people from different walks of life, and not forgetting my family too.

JahArt Kushite born Isaiah Phiri is a Cape Town based Poet who recently came to the limelight through Facebook where he posts his deep soul ,heart wrenching poetry. His first poetry book "Wailing Soul" is currently under revision and working on a second book titled *Tonnes Of Love* to be published soon. Author of selected poems featured on *Spillwords.com* like "Vanity," "Death," "Coiled," "COVID-19," "I am Not Everything" and "Soul Hunter." A contributing poet to an anthology titled *Colours of Love* published by Rock Pigeon Publication in India featuring; "I Am Thirsty for Those Who Love Loudly" and "I Remember Those Moments."

I, VERONICA LEIGH

I have often heard that everyone in life has been given a gift. Some people can sing, others are artistic, many are crafty. Everyone has a secret talent; one they can tap into to release their passion. My family writes. I have a poem written by my great-grandmother Edith, testifying that it began with her. At least, that's the first recorded piece of creative writing in the family. Her daughter, my grandma, Margaret, was a talented poet, producing thought-provoking rhymes. Off and on throughout her life, she submitted her work to be published, but she never had anything accepted. "You kids will probably be the ones to publish my work and make money off of them," she joked.

My Aunt Barbara, an English Lit major, dabbled in screenplays and poetry. My Dad, though not literary in any sense of the word, could spin a yarn and wrote a couple tales that made us laugh so hard we cried. Most of my cousins write: poetry, essays, short stories, devotionals. So, it's nothing extraordinary to write in my family.

I've been writing since I was six years old. My first story was an illustrated book of *Dark Wing Duck*. The great dramatic moment was when a bee stung Dark Wing Duck on the derriere and a welt formed. My family erupted in laughter, not understanding how frightening bees really were to a six-year-old. I wrote off and on, until I was eleven. My Mom shared a story I had written with my Aunt Barbara. On a trip back from visiting family, Aunt Barbara and I discussed my story, and she edited it on the steering wheel, while simultaneously driving on the highway.

"You are intuitive; I think you have the potential to be a writer," Aunt Barbara declared, "I want to invite you to join a writer's workshop I will be leading. It's for senior citizens, but really, everyone is welcome."

It took some persuading, and assurances that I wouldn't have to read my pieces in front of anyone, before I agreed. For six years I attended, and was considered an honorary senior citizen, producing short stories and terribly written novels. Everyone was encouraging, hoping I'd persevere and hone my craft. Perhaps one day end up in print. There is a magical quality to writing. It's a spiritual experience. Christians generally believe God created the universe in six days and rested on the seventh – I could do as much when writing a story. I might not have been the smartest, prettiest, or strongest – but I could write in a way no one else in my family could.

For me, it wasn't enough to simply write. I wanted to be published. No, I needed to be published. For years, it was an obsessive desire. I wanted to do something no one else in my family had been able to do. My first short story sold years after the writer's workshop broke up, when I was twenty-six years old. In the last several years, I've been published many times. Publication is an idol which I regularly bow down to. My self-worth is measured by the number of pieces I sell each year. I'm only as good as my next story. Others in my family write, writing itself is nothing extraordinary, but somehow writing and publishing has become my superpower. It was the only gift/talent I was ever given.

Now my gift is marketable, and though I've achieved something, I've lost something too. The simple joy of putting pen to paper and innocently creating has been forfeited in favor of bylines and payment. In the end, it has become more about selling a story or an essay rather than the art of writing itself. The first love is gone and has been for years. While I hope to continue to be published and perhaps live by my pen, I hope to find my way back to the joy I once had when I was just beginning to write. To relish in the simplicity of feeling the pen scrape across the paper as a new idea takes hold. With writing there is always hope, there is never an end, and always a fresh beginning.

Veronica Leigh has been published in numerous nonfiction anthologies. She is a regular contributor to the blog *Femnista*, she was included in Sweetycat Press' *Who's Who of Emerging Writers 2020 Anthology*. Her fictional stories have been published in *Dark Moon Digest, The Scribe Magazine, Fleas on the Dog Magazine, After Dinner Conversation, ParAbnormal Magazine*, and she will be eventually published in *Only One Bed Ezine, Lumpen Journal,* in the Transmundane Press' *On Time Anthology,* and *Sherlock Holmes Mystery Magazine.*

I, PINA LEYLAND

It is 2010 and I have just turned 50. After a lifetime of focusing on other priorities, I am finally fulfilling a life-long dream, studying creative writing in a Master of Arts program at UTS, University Technology Sydney. I have an essay on literary theory and an experimental piece of writing due for submission imminently.

The jackhammering outside our apartment reverberates in my brain. The minute we moved in, we were given notice of remedial works required to waterproof all the balconies in the huge apartment complex fronting Balmain Cove in Rozelle. Of course, there was no mention or forewarning of this at the time of signing our lease.

By day, there are the building works and by night, there is music blaring and sport on television, loudly enjoyed by the two male members of the household, with no heed to my need for quiet space to concentrate if I am to meet my deadlines. The football. AFL. NRL. Rugby Union. Association Football. Premier League. A League. You name a code and (with the exception of American Football) they watch it!

I give up on trying to write at home and retreat to the University library. I bus it into the city and trek down George Street and Harris Street, lugging my notebooks and research material along with me, then climb up three flights of stairs to find the computer lab. It's been a long time since I have had to resort to such measures. The only available terminal is in a nest of young things sitting on each other's laps, watching anime streamed in another language, most likely Chinese, laughing raucously and feeding each other fried crispy crunchy snacks from little colorful cellophane packets. Trying not to be one of those grumpy old bags, oblivious to their white middle-class privilege, I settle myself down and plug myself in. In Australia, Italians were the outsiders once. Now we are lumped in with the white majority, our "otherness" blended in with the "spag bol" recipes. The key board is all sticky and despite my best efforts, I am overcome with revulsion. I remember when I was a young social work student being glared at by other students and shushed by librarians for talking and making noise in the library—a sanctuary almost as sacred as a church—and we certainly weren't allowed to take food and drinks in with us. How the world has changed.

Fast forward 10 years. It's 2020 and I've recently turned 60. I'm rooting through boxes, trying to find my birth certificate and university degrees. Memories flood in. I recall the difficulties I had completing my Master of Arts course. I nearly gave up. The final stages were so arduous that I was unable to write anything else for years afterwards and took up painting and drawing instead. But 2010 was a doddle compared to 2020, which is proving to be a nightmare on so many different levels.

When COVID-19 hit our shores, my life had already gone "pear-shaped" and I was trying to piece it back together again. March 2020 found me living by myself in a small flat in Wollongong, working full-time as a social worker with the Italian-Australian community, and keeping busy with writing and an active social life. Then the social restrictions kicked in. I was no longer able to perform my normal duties, my hours were cut and I was required to work from home. I became increasingly isolated. Over the Easter long weekend, I went quite mad with loneliness and decided to quit my job and return to live in Adelaide to help care for my elderly mother, who was also living alone and suffering anxiety and depression as a result of the global pandemic crisis.

And so, on 23 July, I arrived at my mother's house and went into two weeks mandatory quarantine and now here I am, six weeks later, living with the consequences of my decision.

I'm sitting at my little white IKEA desk, the same one I sat at ten years ago to write my final project for my Master's degree, thankful that it survived the long train journey from Sydney to Adelaide. I'm tapping on my new white hp keyboard, bought the other day to replace my black logitech keyboard, which was not so lucky. The white one looks and feels all wrong. I miss my old keyboard but I know there's no point. All week I have ranting to my mother about letting go of old, broken stuff. I need to practice what I preach: "Take the splinter out of your own eye…"

I stare at the Word document on the laptop screen and my mind is a blank. I've been trying to finish this essay all week but other priorities have demanded my attention. Helping to care for my mother is more exhausting than I thought it would be, especially trying to keep her spirits buoyed in the face of her anger, frustration and grief over declining functionality and loss of independence.

It's now 11.30 pm. And I'm on a roll. I have written around 2,000 words and need to cut it down to 1,000. My mother went to bed two hours ago. Just as well she can't see that I have the electric heater on full blast and the overhead fluorescent light is on, burning up her solar-powered electricity. I think she may have OCD. She is frugal to an extreme. I hear shuffling footsteps and the hallway door opens. I look up to see mamma in her nightie, blinking at me in the bright light.

"Ancora ess'scti?" (Are you still there?)

"Yes, Ma, I'm writing!"

She harrumphs and shuts the door. I hear her shuffling back to the bedroom.

The spell has been broken. I sigh, save my Word document and put my laptop to sleep. I switch off the electric heater and the ceiling light. F*ck! I may never finish this piece in time to submit to the anthology.

Giuseppina (Pina) Marino Leyland is a social worker, author and artist. She was born in Australia of Italian immigrant parents and currently lives in Adelaide. Pina was awarded a Master of Arts in Creative Writing by the University of Technology Sydney in 2011. Her work has appeared in several anthologies and publications of various genres and her first collection of creative writing entitled

Pezzi Pazzi/ Crazy Pieces was published by Clarendon House Books in 2019. She is now working on a second collection entitled *Pezzi Pazzi 2*, as well as several other writing projects.

I, S. LYLE LUNT

"I was born in a mint." Those are the words that began my writing journey.

I was a five-year-old first-grader when I wrote my first book. I lay on my belly on the floor of my grandparents' old farmhouse, and wrote and illustrated my masterpiece, a story about little yellow-haired Sally who tried on her mother's high-heeled shoes and toddled around, saying, "I am a lady." My grandma, ordinarily stoic, clapped her hands when she read it and saved it until the end of her life.

Two or three years later in the school library, revisiting one of the *Dick, Jane, and Sally* books that had taught me to read, I came to a story about little yellow-haired Sally trying on her mother's high-heeled shoes and toddling around saying, "I am a lady." My heart pounded. I'd thought that was my creation. I didn't know the word plagiarism yet, but blushed in secret shame, knowing that my grandmother's pride wasn't earned. I'm no writer, I thought.

For the next couple of years my writing career was non-existent. Then, in fifth grade, Mrs. Staff gave the class an assignment: we were to write a story from the viewpoint of an inanimate object. Richard, to my left, slumped at his desk and moaned. I sat up straighter. This sounded interesting.

I decided to write about the life of a dime. I remember vividly sitting that night at the dining room table (which was used for actual dining only at holidays; the rest of the time it was a homework and laundry-folding table) with my blank, inviting, wide-ruled sheet of paper before me.

"Dad," I called into the next room. "Where are coins made?"

"In a mint," he answered. A mint. I liked the sound of it.

A couple days later Mrs. Staff stood in front of the class and read a couple of stories that she'd particularly liked. Mine was one of them. She read my first line, "I was born in a mint," and smiled before reading on.

After the readings were over and students were instructed to pull out their social studies books, Mrs. Staff called me to her desk. "This story is very nice," she said. "Did you write it by yourself?"

I was offended. "Of course!"

"I want you to take it to Mr. Martin's office," she said.

Mr. Martin was the principal. Was I to be punished? I knew that boys were sometimes sent there for paddlings. Mr. Martin kept a paddle hanging on the wall, the story went, that had holes drilled into it so that there'd be no cushion of air when he beat children with it. Maybe he'd use the paddle on me if he, like Mrs. Staff, believed that I hadn't written the story on my own. Had they somehow learned about the story I'd written at my grandma's as a first grader, and now suspected me of plagiarism?

But, hands trembling, I dutifully carried my paper to Mr. Martin's office. The secretary ushered me in. Mr. Martin sat behind a huge desk, and yes, a paddle with holes hung on a hook behind him.

He read the folded and stapled note Mrs. Staff had clipped to my story, and then smiled and told me to sit. He read my story out loud. "I was born in a mint," he began. He chuckled when he came to the part about the daily agony of the dime being shaken inside a child's piggy bank. He laughed at the part where the dime bragged to the nickel that she was smaller, yes, but worth more. His eyebrows drew together in despair when he came to the tragic part about the dime being alone in a filthy gutter for many years. When he came to the end he put the paper on his desk and looked at the little, shy, freckle-faced nine-year-old girl in front of him, and said, "You're a very good writer."

"A very good writer." He said that about me. He beat children, yes, but he liked my writing. My older sister was an all-A student. My younger sister was an athlete. I was the little space-case who looked out the window during arithmetic. My report cards always had notes such as "Sandy struggles to pay attention in class." I wasn't used to being "very good" at anything.

That's the moment, I think, that I became a writer. A dime was born in a mint; I, the writer, was born in the office of an elementary school principal.

S. Lyle Lunt had her first short story published in 1979 and has been writing ever since. She lives in Georgia with her husband, and when not writing spends her time working on their fixer-upper, trying to manage the untamed acres it sits upon, and traveling. She hopes to have her completed coming-of-age novel, *A River Away*, ready for publication soon.

I, CATHERINE A. MACKENZIE

In my teens, I wrote poetry, replete with despair and death. Later, I flitted from here to there: sewing, macramé, crocheting, knitting, furniture reupholstering, crafts, woodworking, painting... I was a jack of all trades and a master of none, to use a cliché. Clichés are no-nos in the writing world, but sometimes, as I wrote in a recent poem, only a cliché will do!

In the early 2000s, I despaired of ever becoming a grandmother. I hadn't realized how much I wanted that title until I thought it would be denied to me. Silly, I know. Who craves to be a grandparent? Doesn't that imply old age and death?

Then, in 2007, almost like magic, after several years of shedding tears, my first two grandchildren were born. More amazingly, they were born three weeks apart—one my now-deceased son's, the other, my daughter's. After the birth of my first granddaughter, Taylor, I wrote her a poem that I framed and presented to my daughter and her husband. I did the same after Abby's birth.

These two little beings inspired me, propelling me back into writing. Happy poems this time, not those depressing ones from my teens. I overflowed with emotion, overcome with gratitude and joy, and wrote poems and short stories with a vengeance. I soon had enough "grandmother" poems to publish a book. Even a book of religious, inspirational poems.

I'm not sure if I consciously knew what I was doing. Maybe, as a grandmother, I wanted to leave something of myself behind, something more concrete and meaningful than etchings on a pillar of granite or marble. Perhaps I needed to make up for lost time, knowing chapters of my life were passing, the pages turning faster than ever. I yearned to stay alive forever. I didn't want to miss one facet of my grandchildren's lives.

Despite the joys of successive grandchildren, life had its ups and downs. Writing became my escape to imaginary worlds when life wasn't quite so kind. My worlds were all mine, and I alone could choose life or death for my characters. Make them happy. Make them sad. Total control in a make-believe world.

A couple of years before my mother suddenly passed away in 2016, she asked me, "Can't you write anything happy?" She had read one of my stories published in a *Chicken Soup for the Soul* book. Everyone knows Chicken Soup likes sap, so I made my story a tad weepier than reality. "Yes, Mother, I'm fine. And I do write happy." I don't think she believed me.

Despite my grief over my mother's death, in honor of her, I tried to write happier stories and poems. It wasn't easy.

And when I thought my life couldn't get any worse, my world shattered.

In January 2017, my thirty-six-year-old son Matthew was diagnosed with a rare heart cancer and died two months later. My mother's death had hit me hard, but the death of one of my children was horrific.

How would I continue? I couldn't fathom life without him. I wanted to—somehow—kill myself to join him.

But no! Despite my numerous borderline morbid writings, I was petrified of death. No way would I kill myself to be with *anyone.*

My teenage writings haunted me. My mother's words haunted me, too.

Family members have never been *that* supportive of my writing. Turned out, they weren't even that supportive of my grief, saying that after "x" amount of time, one should be over a death.

How could I be happy with a huge hollow in my heart?

I couldn't concentrate. Couldn't sleep. Couldn't touch my first novel, which had been hours away from completion.

As when my granddaughters were born, I delved into poetry. Again, I don't think I consciously knew what I was doing. It was a coping mechanism. An escape. This time, however, my poetry was full of heartache and bitterness.

Matthew died on the eleventh of the month, and without fail, as if I was bound to a publisher's do-or-die contract, every month I painfully composed a poem to, I guess, memorialize him, which I posted on social media.

Oddly, I couldn't write these commemorative poems until the tenth or eleventh arrived, almost as if I needed to reach that monthiversary first, when the words amazingly flowed.

For a year after his death, I couldn't write anything else but sorrowful poetry. My novel languished. I didn't enter writing contests or submit to publications. I even gave up my local writing group.

Instead, I moped. I cried. I sat in the backyard and screeched. "Why, God, why?" No answers from Him. Or from anyone.

But I wrote more and more poems, most of them worthless, relentless scribbling of misery and mourning.

After the first year, which is, apparently, called "the year of firsts," I began writing again. I finished my novel and published it. I finished the sequel and started the third.

At the end of three years, I compiled these monthly poems, along with others that commemorated a special date or event in connection with my son, into a poetry book to try to help other grieving parents.

I continue to write poems for my son even though every month I despair of words. How many times can one write about grief? But words, as I've come to realize, are endless even though I fear I have nothing new to say. I persevere, for if I don't write these poems, I'll have given up on my son. Foolishness, of course, but doing so keeps me alive. Despite my fear of death.

Catherine A. MacKenzie: Cathy's works appear in print and online, including short story compilations, poetry collections, and children's picture books. She published her first novel, *Wolves Don't Knock*, in 2018. *Mister Wolfe (*the second in the series) will be published in the summer of 2020) and *My Brother, the Wolf*, the final volume, will be available in 2021.Cathy also edits, formats print and e-books, and publishes other authors under her imprint, MacKenzie Publishing. She lives in West Porters Lake, Nova Scotia, Canada.

I, SCOTT MACMANN

Arguably my writer journey began the day the Life Squad came for my mother. Just three years old and the youngest of five, it was not long before my mother's older sister, Aunt Vera, came for me. In 1965 a brain aneurysm was tricky stuff. Maybe it still is, but it definitely was then. The operation was successful, but a post-operative stroke left my mom in a six-month coma from which she never exactly recovered. Alive, but permanently gone.

There's little doubt that novels and stories were the furthest thing from my mind as we boarded the airplane that would fly us from Cincinnati to Chicago, while the stewardesses doted on the blond-haired, blue-eyed little boy, and the captain pinned wings on my shirt. But the dual life I led for the next decade was formative. Summers in Chicago with my aunt and uncle. Winters in Ohio with my father and siblings. Summer friends. Winter friends. My library card up north had their last name, because it was easier than explaining.

Easier than explaining.

And growing up there was a lot of explaining to be done. Where's your mom? Some of my first stories were telling other boys and girls that my mom was dead. It was so much easier than telling them the truth.

Education, knowledge and books were highly valued in both my worlds. My parents were both teachers, and Vera was also a teacher. But whereas my father had lots on his mind, my aunt was retired and had me on her mind. Summer meant math and grammar worksheets, and lots of books from the local library. I did not resent these things. There was no other expectation in my mind. In retrospect, thank goodness for that.

At home the only remnant of my mother was her bookshelves of novels. She loved to read. And although she never got to share that love directly with me, indirectly I read many of her favorite books.

Books fascinated me. They were beautiful things to be treasured. That's probably when I really started to think of myself as a future writer.

Over time, I have come to see myself as one link in a noble tradition of storytelling that stretches back to the dawn of our species. How different are we from those persons sitting by the fire explaining a vast and terrifying universe to their tribes? My sense of my purpose in life is to offer some semblance of explanation to my fellows. To offer a glimpse of order and purpose in an otherwise chaotic and inexplicable universe? Yes. That's the goal.

I have met many along the path. Only a few told me my writing sucked. Others no doubt thought it. Mostly I received encouragement.

Unfortunately, it was not lack of encouragement, but lack of focus that led me astray. Life has a nasty way of intruding on the focus and dedication needed to produce fiction. One day you open your eyes and it isn't years that have passed, but decades.

Having opened my eyes and clambered up the scree back onto the path I might have progressed, but the next fateful day in my writer life was when I built up the nerve and walked through the doors of a Cincinnati Fiction Writers (CFW) meeting. That was 2015.

What I discovered with that group is the extraordinary power that comes from being with like-minded people. I discovered that even though one might not be attracted to a particular genre, that you could always learn more about your craft, which would strengthen your own writing. At the same time, as you learn, you help others learn too.

That environment is powerful, and it encourages and supports when your confidence flags. I am grateful to have found my little group, and of my many hopes for this universe of ours, one of my greatest is that CFW lasts forever.

Scott Macmann helped win the Cold War for America as a U.S.

Army infantry and military intelligence officer during the 1980s and 1990s. Warped by those experiences, his fiction often mixes military, political and social themes with a dash of absurd. *Winter Solstice* is his one published novel.

I, MARLON MARTINEZ

You enroll back into college, after a few years' sabbatical, after working menial jobs, after teaching yourself how to write and being semi-fulfilled by your talent. You're going back because you've been writing stories since the third grade and want to go *pro* and feel that having a degree or three might help legitimize you as a writer. You're usually the oldest person in the room but good genes help you not seem geriatric. You take multiple writing workshop while in college. During one of these workshops, it's your turn to submit a piece. It's a story about a group of people who meet once a month and commit suicide and then get immediately brought back to life. It's hilarious. You managed to make the piece funny and light, and to a certain extent, it is more *Rom-Com* than a tale about morbid and broken people.

The class reads the story and it is met with enthusiastic approval.

Except for one woman.

You never had any interaction with her prior, and in all honesty, you kind of don't know her name, but she *ice grills* you and doesn't move any of the muscles in her face. You look away from her gaze because eye contact, in general, was never really your thing.

The class ends, and all the students hand you their hard copy of the story with their comments. You're on a break before your next class starts, and you begin to read the comments eagerly. It's basically the same praise they gave you while in class but seeing it written down puts a different kind of butterflies in your stomach. Then you get to the paper that is not a fan. The comments begin with the person telling you how insensitive they initially thought the story was. How your lighthearted approach to suicide was insulting. They inform you that their father had committed suicide the month before.

And the butterflies turn into knots.

A deep despair and disgust with yourself washes over you and

190

your hands get to tingling as though *asleep*. The idea that you made a person feel worse, about the tragic death of their father, is something you never thought you'd have to think about. The *high* you got form all the praise and acclaim and pride, it gets flushed out of your system.

You soldier on reading the comments, you feel you owe it to the person, in some sort of backward attempt at respect. They talk about the resentment they felt when the story made them laugh when you described death by asphyxiation as: *a real pain in the neck*. The comments tell you that, while the person was ultimately glad that the *will they/won't they* storyline ended happily, they still wanted to punch you in the face. The comments say that they hated you for making them feel something that wasn't the pain of a father's untimely death. That you made them see that suicide has a selfishness that has nothing to do with them. Then you realize that the woman who was glaring at you during the workshop was this commenter. It becomes clear why she was looking at you in the way she was. She finishes her comments by saying that the story had helped to understand how to cope, not to completely get over, but to see that her father's death as complicated. She asks for a hard copy of the story, in her closing comment she says: *It will help me, and that can help my family.*

This—this gift—this is why you write.

This event, this woman sharing her unimaginable pain, engaging me in a type of intimacy whose only shared physicality between you were a pen and paper, will shape the rest of your life. It is the single greatest affirmation that every decision you've made, every heartache, every firing and quitting, every rejection letter, were all meant to happen exactly the way they needed to, and that following your *gut* had been right all along. Over time, you go on to get your degrees. You get published in multiple journals and magazines. You see your words, in print, appear in an actual, corporeal book. You do not take her gift for granted.

I'm very sorry for your loss, you tell her as you hand her a hard

191

copy of the story at the start of the next class. There's no eye contact exchanged and you think she says: *thank you.* She doesn't say anything to you for the rest of the semester. What was there to talk about? And, in the spirit of being honest, after all these years, after she changed your life, after you've accomplished so much, you *rack* your brain, but still can't remember her name.

Born and raised in Queens, New York, Marlon Martinez' view of the world takes an abstract and unique approach. His writings reflect his curiosity about drugs, sex, death, the forgotten, addiction, recovery, love and other technologies. He journeys to the bottom of the barrel, often at times looking at the obscure hilarity of the underworld, gets into the parts of ourselves we desperately try to hide, and gives the destitute a platform to tell their stories. Marlon gives hope to characters that find themselves hopeless. Marlon holds an A.A. in Creative Writing, and a B.A. in English studies.

I, JAN McCULLOCH

Born in 1961 Jan McCulloch has always been a writer, since she could first scribble a reasonably legible paragraph. But she never showed any of her writing to a single soul. Fear of being ridiculed and teased made her secretive, furtive even. Her stories were quickly torn up and thrown away in order to keep them from the critical eyes of older siblings. Being the youngest of a large brood possibly made her a reasonable target for jealousy, acted out by bullying and teasing. She cried herself to sleep often as a child. Maybe she was too sensitive, but sadly the bullying and teasing destroyed her confidence which led to further bullying and teasing at school.

Her love of animals brought her great joy however, and provided a welcome escape. She often had a hamster in her pocket or a rabbit up her jumper, and dogs trotting at her heels on long walks in local woods and fields.

In her early teens, Jan had started to write a story about a dog, on similar lines to Jack London's Call of the Wild. She had hidden it away in the back of her English homework book. Her English teacher, Mrs. Guest, found the story. She praised Jan and asked her to read it out to the whole class. Jan, blushing beetroot red, crippled by lack of confidence, terrified of the limelight and of henceforth being again a target for bullying and ridicule, declined. But Mrs. Guest read the story to the class. And the class enjoyed it. No one laughed or teased or ridiculed her work. It was the first time in her life that Jan actually felt she was good at something.

Life swiftly carried Jan along, marriage, children, a great many life experiences... Until one day in her mid-fifties she started to write again. It seemed as though the characters were spirits, whispering their stories, begging to be heard. Jan listens to them and tells those stories. These days she doesn't hide them or destroy them. She sets them free.

Jan McCulloch is a shepherdess who spends many hours with her dogs on farms around the UK. Her writing includes *A Little Dog's Prayer* and several short stories and a poem included in Clarendon House Publications anthologies. She regularly contributed to *Urban Tribe* online and is a named author on *Paragraph Planet*. She is currently working on a collection of poems that she hopes will be published early next year.

I, ANNE MERINO

I believe I was always really meant to be a writer. I grew up in a family of writers. My father was a noted writer of a number of well received books and had been quoted by the U.S. Supreme Court in one of their key decisions. My grandmother published serious literary poetry. My Uncle Cyril is the well-known Welsh author, Richard Cyril Hughes, and my lovely Great Aunt Ruth published a collection of short stories in the 1930s – *The Blue and The Jungle* – that was the basis for some short nature films for children in that era. The writing discipline was all around me in my childhood, always tugging at me and demanding to be taken seriously. Indeed, very early on I had the distinct impression that's what adults did once they had obtained their majority – they wrote something. Being published was a rite of passage.

My mother was always very encouraging of the arts in general and during one long Christmas holiday cheerfully suggested "*Why don't you write something?*" So my sister Vicky and I (we were six and seven respectively) spent a few days furiously scribbling down our stories in notebooks that mum had given us. Looking back, I realize she must have really needed the break. We finally emerged to solemnly hand her our notebooks and mum sat down with a large cup of tea to read our finished stories.

I had written a mystery story entitled "Secret of the Thirteenth Pharaoh." It ran about fifty pages and very much in the Julie Campbell Tatham (Trixie Beldon) style – if Julie Campbell Tatham had been seven. My lead characters were thirteen-year-old twins, Chip and Judy Powers who loved a good mystery. Their father was a well-known archaeologist who worked for *the government* for reasons unclear even to the author. The high point for me was giving Chip and Judy special secret government issued driving licenses that allowed them to pilot a car despite being thirteen.

My mother stoically made her way through all fifty handwritten pages filled with plot holes and improbable teenager access to secret government tech. She sipped her tea and finally pronounced that I had talent. *But–* I would eventually learn there was always a *but* in writing – she went on to note that I was in desperate need of great, punchy opening and closing sentences. Mum fetched a collection of Trixie Beldons and Famous Fives, showing me how these crafty writers wrote a catchy opening and closing.

"Secret of the Thirteenth Pharaoh" went into a desk drawer that Christmas and, thankfully, was never seen again. I continued to write for pleasure but my ambitions shifted to focus increasingly on a professional ballet career. Many dancers like to knit or crochet while waiting on the sidelines in endless rehearsals. Utterly hopeless at anything crafty, I'd plop down in a corner to stretch and write. I wrote detective novels that I never finished and the occasional short story but nothing quite as useful as a pair of colorful leg warmers. Still, all those fragments taught me a lot about what I enjoyed writing and helped me start to develop something of a style.

Retiring from the stage after an injury, I knew I wanted to create ballets about *people* with interesting stories to tell and challenges to overcome. Inventing a completely new form of ballet in which spoken dialogue and ballet were evenly divided to tell the story, I created *The Lady in White–* an Edwardian murder mystery – on my ballet company. It's success with Los Angeles audiences, allowed us to continue producing these hybrid ballets. When we realized, after 25 years, that it was time to close the company, we decided as a group to mount one last production --*The Moon Goddess*.

One of my touchstones is World War One. This terrible conflict has always resonated with me almost as if I had been in the trenches myself. I decided to do a ballet about a young Welsh army officer who sees the Moon Goddess – one of Welsh folklore's harbingers of death – pricking her way through the bodies on the battlefield one Christmas Eve. He realizes the Moon Goddess has come for him and reminisces about another Christmas Eve with old friends before the war. I wanted to the audience to see and become involved with him and his friends – all of whom would be heading into war. Britain lost an entire generation of its young men – the best and the brightest. In *The Moon Goddess* the audience sees them fall on the battlefield.

The final performance of *The Moon Goddess* saw tears on both sides – stage and audience -- for a variety of reasons. One of our dancers had a mother in Stage Four of breast cancer and this lovely woman had come to this performance despite being very very frail. After the performance, she made a point to speak to me which was very kind of her. She held my hand –"I just wanted to thank you. Thank you for this story. I was feeling pretty low when I got here but now, after this ballet, I know it's okay to die."

Later, I cried, relating this to my husband, Tom who is a filmmaker. He nodded and said "That's the power of writing, isn't it? You know, you've just been writing novels and screenplays with ballet all this time. "

It was then I understood that I really was a writer and always had been. I picked up a notebook – much like the one my mother had given me all those years ago – and started the first pages of what would become my debut novel, *Hawkesmoor*.

Anne Merino: a former ballerina who danced for notable classical companies both here in the United States and in Europe. While *Hawkesmoor* is her first novel, Anne's feature film screenplay, *A Season For Wolves*, did well in the annual Sundance Institute competition and was professionally workshopped in Los Angeles. She has written a number of plays including *The Dorian Proxy*, *The Moon Goddess* and *The Séance*, all of which have been professionally produced in Los Angeles. On a more scholarly note, Anne has published serious theatre criticism with Salem Press.

I, LYNN MICLEA

Ever since I was a child, I always loved reading. I loved stories and being caught up in a magical experience. Growing up in a difficult and uncomfortable family situation, stories provided an escape from a painful world into a delightful world of fantasy, wonder, and excitement. I couldn't get enough of those stories, and those escapes when my mom read to me, and later when I read books myself, were some of my favorite times.

For years I longed to write stories. However, I never thought I was capable of that and never even entertained the possibility until I retired. My entire working career was mainly in the business world and was at tedious jobs that left me feeling unfulfilled. When I finally retired and had no idea what to do with my time, I took an online writing class, and I was immediately excited and hooked. Motivated and driven with a new passion, and with plenty of free time to explore this compelling and amazing outlet, my creativity exploded. I was like a kid in a candy store. It was finally time to play. But I was still not sure what I would write. Toying with a few different ideas, it finally hit me — a story that begged to be told and that I could not ignore.

My mom had developed ALS years earlier, and after she passed, I had gone to a medium to see if I could get a message from her. Not only did I receive a clear communication from my mom, but I was also told that I needed to write a book. At the time I was not sure what that meant. However, while taking that online writing class after I retired, it hit me that my mom's story was the book I needed to write.

Writing that story was incredibly painful, and I sobbed as I wrote it, as I relived every agonizing moment — but it was so worth it. I knew if it moved me and made me cry, it would touch my readers as well. Not only did I learn writing skills through that, but it helped me move through the pain of losing her, including the difficulties we went through, and it brought me closure.

198

Publishing that first book opened a whole world for me and showed me that I continued to grow, and that maybe there was some hidden talent blossoming within me. It gave me a second life. My confidence and sense of self bloomed as well. Maybe I did have something to offer the world. Maybe I was more than I thought I was. The thrill of being able to express ideas, feelings, emotions, and stories, and also affect others through my writing, was intoxicating. Writing became compelling. A loner through most of my life, I finally found a place where I fit — I found my niche. Creating stories that would open worlds for others, take them on incredible adventures, and stimulate their imagination, was thrilling and exciting.

Since then, I have written and published many books, mostly fiction, and my husband is my biggest fan. He laughs, cries, gasps, and gets excited by my stories. He believes in me even when I am overcome with doubts and fears. When I wonder if I should keep writing, he is the one who tells me that my writing is not only good, but that it keeps improving. His unwavering belief in me helps me believe in myself, and that continues to grow. And I am especially grateful for his support since I ignore him all day long as I type away at my computer, hoping to touch others through my writing.

I find that as my writing improves, so do I. I become a better person each day, as I dig deep inside myself to find that place that is uniquely me and that needs to be expressed in some way through my stories, enhanced with bursts of imagination that always surprise me. And the more I grow and learn, the more I like who I am and who I am becoming. Each day, I believe in myself more and more, and that strengthens my writing and boosts my creativity, and my writing helps me continue to grow as well. Writing is a way to not only touch others, but to also be the best we can be ourselves. And that never ends.

I realize that so much of our writing goes beyond mere words. Words are a vehicle to touch people and make them feel something. And feeling something expands the human experience of life and also connects all of us. And I think that's what writing is really all about and why I need to keep doing it.

Lynn Miclea is a writer, author, musician, Reiki practitioner, and dog lover. Lynn has written numerous short stories and has published twenty-four books with more on the way. She writes science fiction, thrillers, suspense, paranormal, romance, mystery, memoirs, self-help guided imagery, and children's stories (fun animal stories about kindness, believing in yourself, and helping others). She hopes that through her writing she can help empower others, stimulate people's imagination, and open new worlds with her heartfelt stories. Originally from New York, Lynn currently lives in southern California with her loving and supportive husband.

I, LADY C. E. MILLER

I had an unconventional teacher in the second grade. We made Mother's Day Cards and we wrote them in Chinese, and I wrote them perfectly. She realized then because of my normal writing that I might have had dyslexia. My mom took me to a specialist, and I was diagnosed with a severe form of dyslexia. I can't see depth or remember left from right, over and under. Finally, we realized why I had so much trouble with my schoolwork... not to mention athletics which I was never good at like my siblings and I never liked the games anyway.

My mother and I spent every afternoon working with the exercises the doctor prescribed and we moved to a farm where I could have horses. A horse was all I ever really wanted. My mother homeschooled us when I was in fifth and sixth grade and caught me up to grade level. I rode my horses in competitions and I loved the time I spent with them.

I learned to write poetry from listening to my mom read hers to us. Through the years I found out my life lessons could be put pen to paper and not only involve an audience, but my words could hold their hearts, and sometimes heal.

A high school friend recently told me he has a poem I wrote when I was 15 framed on his living room wall. At 16 I was able to interview trainers from the Spanish Riding School of Vienna for an article for Western Horseman Magazine, the magazine didn't publish my article, but it was still a proud moment for me.

I grew up in the smallest town. Less than 300 people with one stop sign on Main Street, one little store, and two gas pumps. The gas station closed and in high school, my friends and I would have poetry readings in the parking lot of the closed gas station. It was a very small town. We would take turns sitting on the cab of the tallest truck and reading our newest poems and everyone's old favorites. Those are good memories for me, and they taught me a lot about how people react to words. Almost like magic, the words could change the mood, bring up memories and we would talk for hours.

After high school, I traveled for a few years, taking jobs on ranches, I broke horses and settled down on the East Coast for a few years. I had a bad experience there and returned home completely unsure about what I wanted to do from there. I had all but abandoned my writing in those years and picked up a little problem with anxiety attacks.

Two years later, I married a man who lives a simple country life on a small farm. The perfect life for me. He loves animals as much as I do. We have been married fifteen happy years. I still on occasion have problems with anxiety. Especially in my mid-twenties and though I found solace in my animals, I had an idea. I began drafting a novel.

I decided to do things differently. Instead of Beta Readers, I had Book Parties! My mom, my grandmother, and two of my great Aunts and some friends would get together and have slumber parties, where I would read my progress. Everyone would add ideas or ask for clarification. We would eat dinner, popcorn and sometimes have a fire. It was a blast!

In 2012, I had a riding accident. It was a serious injury and required surgery and I was laid up or on crutches for over a year. It was then I decided to start writing seriously and my novel became a big story. It is loosely based on the history of the Arabian horse and the research gave me something to occupy my mind.

I am a photographer and an artist as well as a writer. I have received honorable mention for my photographs from National Geographic, and won several local artist competitions. I still ride but only one horse, a gypsy cobb with which I have a special relationship. It took me a long time to get back on... as we say in Texas. It was a happy day when I summoned the courage to ride again. I felt lost when I couldn't bring myself to face that fear. For my entire life my footsteps have been shared with an animal. It's been an amazing journey and as I write my stories, I share those blessings with so many.

Christy Miller writes under the pseudonym Lady Miller, having been given an honorary title from Dunans' Castle in her quest of Ancestry. She lives in southeast Texas on a small farm where they have horses, cattle, sometimes goats... chickens, rabbits, dogs and cats and a general menagerie. She spends her time photographing, writing and painting. Sharing the country life with her husband and their four-legged family.

I, UMAIR MIRXA

The first book I ever read outside of school, if memory serves, was *Adventures of the Wishing-Chair* by Enid Blyton. It was an old copy, slightly battered, lent to me by my uncle. I wish I could say I had asked him for it, I really do, but I wasn't then the reader I am today. I want to say I read it the first time, but as a six-year old, running around the yard seemed far more interesting and important.

Every Sunday, from before I can remember to just after my fifteenth birthday, was spent at my uncle's home, almost without exception. We would arrive there soon after breakfast, spend the day, and leave around midnight or later. The adults cooked and shared gossip, watched TV, played chess, and discussed politics. I was usually bored out of my mind, especially when the only cousin my age wasn't around.

And so, one day, I read the book.

It was like nothing I have ever experienced, before or since. I could not believe such creatures and characters could exist. Never imagined such worlds could be brought to life with a few, well-chosen words. The possibilities which now lay before me were endless – the places I could go, the people I could meet, the adventures I could have.

Most important, perhaps, was the realization that books offered me an escape from a life which was unhappy more often than not, and miserable at all other times.

I began devouring books, hounding my uncle for one after another, and begging my mother to buy me more once he had run out of age-appropriate reading material for me. I read everything I could lay my hands on, and soon, there was no more room on my shelves for any toys or games.

It occurred to me, not much later and encouraged by a few school projects, I could write similar stories of my own. It was possible for me to create worlds of my own instead of simply visiting those sprung forth from the imagination of other writers. I could bring life to all the creatures running around inside my mind, and give stories to each character. I now possessed a power I had never felt or imagined before.

My first attempts at writing a story not assigned to me by a teacher came after I'd read the two-volume set of *Sherlock Holmes: The Complete Novels and Stories*, bought by mom as a present for my 13thbirthday. They were clumsy and childish, and wholly rewarding. One story I remember, the best I can describe it, was Sherlock Holmes meets the *Famous Five* meet the *Swiss Family Robinson*. All on a deserted island. It made no sense whatsoever, not even to me.

I joined a new school then, and began reading Shakespeare, Dickens, the Brontë sisters, and fell in love with *To Kill A Mockingbird* and *Wuthering Heights*. I was appointed editor of the class magazine, and soon, the most wonderful thing happened.

New friends came into my life, friends I hang out with to this day – two decades later, friends who appreciated and encouraged my love of the written word, even if they didn't themselves participate in it. Friends who insist there will come a day when I will abandon civilized life as we know it, and go off to live in a cottage by a lake in a forest somewhere, only to spend the rest of my days writing stories and being haunted by my own characters. I cannot claim they are wrong, for such a day is yet within the realms of possibility.

One of them told me of his desire to one day have on his shelf a book written by me so he could boast of his author friend, and I strive every day to make his wish a reality. I have received similar encouragement and support from other people: mother, siblings, friends, my wife, and most recently, fellow authors I have met in online writing groups. And yet, the journey from being a kid who fell in love with stories to a published author featured in several international anthologies has not been without its challenges and obstacles.

I was forbidden from formally studying literature because it was deemed a poor career choice, one which did not offer a secure financial future. I have been told, countless times, how I'd never amount to much if I insisted on chasing the "ridiculous" dream of writing stories for the rest of my life. Even now, when I tell people I've had a story published, the first question most of them think to ask is how much I was paid for it.

There have also been other doubts and fears along the way. Am I a good enough writer? A storyteller worthy of the rewards I hope to achieve? Not a fortune. Not even fame, not really but recognition, perhaps. But would my skills and talent and perseverance even matter in a world which refuses to let go of hate? Is it possible for a Pakistani Muslim to be a successful, English-language author? I wondered if I should write under a pseudonym, and really considered it for a long while, for fear no one would ever pick up my book off a shelf because of my name.

I decided against using a pseudonym the day I first left a message to Steve Carr, struggling to type as my fingers trembled from nerves, and asked him if he would contribute a short story to the digital magazine I was hoping to launch.

It's nearly three years to the day, and here I am writing this essay for Steve's book, and I have never thought about using a pseudonym since. The constant support and friendship offered to me by him, and other authors such as Shawn M. Klimek, David Bowmore, Mark Kuglin, Patt O'Neil, Mehreen Ahmed, Kelly Matsuura, Pavla Chandler, Dawn DeBraal, Julie Eger, and Jim Bates has meant the sixteen-year old kid who once read *The Lord of the Rings* and vowed he would one day write something similar can continue to dream of being a successful author, and to do it under his own name: Umair Mirxa.

Umair Mirxa lives and writes in Karachi, Pakistan. He is the creator/editor-in-chief of Paper Djinn Press, and has had his stories accepted for publication in anthologies from Black Hare Press, Fantasia Divinity Magazine & Publishing, Clarendon House

Publications, Blood Song Books, Iron Faerie Publishing, The Reanimated Writers Press, and Zombie Pirate Publishing. He is a massive J.R.R. Tolkien fan, loves everything to do with mythology, fantasy, and history, and dragons were real. When he's not writing, he enjoys reading novels and comic books, playing video games, listening to music, and watching movies, TV shows, and football as an Arsenal FC fan.

I, DAVID K. MONTOYA

I'm not like most people.

I never had confidence or people that believed in me for that matter, growing up and I came from a lower-middle-class family, which were considerably unemployed and uneducated. It appeared, just like the others, I was in line to follow the previous generations' footsteps. In that vital time of my life, no one ever pushed me to do my homework or schoolwork for that matter, and because I was always the *tall* kid in class, I was bumped up to the next grade each year.

With the lack of education and being the *odd* kid (I was not into football or manly things), I was considered an outsider within my own family. Some even believed that I was *touched* in the head. Well, you hear that sort of thing enough times, you yourself begin to believe it too.

So, when I entered high school, no one was surprised that I scored below a third-grade reading level on my reading assessment test. I was placed in a *special* reading class and felt less than average. I was an idiot. The tests proved it and, again, I believed it.

That was until something interesting happened.

I had a stack of comic books that my Aunt had given me for my birthday. I could not read them, but I was a fan of art for as long as I could recall. I would spend time looking at the beautiful drawings that exploded from the newsprint paper. That was until one day I decided to find out what the actual story was and begin to *read* the comic.

When I came to a word I did not know, my parents told me to "Look it up," and since *Google* had not been created as of yet, they were referring to a dictionary. I would borrow my Aunt's so much that she eventually just gave it to me (which I still own to this very day). I would highlight the word and practiced it until I knew it and then went back into the story.

Within that first year, I read every comic book I could get my hands on and then branched out into novels. HG Wells' classic *Animal Farm* was the very first book I read for fun. By then, as my Freshmen year begin to close, something else happened that changed my life. I found myself wanting to consume more than I could provide, and the thought of, "Well, I will just write my own story," popped into my head, and that was when I wrote my first story (which that too, I still have).

The following year, while I was still reading everything I was able to get my hands on, I spent most of my time writing stories. I admit they were not very good at all, but for the first time in my life, I *knew* what I was, and that was a writer. That second year, I entered my very first competition. Although I did not even place, I learned a few fundamental lessons about being a writer. You have to have thick skin; everyone has input on your story even if they have never written beyond a classroom essay. Second, that it is okay to fail as long as you learn from your mistakes, and I learned some writing tips from an English teacher that I still utilize to this day.

Over time, I began to craft stories that I tried to sell to big-name companies, but they turned me down once they discovered my age. With tons of rejections, I asked perhaps the biggest question in my life to the same Aunt, who gave me those stack of comic books, "Why don't I just make my own comics and sell them myself?"

Her reply was simply, "Why not?"

In that realm, I began to write and create for me, and just a few months later, I hit the streets with a stack of makeshift comic books that I wrote and drew. To my delight and utter surprise, they sold out (mind you, this was all still while I was in high school).

My confidence grew with each passing story I wrote, and my grades improved as well. I had a purpose, a meaning, a reason in life, to write. To travel to fantastic places and have an incredible adventure all within the confines of my imagination, then return to reality to share them all with anyone willing to consume them.

At the end of my Junior year, I realized that I had not *earned* enough credits to graduate High School. I understood that I wouldn't go anywhere without a diploma. I enrolled in a continuation school for my senior year. They were skeptical about me achieving the One Hundred and thirty-five credits I needed, but when that final year concluded, not only did I do the impossible, I held a 4.0 GPA that entire year.

It was in that final year that I truly found my confidence in writing, and as a reward in doing so, I found a new onset of confidence in myself as a person. That I could sincerely achieve the impossible, even if no one believed me, as long as I thought that I could make it happen. It was the first time in my life that I was proud of who I was. As I walked away as a new person, I swore that I would be there to help anyone that traveled a similar path.

That was all because I simply found the art of writing.

I have gone on to do many wonderful things in my life, and that is saying something since I am only forty-three years old. But the world of writing and telling stories was that catalyst to everything. As I sit here and reflect on everything, one thing will always hold. Even after I take my final mortal breath, and that is, I, David K. Montoya, knew I was a writer.

First published in 1992 with the release of an independent comic book. In a span of a decade, David wrote over 200 comics. At the turn of the millennia, went to work as a producer and co-writer on a horror film. The following year went back into comics until 2003, when he fell in love with traditional literature and begin writing short stories. From then until now, he has written eighty-two stories. That is only the writing side of him, as he prefers to stay private. He lives in Southern California with his three children, dog and his annoying ass cat.

I, RUTH MORGAN

"You're not a writer if you haven't had anything published. Anyway, no one wants to read your stuff!" Pearls of wisdom from the lips of my ex-husband.

I always thought marriage was supposed to be about mutual support, wanting the best for each other and encouragement to follow a dream. I obviously didn't read the fine print on the contract when I got into it at the ripe old age of 19. I thought he was probably right. He was much older than I was, more worldly, and as a man knew what was best for me. In the same way my father had. I pushed aside, to make him happy, all that made me happy.

I'd been writing stories and poetry since I could remember. My mother used to give me a book of stamps, ask me to look at the faces and tell her a story about them. I read from an early age, anything I could get my hands on, pestering my mother when I didn't understand a specific word. Throughout primary school I read and read, and wrote stories, essays, and poetry. This passion got me through the difficult years of high school, saved my backside doing my HSC. An essay question asked for a creative description of the discovery of Captain Bligh beneath the bed hiding from the Rum Corp. My resulting high mark for the subject gave me the first taste of 'success'. A poem published in the school magazine, gave me another. Reading kept me relatively sane as a teenager. I saved up all my pocket money as a thirteen-year-old and bought the first *Lord of the Rings* trilogy. I book I returned to over and over. A book I've had on my shelves for over forty years, and when I reread it, I still discover new treasures.

As a teenager I read romance, adventures, wildlife stories, crime fiction - anything! My father introduced me to Alistair Maclean, and Arthur Upfield. My mother to Pearl Buck and Catherine Cookson. She always liked stories that had a happy ever after. I loved stories that explored the darkness, pushed a character to their limits and beyond.

Birthday presents from my parents were always books. My grandparents would always send me books on wildlife or distant places. The pictures, the weight of the paper, and even the smell would make me smile. As an adult, an afternoon spent among the treasures in a second-hand bookshop is bliss and money well spent.

As I grew older, I started reading stories that were complex, or ventured into difficult subjects and offered new insights. I stopped writing when I got married, and only started again when I was in my thirties. Dark, difficult crime fiction stories where the characters had to confront evil and win through. Inspiration, though I didn't admit it, came from childhood and a manipulative marriage. Writing gave me the opportunity to change the ending.

Planning to leave my marriage, I began to search for my own identity, and work out a way to be financially independent. I decided to go to uni. Living in regional New South Wales, most of my study was done on line - and that suited me very well. Essays would come back with notes suggesting less story and more analysis.

Two years off finishing my degree I walked out to start a new life. My departure had been carefully planned over difficult months. I moved away to a new location, the marital home I loved was sold and gave me enough money to buy somewhere I had chosen. I knew no one when I moved, needed the street directory to find my way around, was alone but not lonely. I had study obligations, and a new life to build and I had books. Many were friends from childhood.

Study finished, I graduated and decided to give myself a couple of months to rest and recover. I quickly got bored and looked around for a new challenge. Tidying up the files on my computer I rediscovered an old novel draft and began reading. Not bad, I thought. Needs work. That was it. The world of writing which had been waiting for me to return wrapped around me like a familiar shawl. I was sunk and increasingly committed to a life that involved writing, writing and more writing. I was incredibly fortunate to be debt free and frugal and set myself a goal of two years to get something into print. At the end of two years, I would review the situation, and if necessary, get a "proper job." At the end of that second year, I had a story published after it won a highly commended.

The decision was made. I was a writer. I would follow my dream. It took another eighteen months of long days, tears, frustration, study and hard work before my next story was published and I was paid for it! Since then, there have been a number of stories published. I've finished two novels that are currently on a hard fourth draft before beta reading, and a professional structural edit. I grew so much as a writer when I started seeking feedback and doing whatever courses came along. Everything I did taught me something about writing, and life.

I look around me now and am content, happy, fulfilled. I have found my tribe - well, several writing tribes and this year for the first time I will put "Writer" as my profession on my tax return.

I write because I am a writer. I have always been a writer. I see the world in stories. Writing is as vital to my existence as breathing. Without words, I am only half alive.

Ruth was born in the Mallee region of Victoria and now lives in the Northern Rivers of New South Wales. She has had stories published in *The Underground Writers Zine, Spillwords* and the *Inner Circle Writers Magazine.* She was fortunate to be part of the Great Clarendon House Writing Challenge. Her preferred genre is crime fiction and is currently working on two novels about police corruption and the theft of uncut diamonds.

I, DIANNE MORITZ

I'm a late bloomer. Growing up, I aspired to be a teacher. I liked little kids, enjoyed spending time with them, and had a cosmic connection with their joyful spirit and honesty.

When I was hired to teach first grade in inner city Los Angeles, I couldn't have been happier. Teaching, writing lessons, planning hands on projects, taking school trips, the three Rs, plus art, music, and PE, was all I'd hoped it would be.

Yet, as many text books were not accessible in the inner city, I began to write my own units of study: science, ecology, social studies, and more. I immersed myself in modern children's literature. I marveled at the poetic genius of picture books. Books like: *Frederick* by Leo Leoni; *Where the Wild Things Are* by Maurice Sendak; *Elmer the Patchwork Elephant* by David McKee were favorites. I loved these little jewels of sparkling prose and began toying with the idea that, perhaps, I could write for kids. So I penned poems to augment lessons, made up riddles and rhymes, told tales, and encouraged my students to write their own stories.

At recess one day, a teaching buddy pulled me aside on the playground. "Dianne, you are so creative," she said. "You should be doing something more than teaching in a classroom. Have you ever thought of publishing your work?"

Publish? Could I actually publish my writings? I was astonished, then intrigued. So I continued to scribble words, words, and more words. My students giggled and laughed at my work, prompting more and more experiments with rhythm, rhyme, and word play. Soon I was convinced I could succeed. I would be an artist, with words as my medium.

In the summer of 1984, I visited my sister in Southampton, NY, two miles from the most beautiful beaches in the world. I found the area so peaceful and inspiring that I quit my city teaching job and moved out to the country to write full-time.

I wrote, wrote, and wrote some more, then submitted pieces to publishers. I had a small smattering of successes: sold three essays to the New York Times, some to other newspapers, published poems and craft ideas to kids' magazines, and created a Country Kids' Crafts column for a local kiddie newspaper. I loved every minute until ...

...my savings ran out. So I started a cleaning service, tidying up after wealthy New York City second homeowners in the Hamptons. I liked cleaning, it was profitable, and offered plenty of time for writing.

In March, 2010, I spotted a call for picture book manuscripts in the *Children's Writer* newsletter. I thumbed through my files, took out a promising story, spiffed it up one last time, and mailed it off. I had a contact from Kane Miller two weeks later. My first book deal! With a publisher! After thirty years of writing, my first children's book, *Hush, Little Beachcomber*, was sold. Beyond ecstatic, I quickly sent them another book and had a second contract several days later.

Both books went on to receive good reviews. My second book, *1, 2, 3 By the Sea*, a bestseller, was selected for Bank Street College's "Best Books List, 2014."

Persistence paid off! After nearly thirty years my dream has come true. I am a children's author.

Yes, I'm a late bloomer, but I'm in full flower now... enjoying myself no end!!

Dianne Moritz, a former K-3 teacher, has published over five hundred stories, poems, action rhymes, and craft pieces in many children's magazines. She is a frequent contributor to *Highlights, High Five*. Her fourth book, *Going on a Ghost Hunt*, is slated for release in fall 2022.

I, PRAKASH NAGARAJAN

I live in a small town, some eighty miles from Mumbai, India. My background is humble. My family hails from the south of India (Tamil Nadu) but have made Maharashtra its home, having settled over there several years back. I belong to a large family - three brothers and two sisters. I'm the second youngest. Over years, my parents have passed away. Education-wise, I'm a post-graduate in Marketing, IT and Business Management.

By nature, I'm quiet. I often like to ponder over the nature of human existence. Being more of an observer, I tend to view events and happenings in the society at large, in a more equanimous and dispassionate manner. Writing allows me the vent to voice my thoughts and feelings. For me, writing is a truthful expression of what one feels inside. As an individual, whatever experiences I go through in life personally usually becomes with me fodder for thought. I like to share through my writings those experiences with my readers.

Many a times I choose poetry as a medium to communicate my thoughts, not because of its intrinsically lyrical form or its concise nature, but more often than not, it helps find an instant connect. I sincerely feel, very many social issues can be portrayed sensitively or highlighted through this lovely medium of poesy. I try to shape or write my poetry in a way, where it will find on its own an immediate successful bond between me as a narrator, with my reader...allowing him or her to dwell on my poem...not simply read it.

Apart from poetry, I love doing fiction-writing. Through my works of fiction as well as poetry, I usually try to bring to fore, thematically, aspects of social ills that plague our modern societies.

How and why did I become a writer? Of course, it never was a conscious decision on my part to become one. But I can tell you, my love for books and literature had begun at a very early age, even while I was a stripling at school. And funnily enough, this passion

216

had nothing to do with the school itself! I still remember, as students, we would be allowed a period of recess in between the day for having our lunch. My mother, having to cater to the needs of a large family, and often busy with urgent household chores, would at times be harried for time to provide me with lunch, and thus sheepishly offer me a few coins so I would be able to buy for myself something to eat during those break hours.

Very near to my school, there used to exist a small shop that dealt in sale of second-hand comics, and books of pulp-fiction. Taking a stroll during those break hours, more often than not, I would be found in front of that stores, gaping with longing at the colorful covers of comics and books put up for display. The attraction for comics and books were so great for me that I would use only a small portion of my lunch money to buy food for myself, and use the greater part of it to buy those novels and funnies. At times, I would even remain hungry, forgoing lunch, just so I could afford to buy some book!

The books I brought and read back then, became my first love. The more I read, the more I used to get enamored by them. Over a period, I began to own a huge collection of books ranging from comics to pulp-fiction, from autobiographies, to history, and also many other books of serious literature. These books held me in great thrall. I would find myself getting carried over by the charm of their words, ideas, thoughts, the magic of pictures they contained, and the mysteries they wove around me.

Books became my friends for life. I became a voracious reader and still am, but never did the idea of wielding a pen by myself ever cross my mind. I was quite content, remaining engrossed in a world surrounded by books. It wasn't until much later in life, when our family business began failing, (We have a small electronics stores. My father had started it, and I used to assist him in running it.) did the thought of taking up writing as an alternate career choice struck me. I toyed with the idea but never got serious about it. In the meanwhile, online shopping sites, and huge shopping malls in vicinity of our stores were playing havoc with our business, having virtually hijacked the bulk of our customers, resulting in very low footfalls to our stores. But the final straw on the camel's back for me was, when I lost my father. It broke me from inside. I revered and loved him to no end. His loss made an even more introvert of me, as I brooded over for months unable to come to terms.

It was around the same period, I happened to meet an old friend of mine who knew of my love for books and reading. It was she who drove in me the idea, to take up writing as a profession. Thus, I began. Afternoon times in our stores remain relatively free of customers. I started utilizing the spare time I got, to focus on my writings. It kept me engaged, apart from the joy I derived from penning my thoughts. Writers from past whom I idolized became my inspiration in this venture.

I still continue with my work in the stores, and which provides modestly for me and my family. I have found a little success as a writer, having authored three books till date. I'm planning to come out with a book of poems soon, and have fond hopes of it becoming a big hit!

We all live with hopes, don't we?

To all my dear readers, I will just wish your dreams come true too.

Prakash Nagarajan is an upcoming author and a poet extraordinaire from India. Though reticent by nature, he is a keen observer of life, and coupled with his penchant for writing, he often puts to paper with a lovely flourish, his thoughts, views and observations. His easy, conversational style of writing makes most of his books a compulsive read, giving insight to his world views, and values that he cherishes utmost in life. When not confined to his desk churning out poems and stories, he seeks pleasure in long walks, is an intense nature-lover, and avid photographer.

I, FESTUS NWACHUKU

I began writing stories and poems when I was eight, in the form of diary entries and letters to my extended family, teachers and friends. I loved to watch their faces beam with rays of amazement as they read those letters in my presence. And sometimes, they drifted towards me and whispered into my ear, "From where did you steal the story?"

It was a talent that my mum briefly nurtured by buying me more illustrated storybooks than my teacher had recommended. And my dad, who worked in a paper mill, would bring home more exercise books and diaries. So, I had many storybooks to read and diaries in which to write my letters and stories.

Though writing has been a hobby I enjoy, it's also an escape route from unexplained, major depression that has afflicted me since age seven. I didn't know what the condition was called at the time, neither did my parents know, but I knew I felt sad, frightened and withdrawn some of the time, so reading and writing stories and poems in my solitude were very good ways to escape the prevailing reality and create another, which to me was a much better world. It was so much fun, that when it goes well, it's all joy and when it doesn't, it's all sadness.

But the whole thing took a sudden turn for the worse a year after I left my immediate family for my maternal family in Enugu, at my own request, because I'd wanted to attend a particular high school, though I was still in primary school. I suffered a great deal of physical and emotional abuse, in addition to school bullying, which exacerbated my depression, rendering my writing adventure a way too difficult journey across a hostile region. Sadness itself, somehow, became my muse. And with time, the inspiration to write fizzled out and left dabbling with other dreams.

After I graduated from the University of Nigeria in 2016 with a degree in biochemistry, I managed to trace my path back to my old dream, almost lost, with just a modicum of idea on how to craft a good story. My writing skill began to shrink with harsh opinions of friends, skepticism of family members and total lack of encouragement. No one wanted to read what I wrote, and not even to hear that I still write – to them, it was a woeful waste of time. Nevertheless, I took up two jobs, teaching in a high school and working in its clinical laboratory. These jobs further shrunk my time for writing, because, really, writing doesn't pay much, unless you're Stephen King or J.K. Rowling or Chinua Achebe. Most people who write, do it for the love of the art, which was the case with me.

In a quest to improve my skill, I joined some writers' groups on Facebook, to learn from others' contributions and meet new writer friends. That's when I met Robert Shafer, an American author, poet and navy veteran, who was really keen on helping me out, though he wasn't an established writer, and he made it known to me that he didn't have much to give. But from him, I learned to carefully select every word in a sentence, to write with simple but powerful words, and to make conflict a vital instrument in my stories, in which there should be a clear distinction between a protagonist and an antagonist, and add suspense with shorter sentences if it would be necessary. It was a memorable experience with him. Unfortunately, he died on the 19th of August, 2020.

But until I met Steve Carr, I wasn't enlightened on the underlying knowledge of crafting a well-written story. The vague and underdeveloped characterization was the first flaw he pointed out, and then lack of coherence. I was just dabbling with different themes in a simple short story with wrong punctuation. He really enlightened me on how to build a story around my characters and give them identities and personalities, and make them interact with themselves and with the world I'd created around them.

My first published short story, "The Water Child," was actually edited by Steve Carr before he recommended it to the Dastaan World editors, who subsequently published it. And to me, that was a massive progress. Since then, I've received so much encouragement and support from him, including invitations to several writing groups, which greatly influenced my growth as a writer. His stories gave me a great deal of insight, on how much life a florid writer gives to a story and the characters therein.

I believe that reading is a very important part of writing; it's like breathing in and out. You become a better writer by first being a good reader, especially when you read like a writer.

Music is so much a pool of inspiration to me, in fact, I find myself almost getting addicted to listening to music while writing. Personal experiences and that of people I know do influence my writing if it should be a realistic fiction. Sometimes, the imagination doesn't fall from the sky like in fantasy fictions. And when I meet some kind of writer's block, I'd leave the story or poem for a while, eat some cheese, perhaps a little nap or scroll down Facebook and Instagram to read some stupid things. And then comes a voice yelling in my head, to keep moving till the end.

At this time, I've come to realize that you don't always have to depend on people to inspire or encourage you. People can only ignite a fire in your heart to write, but only you can keep it burning. Peoples' successes inspire me. I'll always find ways to inspire myself. Growth is a gradual, continuous process. And every writer's dreams are valid. Writing often makes a writer, otherwise, the skills would slowly and inattentively die off.

Festus was born in the Southeastern State of Abia, but grew up in Anambra and Enugu States, Nigeria. He moved to Jos upon graduation, where he taught in a high school, but currently lives in Abuja, where he now works in a clinical laboratory. He has a degree in biochemistry from the University of Nigeria, Nsukka, but loves writing stories and poems. His short story "The Water Child" has appeared in Dastaan World Magazine. He is currently working on a collection of poems and short stories.

I, IKECHUKWU OBIORAH

Initially, the journey of words seemed rigorously operose: the journeyer is always compelled to cope with the fears of crossing rivers in the chest every day. But over time, I discovered that writing has a way of getting me refined in the furnace of affliction. Though I started studying the Michael West and Macmillan Dictionaries from my pupilage, I have always wanted to be a lawyer having writing as another labour of love. Because I love learning about how words respond to stimuli. But I have always apportioned myself some diatribes on how to achieve my goals, since I came from a lightweight background.

My journey of words started with tears falling like the sky suffering from dysentery. I lost my Dad at a very tender age and my Mum just living from hand to mouth. With my talent of advocacy and writing, I cried that I could just become a waste of the person I am, without a sponsor to further my education. I managed to finish my secondary education with my beloved sibling Ogbonna who took a decision to work in a hotel to bankroll my University education. I finally got admission to study law, after meeting up with the requirement, just to have my admission denied under gunfire by corrupt elites in the country. Then, I alternatively chose B.A English, to enable me develop my writing skill. Though my ambition of becoming a lawyer never dies.

My B.A. English course at the Benue State University, Makurdi, Nigeria programmed my mind to write passionately without fear. I joined The Writers' League; a literary club where writers are being groomed in my University, to get acquainted with the act of writing through the anatomy of literary criticism. The young writers in the literary club usually present their works to be critiqued by some professors and fellow students. At the ne plus ultra of my writing life in the University, I emerged as the Editor-in-Chief of The Writers' League, followed by the appointment to serve as a Student

Ambassador of POETS IN NIGERIA (PIN). The intellectual theatre really cooked me to confront the world with a knife between my teeth. It made me bold and brash with great impudence, to submit my literary works without fear of rejection.

My first literary submission in life was accepted and published in *Poetica 2019, Inner Circle Writers' Anthology*, by Clarendon House Publications. Being published in the Great Clarendon House Publications killed my fear, and made me feel that my works could be published anywhere. That actually became a kind of solidification of spine that gave me the lead in walking a tiger. Since then, I have made a lot of progress having my works published in several reputable international anthologies, magazines and journals across the globe.

Though many a people, including my course-mate friends in my University who knew me as a bookworm, tried every negative statement to discourage me from writing. Despite my testimonies of having some of my works published internationally they still sarcastically questioned my financial benefit, to my own dismay. However, my beloved sibling paying all the ultimate sacrifices for my academic has a great confidence in my talents and abilities. He ginger swaggered me up whenever I was down, to make me feel that my writing has value to the world. He is my true Hero who equally made sure that my debut novel *The Black Python Empire* was published.

My hard work has begun to bear fruits. My beloved lecturer has selected my debut novel *The Black Python Empire* to lecture the students in the department of English and Literary Studies, Benue State University, Makurdi, Nigeria. I have won some literary contests, and represented my University in several literary competitions. I have had the opportunity to impact positively on lives with my own social awareness aimed at making people happy, in my own little way. I have learned to maximize my strength and not to conquer everything. I have also learned to be responsible with my choices.

Writing has made me a nucleus of egghead, carrying ammunition of ink to pull down every deceptive industry. Because I have tamed my demon. And today, my University is proud of me!

Ikechukwu Obiorah is the author of *The Black Python Empire*, a Nigerian award-wining poet, and a novelist included in the *Who is Who of Emerging Writers 2020*", and in *The Book of Books* by Sweetycat Press. His poems have been published in *Poetica*, by Clarendon House Publications, *Spillwords Press, Ponders Series, Breaking Rules Publishing, Better Than Starbucks, Cajun Mutt Press, Active Muse Journal, Sage Cigarettes Magazine, McMaster University Press (The Muse), Relocations, Journal of the Asia-Pacific World, University of Toronto, PCC INSCAPE, Bradlaugh Fingers, the Nigerian magazine EroGospel*, and others. Poetry has been his sweetheart for a decade.

I, P.A. O'NEIL

I have always been a writer. What have not always been is a published author, that came much later in life.

My career began in Kindergarten when I penciled a "graphic novel" about people with beaks for faces. I remember my mother laughing. First mistake, I let other people's opinions in regards to my talent get to me.

During my senior year in high school, I became interested in a writing career, when I attended a state-wide conference. Between goofing off as unsupervised teenagers will do, I attended two lectures by a man named Frank Herbert. Seemed he had written some book called *Dune* which had met with great success. I remember his telling about how he didn't start as a master novelist but had worked his way up through various positions in the publishing business, even serving as a script writer, which really piqued my interest. Did you know, he wrote the movie script about the cowboy who was a teenaged werewolf?

My desire to write, especially scripts, carried with me to college where I wrote several commercials for a Radio & Television Production class. I even wrote a radio play which the entire class helped produce, sound effects and all. It was magnificent, in my humble opinion, but when I asked for the original script back from the professor, his response was the college had produced it, thus now it was the college's property. Second mistake, naivete can be painful.

It was another forty years before I wrote anything of worth. I have always had vivid dreams, and some I kept notes about, but I never followed through with publishing them. Besides, where would I begin? The internet was in its infancy and Amazon hadn't even a seat on the stock exchange. In August of 2016, my life caught up with technology when I found myself unemployed for the second time in a year. Daily I would spend hours on the internet applying for positions, but afterwards I needed more than sitting on the couch to watch old movies. Coincidentally, I had one of those dreams, where it stays with you after you wake. I spent several days thinking about what would happen to the characters, the what-ifs, and how-abouts. With a satisfactory ending to their story in mind, I sat down at 8:00 am and wrote until 5:00 pm, for the next two-and-half weeks (allowing for weekends off, mind you). When done, I had a moderate novel entitled, *Finding Jane*, and job offer.

A few of close friends read it and thought it was wonderful, but one had the honesty to tell me, "it was like a runway model, beautiful but with nothing to wear." She was right of course. *Finding Jane* has good bones, and some great passages, but too slight and needed to be reworked. But how was I going to do that—take a class, join a writing group at the library, hire a ghost writer? With my new job, I had neither the time nor the money for any of those options. I did have access to people on Facebook who I was directed to a few writing groups. I joined a wide-eyed novice, sat in the back of the ethereal room, and took notes. I developed relationships with writers, some I consider my closest friends today though we have never met, as I learned about styles, industry standards, professionalism, and genres.

One of them challenged me to "publish or perish." I discovered a fan-group for Jim French Productions. He was writing and producing his own radio plays of *Harry Nile* and authorized renditions of *Sherlock Holmes*. There was a contest for a 1,000-word Holmes story (any time period). My story, "The Good Student," won. Fearing plagiarism, I sent it as a PDF which they transcribed for their newsletter, but the spell-checker used a word wrong and ruined the story. Third mistake, not every publisher is greedy, and this would not have happened if I had allowed for them to just cut and paste the document.

One of the groups advertised open submissions for an anthology. I barely understood how to do that, but quickly popped off a couple of stories, which were both rejected. I wasn't disappointed, I felt lucky to have gotten this far. One of my friends was opening shop as an editor and offered to look at my work. That was painful! He pointed out my weaknesses—punctuation, tense, and overuse of the semi-colon. I reworked both stories as suggested, and bingo, one of them became my first acceptance released in October of 2017. Fourth mistake, thinking my work was the best it could be with only the computer's assistance. I have used an editor ever since.

I'm known for my short stories with over thirty published online and in print. Recently, my own collection was released, but for a time there I didn't think it would come to fruition. Not lack of a contract, I could've self-published at any time, but because in June 2019 I had a mini stroke which set back my production schedule by three months. Feeling reasonably healed, I submitted new stories, and fan favorites, to the publisher in January of 2020.

The year 2020 has been a wild a ride for everyone, but for me it included a cancer diagnosis in March with surgery in April. My book, *Witness Testimony and Other Tales*, was released at the beginning of May and has been met with great success. It's been over half a century for my "writing career" to come to fruition, and at times *life* set stumbling blocks along the way. I understand now, it just wasn't right for there to be earlier success. I had to learn through experience, gain confidence, and be thankful for any God-given talent I might have. I appreciate my life and desire to keep producing stories of worth for the entertainment of others and help new writers on their publishing journey.

P.A. O'Neil has been writing professionally four years. Her stories have been featured in multiple anthologies, as well as on-line journals and magazines from several continents. She and her husband reside in Thurston County, Washington. Her book, *Witness Testimony and Other Tales*, is available in paperback and e-book, from Amazon. For links to other books which feature her stories, look under the Photo sections of her Facebook author page: P.A. O'Neil, Storyteller, or visit her Amazon author page: P.A. O'Neil.

I, EDENTU OROSO

The first time the variegated world of books drew me in with its diverse offerings and stretched my imagination boundlessly, I was barely six-years-old. In primary school at the time, the reality that I could fly literally beyond the boundaries of my perception through the intrinsic power of words on the pages of books, made me feel like I had unleashed a genie on the inside of me. Its swift wings lifted me with ease into distant horizons, or those realms I could easily reach out to or touch by a stretch of the imagination.

Ever since that first impulse of thought about the world of books, the genie of my childhood fancies has remained a part of my adult consciousness, creating impressions of different hues on different canvasses depending on the nature of the inspiration at any given time.

Creative writing for me has always bordered on the compulsive need to explore new frontiers – the inner craving to discern and situate the tenor and temper of human emotions and actions – what these imply and their rebound on the collective.

I have been enthralled several times by the ideals perceptible on the spawn just as I have been repelled too by distress of various shades. While the need to hold up the mirror to society – which is the primary duty of a writer – often tosses me to shout from the rooftops about what's gone awry in society and how these aspects of things could be redressed for the common good, creative writing, or writing of any kind, has remained a catharsis of some sort that has helped to enhance my life's quality.

I'm at my creative best at moments of inner agitation. When my mind is riled and I need an outlet to purge it of the stirring emotions, I pick up my pen or laptop to write. In navigating other shores in its creative bursts, the tumultuous sea on which the ship of my mind sails finds a smooth berth. Focusing on what my mind is trying to create or conjure through the power of words, often banishes the seething emotion and sets me free from the rein of fear or anger.

228

One thing I have also discovered in the course of writing as a novelist, poet, biographer, columnist, or critic, is that words are powerful and carry meanings beyond the physical. This assertion is not religious in context but a product of an experience I had while working on my first full-length book over two decades ago. It's just what it is, the power of the mind unleashed on paper.

An explanation will suffice. In 1996 I started a book project which I titled *Another Hill*. I didn't know the implications of that title until I had an encounter in a trance flight with an elderly woman who called my attention to the title of the book.

"Son, do you really want to complete this book?" she asked, her eyes glazed with concern.

"Sure," my glib reply went.

"I don't think so."

"Why is that?"

She pointed to a quaint hill behind where I stood. "Look behind you."

I did as instructed.

"That's the hill you've created in your subconscious with the title of your book," she said. "Each time you pick up the book and look at the title, your inner self creates a hill because that's the energy you are constantly feeding it. If you want to finish the book, then go and climb over the hill."

I turned on my heels and climbed up the small hill. Half of the hill disappeared as a result.

"Repeat the process, son," she intoned, watching with keen interest.

The moment I climbed the remaining part of the hill, it disappeared.

She grinned. "Now you can complete your book!"

I awoke from the trance flight at that moment with a start. The experience taught me enduring lessons. That as writers we create realities that are not only physical but spiritual with the power of our minds. Armed with this knowledge, I have always paid attention to the things I write or think about because we all live in our consciousness.

I have written some things down on paper and have seen them come to pass with precision. It means I have to exercise care in my thoughts and words because by them I'm taking on the role of a mini-creator…of things both tangible and intangible.

Edentu Oroso is a poet, biographer, public speaker, columnist with *The Nigerian Pilot* newspaper, bestselling author, and publisher. A member of the Association of Nigerian Authors (ANA), Benue State Chapter, he is the author of the #1 Amazon Bestseller *Titan Race; Richer Than Pride; Strides of Destiny;* and *Memories of Yesterday.*

I, A.L. PARADISO

The beginning may be a good place to start. Since I was born in Italy and spoke nothing but Italian until first grade, English truly is my second language. I had the benefit of immersion and, since I was behind by a few years, intense study of English grammar and vocabulary.

My next writer-shaping experience came in college. When I took an extremely restrictive creative writing class and absolutely HATED it, I swore I'd never do any writing again. Yet, I thought I was OK with it and even passed the class. Etymology became a happy hobby even before I knew what that meant. Looking up words in a real dictionary developed into an adventure as one word lead to another and became an interesting trip.

If I must narrow my choices of influences to the extreme, three consistently come to mind. Although I thought, "I really should write these while I can," it took another catalyst to push me there. That was the impressive influence of the *Babylon 5* author and my understanding of the improbability of creating a cohesive tome of 122 "chapters" of one overall arc with several mini arcs. Online discussions with him and his advice and story convinced me to write some forty-eight years after my vow of writing celibacy.

When I found a web site which published stories free and gave me feedback in the form of reader viewings, comments and voting, I started under a pen name. Fourteen years later, I still write for that site and now have 123 stories published there with 4.8 million views. Looking back at my early "good work," I can see I have evolved. I'm leaving the early works there as a humbling lesson for me. A strong grammar foundation has been a great aide, but did nothing for style. Two Psych courses and studying examples of good writing style and tips, especially from *Babylon 5*, set my personal style and direction.

Those three influences I mentioned were all huge personal

traumas. It was years before I felt I could tackle any of them. One, "Black Feline Love," has been published in an anthology. Briefly, it's about one of the closest relationships in my life. It was with a cat I helped birth and her intensely close bond to me. She passed 11/3/98 and I still can't think of her without tears.

The second trauma was about the one who got away. I named that one *Just the LOML*. We met in sixth year French class, accidentally became friends and dated chastely. If only she were not engaged. When I submitted that story as a catharsis and it was rejected, I wasn't sure if I were more relieved than sad.

The third trauma, thirty-six years old, is still unwritten. Twenty-two painful years to attempt an outline, five more to decide a structure, and the rest to add the least painful notes of a total betrayal on that day. Currently, I plan to write it from five perspectives of four people and a totally "objective" observer. Good luck, me.

Three interesting, or frightening, incidents stand out among others. In a chapter of a Pygmalion type story, I couldn't name a new character. Even after searching multiple baby name sites, nothing fit. When I decided to leave it blank, I wrote his entrance, "Hi, my name is – *Valen* –" WHAT! No idea where that came from. The only other Valen I know of is a *B5* character who has zero resemblance to mine. Stunned, I couldn't write for fifteen minutes.

While I was resolving my *Dumbistan* story, I struggled with where to set it. Ultimately, I chose a hot country, near the equator around the Eurasia border. It needed an international airport with dense city roads becoming fewer as they left the city. The roads dwindled to a trident with one road ending in a huge empty area. My character would then walk ninety minutes to find the sole village of about 400 people in the tiny country. I wanted it primitive with hints of modern touches, a creek angled on its left, a large lake about twenty miles East for fish. Once I "saw" that in my head, I opened Google Maps and searched the area for best fit. The second airport I found in that area is in Armenia. When I followed the roads North and East, they reduced to a trident which ended in one longer leg ending at a huge green field. There is a big lake to the East. When I looked West, there was nothing — until I zoomed in to the max and found a tiny dot. It was a village of 397 people with a creek to its left. I got goose bumps.

The third stunning experience was on the day I met my muse floating behind my right shoulder. Arms folded, she was staring sternly at my screen and shaking her head at a scene I tried to shoehorn into my Pygmalion story. Full details are in a story about that meeting called "How I Met my Muse." She had a few words to add to that story and I knew better than to argue with her.

Even more stunning than seeing her — the spitting image of my main character — was that she *literally prevented* my fingers from touching the keys until I agreed to delete that scene. When my fingers reached an inch from the keys, they and my arms froze. When I moved them away, they flexed fine, then froze again an inch from the keys when I tried to continue. Heart pounding, I agreed to delete the scene and I could touch the keys once more. If I recall that meeting in too much detail, I get goose bumps again.

Respect and listen to your muse. Heed my warning.

A.L. Paradiso now lives in upstate New York with three cats. He managed a series of oil company outlets; ran two of his own; became a mechanic, then truck driver, did direct sales; became a Field Engineer for main frame computers. After ten years he switched to software and worked ten more years, receiving worldwide acclaim, as a System Programmer. As of August 2020, he has shared 140 published stories with others online (over 4.8 million views), in thirteen anthologies and three literary journals. We suppose he's one of those who just can't keep a job!

I, LYNNE PHILLIPS

My love of books started when, aged six, I learned to read. I fell in love with stories. I loved the places books took me, places that my imagination hadn't known. I loved tales of adventure, fantasy, and make-believe. I always had my head in a book. I was the kid who read under the covers with a torch after lights out.

To own a book was a treat, apart from *Little Golden Books*, books were mainly purchased as presents for special occasions. For Christmas every year I received a *Girls Annual* which was a thick hard covered book full of the most amazing stories. The newsagent would order it from England which made it seem more special. I treasured those annuals, reading the stories over and over until I received the next one.

Mostly I borrowed books from the school and town library, reading half a dozen books a week. Now I have a personal library, piled high with books, all treasured. I am still an avid reader, having up to six books on the go at once.

At high school I discovered, H.G. Wells and Frank Herbert, and my love of science fiction began. I wasn't into non-fiction and was probably the only student who wrote a history assignment like a work of fiction.

When I started teaching, I became a verbal storyteller. Telling stories to young children was an effective way to teach new concepts, convey rules, and for behavior modification. I never wrote my stories down, although students would recall them years later and tell me what a difference they made to their learning.

I am known as the "Puppet Lady." My collection of puppets help me tell the stories. Students were more attentive when the puppets were involved in their learning. It made teaching and learning fun. I have knitted thousands of glove and finger puppets which I've given to children, encouraging them to make up little plays using the puppets.

I retired as a principal of a primary school when I turned fifty-five, but I missed the children and the challenge. I went back for another fifteen years as a relief teacher.

In my last two years of teaching, I taught gifted and talented creative writing students. Uninhibited, clever students, challenged me to improve my own writing. They were excellent critics because of their honesty and sharing of ideas. My story, "The Soul Collector," published by Black Hare Press in *Key to the Kingdom* was inspired by a character profile written by a brilliant student who was given the task because he was disengaged in class. I was so impressed by it, I wrote a story for him based on the profile.

My published writing journey began in 2017 when I submitted "Magenta Sunrise" under my pseudonym, Isabella Fox, to Zombie Pirate Publishing and it was accepted. My story "Vixen" was later accepted for *Relationship Add Vice*. I thought writing short stories would be easy, but I was wrong. It was difficult, and many stories were rejected and I became dejected. As a high achiever, I hadn't "failed" before. I wasn't tough enough to cope with the rejection and I stopped submitting during 2018, although I kept writing and improving my skills.

Sam, my son, gave me the best advice. He told me short stories were different from novels and oral storytelling. I needed to change the way I told the story. I had to imagine I was in the story, how did it feel, and what could I see? He taught me to use dialogue instead of descriptions. As a lifelong learner, I set myself a task to improve my skills. I read masses of short stories, taking notes, and analyzing the way the story was structured. I listened to Sam's advice and my stories improved and so did my success when I began submitting again in 2019.

My acceptance of "Dragon's Breath" in *Dragon Bone Soup*, my first paid story, gave me confidence. Success with submissions to online magazines and in anthologies with various publishers since then, across all genres, has been satisfying.

Rejections still hurt a little, especially when I love the story, but now I tweak it before I send it off to another publisher. One story was rejected twice before it was accepted by an online magazine and then chosen for their *Best of the Year* anthology. I tweaked it each time it was rejected. You never know who will accept a story.

I have learned rejection doesn't mean it's not a good story, nor does it mean it's a good one. I use every rejection to improve my writing and ask myself, "What do I still have to learn and how can I make this story more interesting for the reader?" Initially, I struggled with writing horror and dark stories until I followed Sam's advice. My stories have improved, as has my acceptance rate.

I only submit to calls that appeal to me, or when I have a good idea of how a story will evolve. I guess the rejection thing is still in the back of my mind. 2020, has been a good year for me, with stories in twenty different anthologies or online magazines, six of them paid.

I get my best ideas when I am doing mundane tasks like mowing the lawn, pulling weeds at the farm, or on long walks with my husband.

Like all writers, I have a collection of stories that may never be published or are waiting until I have my own anthology. Some are too personal to share. Others were written just for the fun of writing about something quirky. I have no burning ambition to write a novel.

Every writer's journey is different. I encourage all writers to enjoy their journey and the destination will be sweeter. My only regret is I didn't start the writing journey earlier, but maybe I wasn't ready earlier. The Universe moves in mysterious ways.

Lynne Phillips lives in the Northern Rivers Region of New South Wales, Australia. Her stories have been published by Zombie Pirate Publishing, Black Hare Press, Fantasia Divinity Publishing, Our Wonderful Anthology, and in various online magazines. She enjoys exploring the craft of writing stories and the challenge it presents. Her priority is spending time with her family while her passions are reading, writing, keeping fit, and spending time at her farm.

I, VAL PORTELLI

"Be careful what you wish for" is an old saying that came true with a vengeance for me. With a hectic business and social life, there never seemed time to do more than write short pieces for the amusement of friends. A freak accident changed all that when I found myself hospitalized for a month, and finally released to be bed-bound for nearly a year, staring at the ceiling and going stir-crazy.

Although my leg was completely shattered and I was unable to stand or walk, it gave me the opportunity to dig out some old ideas, and put together my first book *Changes*. As a newbie I had no idea of the concepts involved, but was delighted to receive an offer to publish it. The euphoria disintegrated somewhat when the manuscript was returned with my words almost invisible under a sea of red pen.

Once I had the courage to look in more depth, it wasn't as bad as it first appeared. Apart from a few typos and other suggestions, it was mainly a case of including more commas, and searching for alternative words to avoid repetition. When the publishers raised the question of ideas for the cover, they were probably surprised to receive chapter and verse of exactly how it should look. I had no idea at the time that the designers usually controlled that aspect, and they wouldn't expect to receive a barrage of emails telling them their job. Despite that, the finished article was very close to what I had envisaged.

My other assumption was that writers wrote books, the publishers did everything else, and the author browsed yacht magazines and details of villas by the sea while they waited for the royalties to flood in. Who knew you were expected to do your own marketing, and that with the thousands of other books available, it was necessary to get out there and get yourself known? Trundling a bed down the high street to attend a book signing might have caused a stir, but for all the wrong reasons. Unfortunately, jet propelled divans were not available at the time, and the inability to walk did rather hamper things.

For all that, my family were proud of my achievements, and all my mother's friends knew what to expect for birthday and Christmas presents. Shortly before she died, my Mother was herself bed-bound, and my sister took to reading her chapters from my book to pass the time. It was a fairly innocent romance, but at one stage my worldly-wise sister blushed at describing the scene where the hero and heroine decided they were made for each other, and went off to the bedroom to do what lovers do. My 93-year-old Mother's response still makes me smile, "Well, if your Dad and I hadn't done the same, you wouldn't be here now."

A second book with new publishers had less red pen, but the major comment was there were too many commas! Back to the drawing board to adapt to a different house style. After months of physio I was at least able to walk a few yards with the assistance of mobility aids, so I was delighted when the publishers arranged a book signing in a local library. How many paperbacks should I order? Would 100 be enough? What hours should I do? I had been told a local lady's group held a weekly meeting in a room at the rear from 2:00 until 3:00, and passed through the library on their way out. They would be my ideal audience, and the head librarian also told me local children visited the library from school, and were collected from there by parents. Perfect.

Friends were roped in to help me distribute posters and flyers in town announcing the event, which was an eye-opener in itself. The local independent bookshop was surly and unhelpful, and finally agreed to take a small advertisement which I am sure went straight in the bin. The fish and chip shop were delighted to display a full-size poster in their window, and were enthusiastic about telling their customers. Research showed a box of sweets was a good ice-breaker, and on the big day I set off armed with 50 paperbacks, Sellotape, book marks and other marketing material supplied by the publishers.

We arrived early to set up, only to be informed the head

librarian had a day off, her deputy waved us to a corner with a complete lack of interest, and the ladies' group wouldn't be there until next week. Undeterred, we commandeered a table, grabbed a couple of chairs, and positioned ourselves directly facing the entrance, using the support poles to display 'Famous local author book-signing here.'

The spot had both positive and negative aspects. My stand was the first thing visitors saw, but with the library reception desk tucked out of sight behind pillars, we spent much of the afternoon directing people where to take their CV, where to inquire if the library loaned out DVDs, and how to obtain a library card. Tucked away at the edge of a park, even a local friend was unable to find the building, and ended up at the bookshop half a mile away, who denied any knowledge of the event. An interesting experience but I did make some sales, mainly to the lovely volunteers in the on-site coffee shop who kept us going through the afternoon.

I've moved on since then, and now know everything there is to know about metadata, blog posts, formatting, self-publishing, algorithms and the millions of things involved in producing a book-well, at least until next week when they change it again.

It's a crazy world, but once you've been bitten with the writing bug there is no escape, so you might as well enjoy the ride. Go for it and have fun. I did and I still do.

Despite receiving her first rejection letter aged nine, from a popular magazine, Val continued writing intermittently until an accident unexpectedly gave her time to publish her first book. Ten years later she has six published novels, with three more nearing completion, and has contributed to two published anthologies. Although her novels tend towards modern fiction, the weekly short stories she writes for her Facebook author page and website, cover various genres including her trademark quirky twist. She is always delighted to receive reviews, which encourage sales, and pay for the upkeep of the unicorns she breeds in her spare time.

I, THANDO POTO

At the age of twelve, I heard my older sister playing the song "When I'm gone." I was with my mother in the kitchen. She was telling me her story about how she developed cooking skills. I wanted her to finish the story so I would run to the bedroom my sister was in, where I'd pay careful attention to the song that was playing. It was the second verse that made me run to the bedroom the music was coming from. The American rapper had allured me with how beautifully he painted his story. With just his words, I already had a descriptive image of what was happening. It was the American rapper who later inspired me to write rhymes. I was more fascinated with the idea of storytelling. In the rhymes I wrote, I was always concerned about the story I was telling. I wanted someone to get the exact image I painted.

Being the last-born child, I was left all by myself when my sister moved out to a different city for her high school studies when I was fourteen years. Although I lived with my parents, I didn't have someone to talk to. My sister and I had formed a bond greater than any bond I had. I did have friends at school but we had different preferences. Boys my age enjoyed playing soccer. I, on the other hand, when placed on the field, played as poorly as a drunk man. I did try fitting in but I just couldn't no matter how hard I tried. I then found something to shift my focus on - writing stories. When I fixed my mind on a story, I wouldn't see anything besides words. With eyes closed, I saw the letters of the alphabet floating. My duty was to just arrange them.

Being the quiet and lonely child, I was always looking for stories. I didn't really hold conversations with imaginary people. However, I looked for stories in uncommon ways. I was always fascinated by nature. I'd always look at dogs and trees then wonder what kind of stories they would tell if we understood them. When a leaf would descend from a tree, before it reached the ground, I'd hear a story.

I was either listening to rap music or reading novels or writing stories. At the age of sixteen, I wrote my first short story. Unfortunately, I don't remember anything about it. Ever since then, I haven't stop crafting stories.

I wanted my stories to always have a sad ending. I didn't like happy endings because I believed life wasn't all about that. As I progressed with my writing, I decided not to detect the ending of my stories. I allowed the story to take control and tell itself. With my stories, I wanted to capture and reflect the beauty of life. I wanted to write the stories that people were uncomfortable with telling. Growing up in rural areas, I realized there were things I couldn't just talk about. I couldn't just throw my feminist opinions out there. With my writing, however, I could make my characters be whoever I wanted.

Being a writer made me realize the conversations that were not mostly talked about. I had to travel roads I was not ready to travel. I had to remember it was not about me but about the stories that needed to be told and heard. As the shy person I was, searching for a story led me to be great at eavesdropping. With my head down and ensuring my spectacles did not fall had always made me go unnoticed. I've always made certain that I did not judge. I always listened to a story and wrote it as is. When writing, I've put aside my personal views. I just focused on the story that needed to be told. Being an observer of people and listening to the words not spoken has made me a great storyteller. There's nothing I've always avoided than telling a single story.

Being a writer taught me patience. I recall in 2015 when I wrote and finished my first novel. I submitted it to publication houses. I had to wait for months before I received their responses. The first house I submitted to hasn't responded to me even to this day. The other houses rejected my work. As much as I was sad and hurt about the rejection, after a couple of months, I understood why I was rejected. Regardless of the number of rewrites I've done, I've always felt that novel still needed some working. I've never been comfortable with it.

Ever since deciding to focus on my short story and novel writing at the age of twenty, I've never been concerned with making friends. I've always used words to escape. I've never been concerned about making friends who were not readers or writers. There's nothing as special as having a friend who's walked with me on my writing journey. Having someone to send my work to critique. I had a friend who would always remind me of how much he was not a reader but always made time to read my work and provide me with beneficial feedback. Having someone to talk to, someone who listened, has made me a great storyteller. It's those people I chose to show in my work.

Thando Poto was born on the third of March 1995. He was born in Umtata, in the Eastern Cape province of South Africa. His short story collection, which will be his first published work, is set to hit the bookshelves soon. He has completed his undergraduate studies in the field of Accountancy.

I, M.K. RAGAB

When I worked as an English teacher (Even though it isn't my first language) people used to tell me "Ah you're an English teacher! That's why your English is really good!"

My reply was always the same: "I am an English teacher *because* my English is good, my English is *not* good because I am an English teacher!" with an irritated smile that showed my contempt for the remark!

Being a writer is usually perceived in reverse as well, people think you can write, so you write! But the truth is it is usually a path you find yourself walking, not a totally conscious decision!

Growing up in an abusive house in Egypt was one of those factors! When you want to avoid a beating or a horror-film type of punishment, books and TV become your best friends, windows to the outside world that you wish you could interact with but can't. Then the internet happened, offering a magical gate into the unknown and the exciting!

You close your room and ignore the screaming and breaking of things, and you live among movie characters, book protagonists, and chat with strangers online to prove to yourself that you still have a place among the living.

Your mind starts to resent your surroundings with all their attachments, culture, music, even jokes! So you start looking for other cultures to enjoy, to escape your nightmarish reality.

That's what you do! How else could you go on?

Years of swimming in foreign cultures, dozens of types of music, and creating mental constructs that only include things in the language I have been using! English!

I almost went to military prison during my service because my reply to an order from the Captain was "Okay!" instead of the Arabic version of "YES, SIR."

My language, my second first language as I call it, has been my tool for communication for years, it was the only way I knew how to speak, and the language that enabled me to enjoy life.

To other Egyptians, I was usually considered a heretic, an alien, or a circus freak! I had no place I could call home except the streams of digital data floating online. I had very few friends due to my communication problems, some of them were not even a choice for me, I just talked to whoever could talk back to me!

But I did make a few good choices, or maybe I was incredibly lucky! During the high times of the emergence of blogs, I decided to overcome my Greek tragedy of a life by making others laugh. So I posted funny jokes and stories on my blog whenever I could, maybe I would make someone's day better!

A.D., a close female friend of mine, pushed me to send articles to some English magazines here in Egypt asking for work. Reluctantly I did, and that was my first publication at the age of nineteen.

I was so excited someone replied back, and I jumped up and down when I saw my article published for the first time. I had a voice, and it was out there in the world, as I had always dreamed!

It went on for a couple of years before I realized my "voice" is being audited! Edits that made no sense for me (As someone soaking in English for years Vs. my supervisor at the magazine who got her English certificate from a mall!) became expected with every article.

"Why don't you just make your own magazine?" Loyal A.D. innocently suggested. Neither of us knew anything about it, but I thought "Hmm, I study Business Information Systems, that's basically how to create a business online from scratch!"

So I poured all my knowledge and then some, into creating an online magazine that I named *CrazyMag*.

I assembled a team of writers and editors and designers, printed flyers and made deals with SMEs for marketing, and for a while, I had my voice again, or so I thought!

The call for duty took a year out of my life that I had no control over in any way. My voice was the least of my concerns! And after a long struggle to try to revitalize the magazine, the daily "Why is it crashing again?" routine became less fruitful ending in a shutdown.

Years later, with a revolution, a pandemic, and a lost career as my most recent memories, I found myself sitting at home, jobless, bored, and thinking about my voice again!

It had been years since I even thought about writing, I had lost hope of getting back my voice, and I was just happy with the few good friends I have, the closest being M.R. my best friend, and my neighbor.

Two months on a couch, waiting for the virus to knock on my door, eating junk food, and watching TV shows, I had developed a habit of critiquing what I see in terms of structure and writing.

One day I decided to write what I wish I would read or watch. It started as a short story, maybe I could have a blog again! Worst case scenario? I wrote a story for my best friend to enjoy during quarantine! So why not? I have a free schedule anyway!

The short story decided to attract more ideas and characters, gaining a life of its own. It became too complicated for a short story, possessing me for ten days where I turned into a typewriting machine that eats occasionally! 70k words! Did I really do this? In 10 days?

Two months, 7 draft edits, a cover design, and a PhD in self-publishing later, I found myself feeling something in my throat as I googled the name of my published novel and found 12 links for it. I didn't know what it was at first, but then I remembered it was something I didn't have for a while … it was my voice!

M.K. Ragab is a serial entrepreneur, aspiring author, and psychologist with a passion for quantum physics and spirituality. Ragab has been working since the age of seventeen in multiple industries that enabled him to gain knowledge in many fields. He earned his psychology certificate at the age of nineteen, his Kung Fu red trainers belt at twenty-two, and his Graphics Design and Film Making diploma at the age of twenty-four. He shifted his career from Talent Management to Writing in the aftermath of the COVID-19 pandemic, and his novels are now being sold over sixteen global distributors and online stores.

I, D. RAYE

The sun made its way up and over the horizon, flickering through the forest trees. The train rocked back and forth along the long and windy track through the lush German countryside. With each new valley, small villages seem to come to life. Smoke from chimneys billowed into the air, and windows glowed faint yellow hues. Grand church steeples stood erect as though they were the protectors and clock towers rose high as though time had stood still.

Each turn revealed a scene from every child's favorite fairy tale. Castle ruins nestled in the rolling hills and deer grazing upon the morning dew-covered grass—fog rising, causing your imagination to run wild.

At this point in time, I realized I wanted to be a writer. However, I had zero education and absolutely no confidence in taking on such a task.

I was born and raised in a small town in Kansas to parents that were not ready or prepared to have children. To say I experienced hardship would be an understatement. My mother left when I was only three, and my father did his best with what he knew how. My father could barely read or write, and to him, education wasn't that important; farm work always came first. Needless to say, I was the "only boy" my father ever had. (I'm really not a boy. I was born female and still very much one) I hauled hay, cut wood, worked in the garden, heard cows, and knew how to ride a horse before I learned how to walk.

School wasn't as bad as you might think. It was small; I believe 48-52 in my graduating class. I was a cheerleader, ran track, and made lifelong friends. The downside, I struggled to pass. Back when I was in school, being dyslexic wasn't a thing. Therefore, I was put into special ed, labeled a slow learner, and just pushed through.

Life after school was a nightmare. I could not fill out a job application to save my soul. So, I did the next best thing. At

246

seventeen, I married the first guy that came along. As you can imagine, a loveless marriage is nothing short of living hell. I was pretty, and my new husband treated me like I was nothing more than a piece of property. He was verbally abusive and continually reminding me I was too stupid to survive on my own and that I owed him.

Right away, I gave birth to my first baby. Can you imagine holding a child's book in your hand and not being able to read it to your toddler? I cannot tell you how heartbreaking it is. But then Disney came out with books that came with cassette tapes. I would follow along with the words until I memorized them until I could read to my child without the tape. However, life for me did not get any easier, and I gave birth to two more children before finally getting out.

As a single, uneducated mother, I made many horrible choices; some still haunt me to this day. But I did the best I could, and I will never regret that.

In my late twenties, I met a man that taught me I was worthy and that I was not stupid. He took my three children and me in, and life has been one whirlwind after another. In the twenty-five years that we have been together, I have learned to read and write somewhat. I have owned my own business, and we have traveled to many wonderful countries.

I have dealt with childhood traumas (some too personal to mention) abandonment issues and feeling less than. I am an overcomer. I am loved; I am smart, and I published my first novel in November 2019.

Not everyone is going to like you or encourage you, and that's okay; your worth is not based on their opinion. Dance. Travel. Read. You are worth it.

D. Raye was diagnosed with dyslexia in her early twenties. Eager to overcome this adversity, she continued to educate myself. Her love for art and culture has taken her to many countries where she have explored her talent for photography, the very thing that inspired her to write her first novel, triggering a new adventure. She believes dancing and music are the universal languages and as long as we have them, there are no barriers. She plans to make a difference in this world, even if only to inspire one person. Because that's one person more than when she started.

I, SULTANA RAZA

If people see someone giggling on a bus for no apparent reason, they tend to back away, wondering how crazy that person might be. Unless that person happens to be typing away on their mobile phone, oblivious to her surroundings. Depending on how strong the flow of words is coming, I can type my stories in buses, trams, trains, or planes. Sometimes even in crowded cafés where no one knows me, which is the case right now (in sunny Andalusia), with a 90s song blaring away in the background. Usually though, I tend to type away at night, when I have the impression I have unlimited time, and no interruptions.

However, as soon as I go on the Internet to research something, it's easily an hour before I notice I've been page surfing. So I accumulate a few points to check before I dive in research's whirlpool. Once I asked a taxi-driver so many questions about his job, he asked if I was going to start my own taxi company!

Usually I have quite a few open projects, though other writers should avoid this situation. However, after a few months, or even years, I find out that most of my stories are inter-connected. That's why I need to reach a certain point in story number 3, where I realize how certain elements in it will affect story number 1. Or I gain new insights into story number 1. However, I'd strongly urge writers to finish their first project before starting another one. Luckily, most writers actually manage to finish and publish their books.

Though I've been writing from school days, my very first not e-book got lost when I moved away from India to Europe, where I live now. My first story ever published came as a total surprise. One day, I received a magazine in the post from the US. I assumed it was some sort of business journal for my former husband. But on perusing it, I was delighted to discover my short story in India Currents, published from California. Since I'd heard nothing from them, I'd assumed they weren't interested in it. But that wasn't the case.

So I'd urge writers to never give up hope. My next short story was translated and then published in French in a journal for foreigners called ensemble (meaning together) in Luxembourg. At that time my French wasn't all that good, so I had to rely completely on the translator to do her job. Those first feelings of elation at seeing one's name in a journal are difficult to capture in subsequent instances. Though it's always a thrill whenever one receives an acceptance. I suppose it's the fact that someone you don't know from the human race has read and understood your words. That your characters have managed to hold an editor's attention long enough for them to decide to stamp your work in their journal.

After that, I published lots of art exhibition reviews both in English and French. Also, I honed my writing skills by publishing lots of articles on film, social issues, and even finance. In a way it's been easier to get my poems published, as they're much shorter to write, edit and also easier for the editors to read and to decide to pin them on their sites. However, rhyming poems tend to crop up at night. Lots of time I've had to let them go, as otherwise I wouldn't have slept at all. Did Proust know how privileged he was to be able to write at night in a sound-proofed room? Most successful writers of the past didn't have to juggle jobs, and/or household chores with their writing life like we do.

Since I've been living in Luxembourg, where English isn't an official language, it hasn't been all that easy for me to get published. Internet has made submitting so much easier. Of course, I could submit a lot more than I do. That's why it's so encouraging when I see other writers, including members of the Facebook Group of Sweetycat Press getting published. It's motivating to submit yourself when you see that others are much more active than yourself in that regard.

It's hard for the emerging writer to have any sort of creative and business plan. So I just write. Revision is a little difficult, as I tend to start adding to the back story, or expanding on details at the same time.

What I enjoy the most is when a character surprises me. Usually I watch my story like a film in my head when I'm writing. And when a character starts saying or doing unexpected things, then I'm really gripped by my own story. Sometimes plot points will be revealed that hadn't been obvious before. This is what makes the whole creative process so fun and exciting. I think there are currents of sub-texts and inter-connections hidden beneath the surface of most stories. We, as writers just have to dig and find them.

So, what keeps me motivated? I think on the one hand fiction allows us to encapsulate moods, characters, or situations ways that can't be done in real life. It gives us a satisfying overview. On the other hand, by exploring other people's psyche, we're exploring our own as well. In a much broader sense, we're also painting vignettes of particular moments of our lives and times. If it's about contemporary times.

That's not always my case, as I like to delve into the mythical past, as well as the eighteenth and nineteenth centuries, outer space, and parallel worlds in between. While I studied mainly 'classical' Literature when doing my Masters in English Lit in India, I've been fascinated by fantasy and soft sci-fi ever since I first encountered it in Europe. And it shows in my writing choices. Creating new worlds and characters comes with its own sense excitement and adventure, so I suppose that's why I love writing fiction.

Of Indian origin, Sultana Raza's poems have appeared in 60+

journals, including *Columbia Journal, The New Verse News, London Grip, Classical Poetry Society, Spillwords, Poetry24, Dissident Voice,* and *The Peacock Journal.* Her fiction has received an Honorable Mention in *Glimmer Train Review,* and has been published in *Coldnoon Journal, Szirine, Apertura, Unlikely Stories, and Entropy.* She's read her fiction/poems in India, Switzerland, France, Luxembourg, England, Ireland, USA, and at CoNZealand.

I, MICHAL REIBEN

My first attempt at writing was when I was about thirty-five years old, and I used it as a means to ease my pain. I wrote about the car accident which had left me paralyzed and in which I'd lost my five-month-old fetus and also about my husband leaving me. Eventually, I typed out my scrawling's into a book, did several prints of it, and sent them off to publishers. Needless to say, I never managed to get it published. I was bitterly disappointed, became disheartened, and stopped writing.

My second attempt at writing was at the age of sixty-eight and this time I used it as a tool to help me deal with my angry feelings. My well-to-do father had recently died and disinherited me. I'm sure my stepmother had influenced him. I decided that since he hadn't left me any money, I'd use the only thing he had left me, the freedom to write stories about him. Since the book I'd written in the past had been a failure, I now decided to write short stories instead. After I'd finished writing resentful stories about my father, I went on to write a whole bunch of other stories and caught the "writing bug."

I wanted to show off my new hobby and so I printed out some of my stories, although of course not the ones I'd written about my father, and took them to a family meeting. I proudly handed out my stories to family members but they were received extremely grudgingly and one member said, "Who do you think you are, Joanne Rowling? You're wasting your time you'll never get anything published."

As luck would have it a cousin of mine who lives in Yorkshire and to whom I corresponded regularly wanted to read my stories. She loved my stories and urged me to try and publish them. Over the next few months, I spent many arduous, boring hours scouring the internet for suitable publishers for my stories. I never managed to get a single story published.

One evening as I was using Google to look up a school I used to attend in Forest Row, a beautiful photograph of a snow-covered garden in Yorkshire appeared on my screen. The post belonged to Grant Hudson who was a writer. This struck me as a good omen both because my birth mother had been a Yorkshire lass and also because he was a writer. I gave his post a heartfelt "like" and I then discovered I'd become a member of his writing group, The Inner Circle Writers' Group.

I was overjoyed, it was exactly what I needed. Later I learned that Grant had been headteacher of the school where I'd been a pupil in Forest Row but long after I'd left. At first, I felt like "a fish out of water" in the group. Everyone seemed so talented and I was baffled by some of the words or phrases which the writer's use. The authors were kind to me especially the famous author Steve Carr who constantly encouraged me and gradually I became integrated. From the members of the group I learned which publishers were suitable homes for my stories. I'll never forget my first acceptance; I was delirious with happiness for the next two days. Now two and a half years later I've had fifty-five stories published.

Once I wrote a fictitious story about a man who was going blind, he enticed and befriended lots of exotic birds into his garden so that when he became completely blind, he wouldn't be lonely. Since the birds who visited my garden were rather ordinary, I decided to do what the man in my story had done. Thus, every day I'd go out and throw bread and bird seeds into my garden. However, the only thing I managed to lure into my garden was an abundance of hungry stray cats who ate the bread and who also constantly came slinking into my house. Finally, my house became so infested by fleas and mites that it took three exterminators and throwing away all my furniture to get rid of them. Thereafter I learned never to try to live my fictitious stories in real life.

My dreams for the future as far as my writing is concerned is to have my favorite story, it's a fantasy YA story made into a film. I'm allowed to dream! Also, to have my short stories published in a book.

Someone once asked me, "Why do you write stories if you don't make any money from them?"

I answered, "For the same reason I grew flowers in my garden because I enjoy them and I hope they'll make the world a little bit more beautiful."

Michal Reiben has lived in Israel since she was a teenager but she still misses the countryside and the log fires of England where she was born. Besides her two boys and six grandchildren, she loves gardening, reading, and writing stories. She writes fiction, creative non-fiction, and children's stories. Her short stories have appeared in various online publications, magazines, and anthologies. As a result of a car accident at age twenty-five, she is a paraplegic. She lives in Jerusalem.

I, ALANNA ROBERTSON-WEBB

When I was growing up, I babysat my ten younger cousins regularly, and whenever they were sad, I used to cheer them up by creating stories that starred them as the main character. My desire to make others happy through storytelling was a central theme for me, until the year I turned eleven. Three days before my birthday my grandma succumbed to ovarian cancer, and for the next six months nothing else mattered as I cloistered myself away in a comfort zone made from lined notebooks and chewed-on pens.

I spent hours creating worlds where she hadn't died, worlds where cancer didn't steal the ones we love, and my words eased my heart in a way that speaking out loud just couldn't do. Then, on the first anniversary of her death, I found myself challenged by severe anxiety. I got so angry, so bogged down by grief, that I shredded everything I had written. I stopped making up stories for my cousins, and I lost interest in trying to share my creativity.

If my stories couldn't bring Nana back, and couldn't save anyone else, then what good were they?

It was nearly a decade before I began writing again. Outside of school projects I hadn't sat down to write a story in years, and if my classmate Abbey hadn't asked me to submit a piece to our college's literary journal then I question if I would have found my way back to writing. At her behest I wrote a short story for the *Chameleon*, even though it was nerve-wracking to try and come up with something both humorous and unique that hadn't been featured in a previous edition of the journal.

My submission was a short, fun take about what happens when the Egyptian goddess Bast gets released from an urn after thousands of years, and the euphoria that I felt when it was selected by the committee was indescribable. My words weren't directly helping anyone, but for the first time since I was little, I believed that they could at least make people smile.

A little while after I graduated, I stumbled upon the Author Alliance Facebook group, and thanks to the posts people would make about open submissions I slowly began writing a piece here and a snippet there, eventually building myself up until I was successfully reaching my goal of submitting at least one story every two months to various calls.

The Author Alliance was a great starting platform for me, and thanks to the connections I made there I've recently become the editor-in-chief at Eerie River Publishing. Not only do I still write stories whenever I can, but now I get to help other authors achieve that thrilling, wonderful burst of joy that comes from seeing one's own work in print.

My fiancé Hunter, along with my friends and family, have all been my cheerleaders during this crazy ride. They know that sometimes I still doubt myself, and that I wonder if what I create is worth the time and effort that I put into it, yet they keep reminding me that I can do it. They believe that I can reach those deadlines, that I can try writing in a new subgenre or that I'm capable of achieving a million other things that I set my mind on.

I'm blessed.

When things get really tough for me, when I forget that I've come such a long way, I hear a little voice in the back of my mind. It's my Nana, and she tells me one simple thing: "You can do it!"

I may not become the next famous author, and I may never have a movie made about my work, but I'm always going to write. The world will forever need stories to thrill, brighten and entertain it, so I plan on lending a helping hand.

Alanna Robertson-Webb is a Pennsylvanian author who enjoys long weekends of LARPing, is terrified of sharks and finds immense fun in being the editor-in-chief at Eerie River Publishing. She lives with her fiancé and two cats, all of whom like to take over her favorite cozy blanket when they think they can get away with it. She is currently a receptionist at the Exeter Veterinarian Hospital by day, and an editor and author by candlelight. While she loves that she has had over eighty pieces printed across fifty different publications, and that she has edited eleven different books, Alanna one day aspires to run her own nerd-themed restaurant.

I, DANIEL CRAIG ROCHE

Dear aspiring writer,

Do you remember reading Shakespeare in high school?

You do?

Then perhaps you're familiar with the famous line, "To be or not to be."

I ask because this simple line, the longest word being no more than three letters, is easily one of the most important questions you can ask yourself.

So, before you put pen to paper, look yourself in the mirror, purse your lips tightly, and ask the person before you, "are you a writer, or not?"

As I'm getting on in years, I find it harder and harder to tear myself away from the word processor. Therefore, I can safely conclude, the craft of writing is not a fling. It is not a fad. It is not something I can outgrow. It is a lifestyle.

I am a writer. Period.

And that's the kind of dedication you'll be needing if you choose this path, because you're going to pound on that keyboard for a thousand lonely nights, wondering if it's ever going to pay off. Then, that one glorious day will arrive, where you finally write something you're proud of. You're going to go over it with a fine-tooth comb, deleting unnecessary words, sentences, paragraphs, pages, and even entire chapters, until your precious little manuscript is perfect. Then you're going to spend another several days at your keyboard, researching all the magazines and publishing houses you're going to send it to.

But here's where things start to get a bit tricky. You remember that precious little manuscript we talked about? The one you slaved over, worried about, and lost sleep and friends over? Yeah. It's going to receive about a hundred rejections. But don't worry. You've just learned what every writer before you has already learned:

The best thing you've ever written is total garbage.

How did you not see it? How could you let this steaming pile of crap sit on top of your desk for all this time, and mistake it for anything other than the failure it is.

And that's exactly how you're going to see yourself afterwards. As a failure.

I mean, honestly. How much time do you need to spend writing, rewriting, pulling your hair out, and crying over this simple stack of papers? You could've spent that time doing something more productive, like cleaning the living room, or painting the house. Maybe you could've found a nice part-time job, and now you'd have a nice little nest egg in your saving's account. But no. You decided to sit at your desk, wasting your life, when you could've been out with friends, meeting new people, and possibly even getting laid.

No question about it. You're a failure.

So what do you do now, my dear aspiring writer? Do you toss all your manuscripts in the trash? Do you call it quits and focus on something you're better at? Maybe it's time for you to clean the living room, or paint the house, or finally got around to meeting that special someone.

But chances are, if you're anything like the other writers I've met, these thoughts never even occurred to you.

Because you're a writer. Period.

So allow me to introduce you to the rest of your life:

It's lonely. It's stressful. It's filled with rejection, and there's no one in your family who will understand you. Sure, there's writer's groups, but they're filled with people who are as equally downtrodden as you. They have their own pile of failure stacked up on their desks. And they're too focused on their own misery to care about you.

But can you blame them? After all, aren't you too caught up on your own misery to give a damn about them?

Of course, you are, but don't worry about it too much. This is just the way it is, because writing is long nights spent in darkness, where you'll bite your nails worrying about people who don't even exist. That's right. Your characters are your only friends now. And do I need to remind you how awful some of your characters can be? They're relentless, always begging you to let them finish the story. And sometimes they don't finish it the way you'd like. Sometimes they murder your favorite character. Sometimes they don't leave a happy ever after. And worst of all, sometimes, they're writers, too. Imaginary, yet well-worded reflections of yourself. A daily reminder of how long you've been at this. A daily reminder of all those rejection letters. A daily reminder of how hard it is.

But don't beat yourself up too much over any of this, because if given the chance to do it all over again, you would.

I know it sounds crazy, but never forget, you're a writer. And as a writer, someone who spends their days living in darkness and solitude, you wouldn't have it any other way. Because darkness is romance. Loneliness is your companion. And hatred is love.

"To be or not to be."

I say "to be."

And you, my dear aspiring writer, will say the same thing. Because being a writer isn't the life you chose. It's the life that chose you. And I, along with every other writer who has ever existed, am glad you're here.

Daniel Craig Roche is a New England native who has published over thirty short stories, essays, and poems in both print and on-line magazines. His debut novel, *Corpse Lily*, is available for preorder, fall of 2020, and his debut novella, *Yesterday's Wounds*, is included in the *Love Askew* box set, which is available for preorder as of the publication of this book.

I, BRUCE ROWE

I've never considered myself an author but a storyteller. Ever since I was young, I have always enjoyed making up stories to entertain my friends and family or add embellishments to the ones I heard. I always wanted to write a book but was so horrible at grammar, syntax and the like in writing that it was too intimidating for me to even consider it. No doubt, a result of believing school was a total waste of my time.

What slowly set in motion for me to write was the nurturing of my fantastical way of thinking. Before my father's death, I wrote him a letter of appreciation for all he had done for me. In the letter, which now resides in the coffin with him per his request, was the family trip to California when I was around twelve years old. For a twelve-year-old with an already fantastical mind, Disneyland was a mind blower. Rides such as Pirates of the Caribbean and The Haunted House were big influences on me. And if I could've lived on Tom Sawyer Island I would have.

Returning home to Blanchard—a small Podunk town that lays on the outskirts of Shreveport—my two brothers and I made trips to the nearby woods where we went on hunting expeditions, fought Indians, and destroyed creatures that haunted the forest. My story, The Water Witch, is a direct result from some of those excursions. In addition to Disneyland and the woods, living in the land of Hoodoo and Voodoo and some of the most bizarre folklore this side of the Red River, has played a key part in my writing today. It gives me great pleasure when I can write about a tidbit of Louisiana lore that's virtually unheard of in other parts of the world and the question inevitably comes, "How did you come up with that?"

At the self-publishing of my first book, it was mainly my immediate family that read it. Though my grammar and syntax were slaughtered in the most grievous way possible, my parents and siblings encouraged me with the grace, and forgiveness, of the gods.

The discouragement came by low sells…very low, like less than hundred. And most of those purchases were from family members. So I set aside writing for seven years.

It wasn't until 2018 that I decided to give it another go. I joined several writing groups in hopes of sharpening a very dull pencil. Because of the political and religious debates that I saw overshadowing the topics of writing, I left those groups. It wasn't until I met a person who kindly guided me to the Inner Circle Writers Group where writing topics were actually discussed and encouragement abounded that the writing worm turned for me. This person's name is none other than Steven Lester Carr. By that one simple guiding suggestion, I have met the most wonderful, kind and loving people from all parts of this world in which we live.

I still get the occasional encouragement from my family, which I highly appreciate. But the cheerleading section found at ICWG and the numerous other groups in which I belong are beyond comparison. At times it can be overwhelming which is a credit to all those wonderful people who are too numerous to mention.

Bruce Rowe was born in Shreveport La. He has short stories published at *Spillwords.com, Dastaanworld.com* and Cafelit.com. "The Rider," his first short story, was nominated Publication of the Month at *Spillwords* in October 2018. "Grandfather's Clock" was featured at *Spillwords*. "The Lonely Traveler" received a special mention at Cafelit. He has been nominated twice as Author of the month at Spillwords. His poem, "Twiggy Thin," is published in Clarendon House Publication's, *Poetica*. His story, "Hair of the Dog," is published in Zombie Works Publication, *Monsterthology 2*. He presently lives in Oceanside California where he writes, body surfs and plays guitar.

I, SATABDI SAHA

Sometimes I dream of pleasant things heard long ago from my parents. A big mansion in Dhaka (Lalbag) of the 1930's, once a part of undivided Bengal, their place of birth. My brother and I were Calcutta born, so we savored the details of our huge mansion, of grandfather's elephant and horse, of servants and sycophants. But the best were their paranormal experiences.

Both my parents came as refugees to India just before the partition of Bengal in 1947, the year of India's independence, leaving everything behind. In 1946, the riots started. At that time my father was away and ma was entirely alone, for the servants had already left. Those were vicious times of fire, fear and blood. Dhaka was seething with murderous violence. Outside my maternal grandfather's house, my uncle, running to reach home, was stabbed on the doorstep, in front of my grandmother! In this turbulence my baba, stranded, had to send his friend to rescue ma. Ma oblivious of her brother's death, threw her medals and jewelry into a well, rubbed off the vermilion on her head, wore a burqa and fled with him. Savage mobs with bloodied swords accosted them on the streets, drenched and dotted with blood and bodies. Women and young girls were widowed, raped, abducted, mutilated, murdered, and babies slaughtered. The arsonists lifted ma's veil, saw no red on her brow, then let her go. How baba and ma eventually met is another story.

After returning from East Bengal (now Bangladesh) my baba and uncle set up a business. They also bought a house in Park Circus with two rooms, study, kitchen and bath. Desperate for shelter, they had to share it.

I grew up to observe that our room was always overcrowded. Thanks to baba and ma's philanthropy, there wasn't any dearth of helpless people seeking a single destination! When four, I was admitted to a convent school, a prey to the 'etiquette' of academic discrimination. I wasn't a good student and hated math. Studying for my exams was impossible in one multipurpose room filled with refugees seeking a free haven. At one time, I counted fourteen people staying together, eating, chattering, sleeping!

After school, I read fictions and poems by renowned Bengali and English writers since methodical learning wasn't possible. This habit instilled in me, the proneness to originality. Just before my major exams, I studied inside our dimly lit corridor, sitting on the floor preparing, for four, five nights continuously, in fanless summers. We never got to sit in the study, for my aunt took care to padlock it, or made sure it was occupied by her sons. When the floor heated up, sitting became unbearable. I used to take a lamp to study in our room, apprehensive of disturbing others. I tried defiance by breaking the padlock open, but the operation fell flat by ma's weird insistence. It was impolite and disrespectful. Ma's idea of 'moral victory' seemed unconvincing. I couldn't figure out why I would suffer in my own house, when others were preventing me from doing well in my exams! Actually ma was emphasizing on sacrifice. But at that moment I was too incensed to see 'sense'. Euphemistically said, she meant, 'fight your own way out of this mess without troubling others.' This lesson helped me develop patience. Baba consoled me differently. He provided comforting sweets and coffee. Heaven knows, how badly I needed those, in my waking nights!

Eating glued me to the books I rarely touched! Remembrances still spawn yearnings for those moments of love and lessons of life. When I visualize ma giving food to beggars, making them clothes, and baba helping the needy, with little to spare, I thank God for making me their child!

When in high school I witnessed the Naxalite movement, which started in 1967 in Naxalbari, West Bengal. This Maoist communist group, flamed terrorism which impacted the lives of many students and youngsters. The fallout was mindless decimation (steered by the Congress government, under C.M. S.S. Roy) of unnumbered youths, the best brains of Bengal. Fear pervaded in families, having youngsters. Streets were traps, littered with bodies and bloodied by unfair policing. My cousin who was in the fray, absconded, and was sheltered by baba, at his life's peril! He came at night and shared his gruesome experiences which haunt me still. We were allowed to step outside only during school hours, strictly manned. Gradually the movement spread, but massacres of the young, quelled the revolution in West Bengal.

From an early age I was handicapped by illness. I couldn't socialize much, but discovered friends amongst the academicians. Colleagues inspired me, I gleaned writing techniques from them. Impeded by excruciatingly painful diseases it was only in bed that I could write my dissertation, unable to go to libraries, shackled by numerous operations. But these too I believed, added to my personal experiences. Even if I failed to go out, the world came to me in the shape of various people. Apart from observing our neighbors and friends (who were from all walks of life), rearing up my sickly child and being a doctor's wife were challenges that helped me confront my inner world of light and darkness. Having no mentor in academics or creative writing, I fended for myself, with immense support of my family, my brother, and a friend. Without them I wouldn't have managed to attend a certification course in films from Pune's IFTI, for which I was nationally selected. I stayed there for a month, attending classes, making friends and enriching myself immeasurably. These were real inputs in my life, the nourishment for creativity, the platform on which I appeared, though quite later in life. But I will carry on till the end.

Satabdi is an ex-professor, a bilingual poet and author. She was born in Calcutta (Kolkata), living with neighbors from all walks of life, gaining experience mostly from observing them closely. Though spiritually inclined, she protests against injustices, and is drawn to the factors that determine human happiness.

I, LAURA SAINT MARTIN

I often tell people that my writing journey is that of a liar, and that fiction gives me a more socially acceptable outlet for this propensity. I was blessed at an early age with an advanced reading aptitude and skill with composition, as well as an overactive imagination, which continues to get me in trouble at my advanced age. My childhood essays won me special favor with teachers, and had my peers rolling on the floor in laughter. After a violent sexual assault in my teens, I began journaling as part of my recovery, a daily habit I kept up for over ten years. I wrote poetry in college and was published in my junior college's poetry anthology, the only student featured. I was right next to Shakespeare, y'all! At nineteen!

But I did not pursue a writing career. I majored in music, then premed, then my drinking career took the lead. I needed a job, and fast, so I went to nursing school. I supported myself through numerous odd jobs and a year of prostitution before I finished school and got my license and got a real job. I worked at state hospitals for 32 years, and pretended I was like other people. I wrote occasional poetry, but immersing myself in writing seemed to trigger my isolationist tendencies, and I would quickly find myself lost in my inner landscapes. It was a dangerous place for me, already on the fringes of acceptable society. I opted for as much normal as I could, because I hated my differences. I put one foot in front of the other, and used jewelry making for a creative outlet. And I still told lies.

When I retired, I felt like a failure. I was never much of a nurse, I was a flop at marriage, and I couldn't find a new career. Then my sister encouraged me to join a critique group. Since writing seemed to be the only thing I was ever good at, I opened up my laptop and started writing. I wrote anything and everything, planned out a series of books, wrote my opinions on a variety of subjects, went bat poop crazy. When I returned to work as a retired annuitant, I found ample literary fodder in the stories and antics of the criminally insane. A long-time fan of thrillers and procedurals, I began a mystery series about a mounted equestrian patrol, some of which is set in a state forensic hospital where one of the equestriennes makes her living, and where some of my villains find themselves after their proverbial day in court. I wanted women's stories, I wanted neurodiversity, I wanted flawed protagonists and trauma-informed antagonists. I wanted to show life in a real psych hospital, free of the dark, dank, scream-filled tropes other procedurals rely on. Most of all, I wanted horses, and I wanted their voices in the stories on my pages. I wanted their rich and diverse histories, and I wanted to show my appreciation for all they have done for us.

I joined more critique groups, bared my fragile literary soul, and survived, even thrived. The best critiques, I've learned, are the ones that leave me in tears. I've learned to listen and sort through the critiques, and savor the rough ones for the tools they are. My writing grew the hell up. Being free to lie my keister off on paper, I slowed down on the real-life fabrications. I didn't need them anymore. I had this magical cure called fiction.

Next step: getting myself out there. I posted poetry, which I also picked up again, on Facebook. I submitted occasionally. Then I encountered a gentleman, Steven Lester Carr, who was always posting acceptances of his short stories. So many stories! Inspired, I began sorting through some of my favorite chapters and scenes and modified them into flash and short stories. I gathered my poems as well. I saved all the posts listing calls for submissions. I started submitting. I collected rejections, and I coached myself to "keep my dobber up," as my dad would say, but my dobber was drooping pitifully. Then acceptances started trickling in, then a flood or two, and I discovered one of the true chores of writing: informing other publications of your success. I had to get my submissions in order, keep track of my submissions and my rejections and acceptances. You know you're on your way when you read a rejection letter with a sigh of relief!

I have had some top-notch support along the way. My father

collected my poetry and encouraged me to write more. My college professors promoted and published me. Today I have the support of a wonderful online writing community, and the mentorship of authors who dedicate much of their time helping us fledglings. I have a smart and kindly critique group that keeps me in check and helps me round up my not-so-Oxford commas and hyperactive hyphens. I have my sister, also a writer, who reposts all my announcements and introduces reality checks when my computer makes me crazy.

My writing journey has been my therapy, my grade point booster, my Hail Mary in times of tribulation. It has allowed me to accept my differences, some of which I strongly believe stem from undiagnosed autism, and to find a place for my frustration, anger, futility, as well as my natural exuberance and unflagging hope and joy. My writing is chaotic, profane, political, infuriating, humorous, glorious, boring, offensive, thrilling, ridiculous. My writing chronicles true events, figments of my imagination, injustices and unbearable beauty. My writing has, and continues to save my life. Now that I can embrace my neurodiversity, my writing saves my sanity, or maybe just allows me to enjoy it fully. Writing makes me happy. And it can make others happy. They just don't know it yet.

They will.

Laura Saint Martin is an emerging writer, currently working on a mystery series set on a horse ranch in Southern California. She also writes poetry about mental illness, blue collar struggles, animals, nature and life on the autism spectrum. She works for Patton State Hospital and Rover.com. Due to her turbulent childhood, numerous and contradictory psychiatric diagnoses, and sensory processing challenges, she has determined that she is on the autism spectrum. She lives with her family and numerous spoiled pets in Rancho Cucamonga, CA. She has only recently started submitting short works to online journals and print anthologies, and has several poems and short stories awaiting publication.

I, ELIZABETH SAMS

I am a product of two very different worlds – Wild Wales and back roads Canada. How did these dichotomies come together, to make the writer that is me? WWII is the short answer. My father took his leave from the Canadian army as a printer in London, England, ending up at Cambridge University Press. My mother was a nursing student in London. They met at a dance while bombs were dropping and the war was raging and, to his death, he remembered her chestnut hair tied up, haphazardly, in a navy velvet ribbon and how she kept her arm very stiff so he couldn't get close. He was smitten; he knew he would marry her. But she wanted no part of him.

My mother grew up in mid-Wales; we didn't know where my father grew up exactly. My mother's father was a published poet in Wales, and she won silver cups at the National Eisteddfod for writing. My father's father remains unknown, and the closest he got to a cup was being "in his cups." My mother grew up in a happy family with two parents and three brothers; my father raised himself, his brother and his mother. My mother learned at her mother's knee about charity work, community and family. My father learned to survive with no family compass. My mother grew up with stories of giants and fairies and ghosts and gypsies in Wales. My father managed life on his own; it is that life, once researched, coupled with my own, that is the stuff of my memoirs!

And so, these two opposites married. My father became civilized over the next four years, fathered two children, and made a name for himself in Cambridge. He became an insatiable reader and writer and collected first editions. My mother said "he could talk with anyone about anything in those days, or even have tea with the Queen and not bat an eye." He came to the attention of Lord Beaverbrook and was offered a job in Eastern Canada or South Africa. They chose Canada and my sister (born in England) and me (born in Wales) came to Canada on a post-war German battleship-turned-ocean liner as guests of Lord Beaverbrook. My mother was beyond excitement; however, life was about to change dramatically.

My father was brilliant. He was a brilliant high-functioning alcoholic. Where he would stop at the corner pub for one pint in England, and then settle in at home reading or playing music, his drinking behaviors changed once back in Canada and worsened through the years to become uncontrollable. After two more children, several Canadian newspaper jobs, losing our homes and disappearing for days, he gave up. My mother raised us, using all of the teachings of her parents to keep our home stable. I finally left that chaos when I was eighteen and entered nursing school. My mother carried on, although she faltered once and nearly died. She wanted to. She intended to. But, when she awakened from that episode, she packed her carpetbag and left. She was finally free. And so was I.

Or was I? No, my baggage left with me; it was mine, not his. I captured it all in poetry. We had been emotionally robbed, psychologically bereft, spiritually drained and physically abused for many years by our father, our childhood stolen, our defense mechanisms entrenched. But what rich fodder for writing poetry! Perhaps my most significant influence at first! I could write out the pain and hurt and disillusionment. I could imagine a beautiful fun world. I could imagine a father's love, all lacking at home. My early poems were about my feelings and my journey, and I started writing them prolifically at about twenty-three-years old after a counselor helped me put everything in perspective.

One surprise for me was that I blamed my mother for not stopping the train and getting us off. A poem handled those hurts. She became my first cheerleader, and I remember one dark and stormy night, standing by my bedroom window, crying. She listened while I poured out my angst about nursing ethics; what I was learning did not match what I saw. She looked at me and said something I never forgot, "You will never change things from the outside. Work ·from the inside and write it out." I did and had a fabulous international career. Wise advice! And great experiences to write about!

At home, slang was never an option. My father demanded "proper" King's English. There was always a concise Oxford dictionary at the ready. My mother shared my father's love of words and helped me understand what I had learned from him in a reversed-learning way; his love of words, gifted to me. She shared my grandfather's poetry with me (translated of course - only a speaker of Welsh in Wales could learn that language!); I appreciated the gift of poetry. My two degrees in nursing and health taught me how to write an essay with syntax and style.

My husband of many years taught me about love, laughing, a cohesive family, and cheerleading. My son, a Buddhist, teaches me every day about living in the best possible way through mindfulness and compassion. My husband's white rabbit, Jefferson Airplane, teaches me every day about freedom, nourishment provided by Mother Nature, and gentleness. Poems emerge with all of these experiences.

My friends nag at me to "get going" with completion of even one book, but the perfectionist tendencies from my childhood are still alive and well; I can't stop editing! Old fears arise, and I sometimes fleetingly wonder whether my work is good enough. Having ten poems published in the past three months as a new poet has given me confidence. And, I can take rejection now. I know it is not my work quality, or me, that is rejected. It just may not be the time. I know about the right time for things.

Elizabeth is a writer of poetry and non-fiction. She lives on one of the Gulf Islands in British Columbia, Canada with her husband and his white rabbit, Jefferson Airplane. Hummingbirds and deer on the doorstep are her audiences. She is a retired nurse educator who brings mindfulness, wonders of nature and the allure of impermanence and emergence to her writings. She thanks *Plum Tree Tavern Journal* for her first poem published in May 2020. Thanks also to *Ariel Chart International Literary Magazine, The Writers' Group/Grey Thoughts, Spillwords Press, Academy of Heart and Mind, The Drabble Quarterly* and *Gabriola Arts*.

I, MARK SCHEEL

Looking back on the long road stretching behind now, I must confess that pursuing writing as an avocation has been both the most frustrating and the most exhilarating life course I could have selected. That's true for several reasons, but mainly because I'm a "literary" writer who aspires to make people think as well as be entertained. And over time, experience has taught me that people in general really don't like thinking that much. Those who do, however, and get what I'm trying to convey, form an instant love bond! That's the exhilaration. Not being published more, the frustration.

I was born and bred on a Kansas farm, and early on I exhibited an interest and aptitude for pencil drawing. My mother, Ethyle, had been a school teacher, an artist and a bibliophile before marrying my father and redirecting her talents to homemaking. So her abilities in creative realms nurtured my own. The presence of books galore in my surroundings seemed as natural to me growing up as the cows and chickens and rows of corn.

In high school, I was a conscientious and intelligent student, but was also shy and at times a bit lazy. Mrs. Sullivan, our teacher in honors English class, saw potential with words in me and pushed to bring it to the fore. The same with my art teacher, Richard Stauffer, and my drawing. My debt to them both will follow me to the grave.

The smartest decision I made in college was to change my major from engineering to psychology and transfer to the University of Kansas where the liberal arts ambience affected me like an elixir. I read Orwell, Wolfe, Bertrand Russell, Rand, Voltaire and Euripides to add to my earlier acquaintance with Hemingway, Steinbeck and Frost. It was there the desire to write took over beyond disavowal, and my experiences began to be chosen as to what might translate well onto the page.

I'm sure that's partly why I volunteered to serve in Vietnam as a Red Cross worker. I kept a daily journal highlighting what I encountered. In a hostile fire zone, one comes to witness the absolute best and the absolute worst in human nature—courage and cowardice, sacrifice and greed, love and hate—sometimes in the span of one day. Then, too, my work necessitated recording in narrative detail each client case, which in turn provided a day-to-day typewriter discipline that thereafter always served me well.

Friendships were formed in those years in Southeast Asia and Europe that lasted a lifetime. Andy, the WW II vet I worked with in Bangkok, became a character in a short story. Noel, the school teacher rooming across from me in Germany, collaborated with me to produce my first published article in a major magazine, *Cycle Guide*. (Later, stateside, I was his best man at his wedding.) Two women I'd known in Germany provided me living space in California when I left my Red Cross employment and commenced my fledgling attempts at fiction.

A short time later, my mother's diagnosis with cancer constituted a watershed event in my journey. Being the only living child, I felt it my duty to remain in the home area—Emporia, Kansas—and assist my father with my mother's care. Consequently, I enrolled in literature classes at a nearby university to help sustain and progress with my literary ambitions, and it was there I met two unforgettable professors—Keith Denniston and Green D. Wyrick.

Keith welcomed me into his creative writing circle and the Quivira Literary Club. I took his poetry class, which gave me an invaluable grounding in the art of poetic composition. Professor Wyrick directed my graduate study in the writing of my first novel. He had a circle of friends drawn from AA that I came to know, one being a priest of extraordinary poetic ability, Fr. John Kumli, a master of the sonnet sequence.

Following my mother's passing, I moved to the Kansas City area and secured employment with the Johnson County Library as an information specialist. It was an ideal situation for a book lover, and the training I received in technological advancements was superb. Dealing with differing reader interests day after day exposed me to a

275

fuller range of book genres, and I came to respect even well-crafted romance novels!

Over time I connected with other writers in the region and helped found The 5th Street Irregulars, a writers' critique group. I was invited onto the board of directors of Potpourri Publications Co. as well as the directors' board with Whispering Prairie Press whose magazine, *Kansas City Voices*, took me on as prose editor. During those years I formed lasting friendships with other creative souls like the late Glen Enloe, a terrific cowboy poet and Western novelist, and the "ecstatic " poet Paul Goldman, writing in the tradition of Rumi. We all dreamed together, created together and published together too.

I had qualified for membership in The Kansas Authors Club right after moving to Kansas City and that association eventually led to my securing a literary agent, Stephanie Hansen, with Metamorphosis Literary Agency. Her assistance has been beyond words—placing my fifth and sixth book publications on a traditional royalty contract.

So, concluding with candor—the thing I always sought was to write well and be read, not achieve celebrity or fortune. I couldn't care less about Dick-Cavett-type interviews or sycophants groveling for an autograph. I wanted the words I put on the page to reach out to people and do the talking, and give those people something worth their dime. To know that across miles and time my words on paper might inspire another human being, whom I'll never meet, to an accomplishment of their own is my reward. My written words are my children and all I desire is that they have the opportunity to live their lives productively long after I've departed the building.

Mark Scheel grew up in Kansas farm country. His short stories, poems, articles, and essays have appeared in numerous periodicals, and his 1997 book, *A Backward View: Stories and Poems,* received the J. Donald Coffin Memorial Book Award. His blog series appeared on *The Grant Journal* and *Scriggler,* and in 2015 sixty of the entries were collected in the book *The Pebble: Life, Love, Politics and Geezer Wisdom*. His fiction collection *And Eve Said Yes: Seven Stories and a Novella* appeared in 2019 from Waldorf Publishing and his poetry collection *Star Chaser* launched 29 July 2020 from Anamcara Press.

I, PAULA SHABLO

I learned to read at a very young age; by the time I started school, I was reading books above my grade level. My love of reading led me straight down the "I want to do that, too" path.

I wanted to tell stories, and tell them in a way that would get people to take a moment to sit and listen—or read—for the sheer joy of it.

I am the oldest of five children, so I had a captive audience from the start. Mom would read a bedtime story and leave the room. Then my siblings would climb up on my bed to demand the "real" story.

It was a challenge. Kids are so demanding. They didn't want to hear the same story night after night, although after a while there were some requests for favorites. It irks me now, at my greatly advanced age, that I didn't have the foresight to write many of them down.

I ventured into "publishing" at the ripe old age of nine, when someone showed me how to assemble my own chapbooks. I would write a short story, illustrate it, design a cover and clumsily sew it all together. I thought they looked great, and I sold a few, too. Then, Mr. Grumpy Neighbor informed me that door-to-door selling in our town was actually a misdemeanor offense and I could get into trouble. Not only that, I might have to pay a fine. What? Give up my hard-earned quarters? No way!

Throughout my school years, I continued to be the teller of stories, and I ventured far beyond "write what you know," because I was a kid and I didn't know anything. I was fond of science fiction and fantasy in those early years. I didn't sell anything, but I had a few friends who were willing to listen to a tale now and then. And my siblings, who were less inclined to do so, still got suckered into it from time to time.

In high school I started a love affair with poetry. I even sold a couple to some teen magazines. It was silly school-girl stuff, but it made me happy.

Then I got married and life became…busy. I had kids. I discovered that my husband was a lying, cheating cad, but I had kids. Then he started beating on my son, and it no longer mattered that I had kids, no good job, no experience—I got us out.

I never stopped writing, though. Most of what was written during those years was a conglomeration of depression-inspired poetry and angry, hurt journaling. But they were words on the page, and that kept me from going completely insane.

The life that followed was one of working two and sometimes three jobs at a time, chasing teenagers around so they didn't end up in some sort of trouble, worrying about rent and food and clothes and trying to at least appear happy.

"Write what you know" became a real concept to me, and stories were written. I was building up a bit of a portfolio that I planned to get around to editing someday. I entertained thoughts of trying to submit something for publication.

Then the house burned down, and everything was lost. Not just the stories—everything.

It was a struggle getting us back on our feet, and then I was injured in a car accident. I felt like the whole world was out to get me.

Thinking back on it, I probably had plenty of fodder for some decent stories. What I didn't have was a desire to write. During my recovery—which took far too long, in my opinion—I turned to reading as a way of surviving it. I read everything Stephen King had written up to that point. I read biographies, westerns, even sappy love stories, which I had thought I'd outgrown in my twenties.

When I was finally ready to go back to work, I was also ready to write again. Reading so many other writers' works had inspired me, fired up my tired imagination.

By this time, my captive audience was mostly my son, the oldest of my four children. He read a lot of my stories and essays, and finally told me it was a waste of my time to write if I wasn't going to make any effort to share the work beyond my own four walls.

"I'm too old," I argued. I was fifty-six.

"Bull," he replied. "Publish it yourself."

"How?"

"Hey, what do you always tell me, Mom?" he said. "Look it up!"

Ah, research.

I self-published my first novella in June of 2016. I have never become even close to a best-seller, but everything I have published since then has sold a few copies. I have even been published in anthologies now.

Living the dream.

I have a couple of blogs and a few followers, and I do write what I know these days, because I'm a little old lady now, and I know some things.

It is still a joy to tell a story, and know that no one else could tell it the way I do. I have grandchildren to adventure with, whether with a spoken story or a written one.

I enjoy what I do, and I never worry about a bottom line, because I don't have unreasonable expectations and I remain eternally grateful for every sale or read or follow.

I honestly do it for love. And for my sanity. Let's face it, life is a kick in the pants with a pointy steel-toed boot sometimes, and we must have our saviors. Writing is mine.

Paula Shablo, an American writer, has loved writing stories since she was old enough to hold a pencil. Born in Idaho, she moved to Wyoming with her family at the age of six. She grew up there, but now calls Colorado home. More recently, she has been spending most of her time in Wyoming in order to care for family. Mother of four and grandmother of nine, she is happiest when surrounded by family and close friends. Paula enjoys writing in many genres. She is an avid reader and a staunch supporter of public libraries.

I, AMBER M. SIMPSON

When I was about six or seven, I got in trouble with my mom (the reason why now lost from memory) and she was really upset with me. I decided to write her an apology letter—complete with dried up tears on the page—and fell asleep with my face on top of it, my hand still holding the pencil. I don't recall the exact words I wrote, but what I do remember is the instant forgiveness I was awarded once my mom read that letter. No amount of my *telling* her I was sorry could make things better, but something about my *writing* it seemed to do the trick.

That was my first lesson in understanding the power of the written word, and how it could be used not only as a means of expressing myself, but as a means of making others feel something they may not have before. Even at six or seven years old, I realized what an amazing discovery this was, and on that night, my love of writing was born.

I grew up a bookworm, devouring just about everything I could get my hands on. I particularly loved stories that were character driven, as most of my daydreams consisted of conversations and experiences involving the people I read about. A lot of my early writing as a teenager was what would be considered fan fiction, and this was simply because I didn't want to let the characters go. A strong, well-rounded character can make or break a story and that is one key element I try always to achieve in my own writing to this day.

Though I've considered myself a writer since around the age of 11 when I started my first notebook of poetry, it wasn't until well into my adulthood that I felt comfortable enough sharing my work with more than a few trusted people. My greatest fears were that no one would like it, and that I wasn't as good a writer as I thought I was. Writing brought me such pleasure and happiness that I was afraid a few bad critiques might ruin it for me. I allowed my fear to stunt my growth as a writer without even realizing I was doing it.

That is why I am so thankful for the creative writing course I took as a returning college student in 2017. With a final assignment of writing and sharing a short story with the class for feedback, I was given the push I needed to put myself out there. The positive responses I received gave me the confidence I needed to continue sharing my writing, which eventually lead to my first submission and acceptance with an indie publisher that same year—with the exact story I'd written in class! That publisher was Fantasia Divinity Magazine & Publishing, and I credit them with being the springboard to where I am in my writing career today. Not only did they publish my story, but they took me on as Assistant Editor as well, and through that responsibility, I believe my writing ability has grown exponentially.

Since that first acceptance back in 2017, I have had enough publications to fill a small bookcase with books. I have it front and center in the family room of my house where I can look at it every day and be reminded... all those fears and insecurities I struggled with inside as to whether I was good enough... all those long nights of staying up late after putting my sons to bed and slogging through the day dog-tired just so I could write... all those years I dreamed of being able to do exactly what I'm doing now. I look at those books and I am reminded that all my hard work has begun to pay off.

I'm not all the way where I want to be just yet—finishing and publishing the novel I've been working on for years being my ultimate goal—but I'm getting closer every day. And every day that I work on my craft only makes me stronger and more confident as I, the writer.

Amber M. Simpson writes from Northern Kentucky, with a particular interest in horror and dark fantasy. Her work has been published (both fiction and poetry) in multiple anthologies, in magazines, and online. She assists with editing for Fantasia Divinity Magazine & Publishing, where she has gotten to work with many talented authors from all over the world. While she loves to create dark worlds and diverse characters, her greatest creations of all are her sons, Maxamus and Liam, who keep her feet on the ground even while her head is in the clouds.

I, CHRIS SMITH

Writing was always just a dream, something unreal. I never thought that I would write a full book, never mind have it published. But here we are...six years later!

I started writing as a hobby. I've always written poems and writing a full novel was on my bucket list: things I'd like to do but probably won't ever get around to. Anyway, I started writing for fun and decided on a Western because I've always loved Louis L'Amour. There's just something awesome about a stranger arriving in town and bringing law & order to it with nothing but courage, his fists, and a six-shooter.

Writing is relaxing. You can escape into your own world and I get immense satisfaction when people read a bit of what I've written and say "What happens next?" or "Hurry up and get the next few chapters done, I want to know what happens to her."

Being able to evoke an emotional response from your readers is special. You connect with them and your characters come to life. I'd probably have never discovered this joy without the support of my family and friends. My twin brother, Steve, was a huge support. he pushed me to write when I felt like leaving it, he edited my work for me, and he even acted out scenes with me when I wrote myself into a corner. Nothing quite like two grown men playing guns at work!

Mom and Dad have also been fantastic. I had about two hundred rejections from publishers and literary agents and it really got to me. I doubted my abilities as a writer, and I pretty much gave up on my novel. My parents never let me give up though. They were always there to encourage me and their love is amazing.

I have a friend in South Korea, Plumpy, and also acted as an editor for me. Her responses and comments always made me laugh and were a big encouragement to keep pushing.

I eventually gave up on getting my book published and went the self-publishing route on Amazon, using KDP. The book received a few five-star reviews and then I got an awesome comment from a Texan, named Karl Rehn. I found him on Facebook and we chatted a bit. With his guidance and encouragement, I contacted a publisher in the USA, submitted my manuscript, and landed my first contract. Job done...MONEY TIME!

Not quite.

I learned a few valuable lessons from signing that first contract. Writing a book is only half the job done. You need to market it or nobody will know about it. The second lesson was that not all publishers are equal. Some will have your best interests at heart and others will just slap your book onto their website and Amazon without doing any marketing. I ended up with the latter...

Sales were terrible and I lost my motivation to write. I could never get replies to queries and I had no idea what my sales figures were because that information was deliberately withheld from me. I still have no idea how many copies of *Blood On The Range: Caught In The Crossfire* were actually sold. I gave up on my dreams and was left wondering why I'd wasted three years of my time.

Eventually, during lockdown, the publisher went under and the rights to my book reverted to me. I considered self-publishing and I definitely WASN'T going the literary agent route again. More rejection...no thanks!

I decided to Google Western publishers and I was rewarded with a list of about 19. I emailed them all and started getting more rejections until, one Friday, DS Productions got hold of me. Within an hour I was on a Zoom call to a publicist from the UK. The marketing proposals were fantastic, I was treated with respect, and my faith in literary humanity was restored. The next day I signed with them and the support from them has been incredible.

Writing a book isn't easy. Selling a book is even harder!

I've gone through a rollercoaster of emotions. Frustration during writer's block (it's a real thing), a warm fuzzy feeling when people got excited about the latest chapters, elation when I finished the book, annoyance when I had editing corrections, amazement and more excitement when I signed my first contract, and then depression when sales weren't good and some friends and family didn't support me.

Writing has broken me down and built me up a few times, but I don't regret it. I've written a book and had it published, and, if nothing else, I can tick that off my bucket list.

Chris Smith was born in Pietermaritzburg, South Africa, and grew up on the South Coast, near Margate. He studied Accounting at The University of KwaZulu-Natal, Durban campus, and now works as a financial planner. He's an avid fly-fisherman and a rugby enthusiast. *Blood On The Range: Caught In The Crossfire* is his first novel and the culmination of six years of hard work and prayers. He has a number of sequels planned and is also trying his hand at a police procedural.

I, LINDA SPARKS

Long before I learned to write words, I crouched down, drawing stories in the wet-rain earth. My mother snapped a photo of me and I was so pleased because I remember that moment, not only because of the photo, but because someone else saw my story. In the photo, I was 4 years old. Stories were essential in my young life as both my mother and father read to me and I learned to love words. I even created a race of people called the Gulagingas. They were my imaginary people and the world in which they lived and I controlled was totally mine. My father would laugh and call me the dreamer. Both of my parents were readers and so I also became an avid reader but I preferred writing my own tales, even at that very young age and as soon as I was given the skills to write words, I filled reams of white paper with my stories and my drawings. I wrote my first novel in a composition book at age 8, complete with chapters and illustrations. I still have it as my mother proudly saved it for me.

Throughout my life, writing has been my survival. Even in the darkest times, I wrote poems to capture the pain and somehow overcome it by expelling it onto the page. While we were heading on a cross-country trek to be there at my father's hospital bed as he'd had a massive cerebrovascular accident, I was writing en route, to keep my sanity. I wrote the greater portion of a novel during that trip. The terrible angst of not knowing if he would be alive or dead when I arrived, maddened me, so I poured my grief into words. This ability has, thus far, kept me from banging on the doors from within the asylum. Yet, I am unafraid of madness and would find some way to write about the experience.

My formal study was completing my English major with emphasis on writing but, as fate often rules our lives, I spent 44 years working in the medical field at various hospitals throughout our country. Even as a traveling consultant, I brought my writing with me to create great tales from my various hotel rooms. I felt particularly emotional when I was working in New York and the Twin Towers were taken down. The odor of jet fuel and burned flesh permeated the air for months. I wrote about it.

In my younger years, as mother to 4 young children all below the age of 4 and 1/2 and being only 24 years old, I found a way to destress by writing and I worked from home as an Associate Editor for *Valkyrie Magazine*, publishing many of my short stories and poems at that time.

I began my second novel when I was 18, and then I married, and my life was off to a very busy time and I was only able to write 3 chapters of that novel. Yet, I scribbled my poems and stories and still aspired to write that novel. I gave myself an ultimatum and promised I would finish that novel by age 35 and I did. (By that time, I had 6 children and was working at a hospital, for a doctor's office, and as a county commissioner). Thereafter, it seemed I had broken through a barrier and I had freed myself to create, regardless of the things that sometimes keep us from writing. I wrote 3 novels the following year, writing 1 scene in the middle of the night in the bathroom so I would not disturb anyone.

My early life gave me a great foundation for writing. I grew up in California and learned that everything was possible. That is essential to who I am today. I have never felt that anything was too hard or impossible and if it seemed so, I knew to push forward and run faster and leap higher and do whatever it took to meet my goals.

As a dreamer, (as my father called me), I have often written about my dreams as I believe I am one of the fortunate who remember my dreams. I have written poetry, stories and 3 novels about dreams which were haunting and had to be written. I often believe that I am hearing these stories whether they are from the future or from the past but it is a voice I cannot ignore any more than I can stop my breath.

My inspiration is constantly firing and I feel very compelled to write even more quickly now that I am a short-timer. My life has been full and beautiful and filled with wonderful things and terrible challenges and so I wrote them. When my eldest son, Jessi, died last year, I knew the madness would take me if I did not write and so I wrote a book for him and his tragedy spilled onto the page onto a world of space travel and a possible future where the soul survives even the death of the mortal flesh.

Jessi and all of my children love my books and they are my greatest fans and they proudly bring my books to be autographed and I feel like I am the most blessed person in the universe, as my family has given me endless love and purpose and my writing has etched my tale forever upon the stone tablets of my own history. Will someone find this story one day a thousand years from now and wonder why I felt so compelled to leave my footprints behind forever? A trail of a life that had to not only be experienced and lived to the fullest but also to be written.

Linda has published seventeen novels, short stories and poems. She has worked as Associate Editor for *Valkyrie Magazine*. She has a degree from Western Michigan University: English major with emphasis on writing. She has an Accredited Health Information Technician certification. She was elected County Commissioner.

I, CHRISTINA L STEELE

I'm an Edger. That is my chimerical for a person who lives on the edges in life. Most authors live on edges. Here are a few examples from my path toward owning my writing soul, which might explain writers as Edgers.

Embracing My Life Purpose as a Writer

As a child, my extended family lived in rented homes with holes in the roof, where you could reach out your window and touch the window of the house next door. The grass would be tall, the gas bill unpaid, and yet the stray cats fed. Life over money seemed the theme. In the ultra-modern leanings of the 1960s, my grandmother's home was a rundown rented farm with a potbelly stove in the living room as the only source of heat. Poor is always out of step with the times. Poverty forms a hard edge not easily overcome. My immediate family clawed its way out of pure poverty. We grasped the edge between dirt poor and living paycheck to paycheck and hung-on. I was a lucky girl. My path was safe – a witness. This life-quake I was dealt created the people-watcher in me, and the plot deviser.

I found the writer in me early. Waking from my sister-shared bedroom where the queen mattress went from wall to wall just missing the door, I announced to my family that I would be a world-famous author. I'm not sure how I knew other than through a dream. But I knew. My odd affinity for reading, and daydreaming, and creating stories to entertain wasn't encouraged. Introspection, however, remained my true nature. We all have our purpose written in our souls. It's an edge we discover that allows us to reach higher.

My grandmother had given me a bubble-gum-machine necklace that said "to thine own self be true." It would be a decade before I knew who wrote that and longer before I understood the words. I fell in love with Shakespeare and Austen and Emily Bronte thanks to my

English teacher. And thanks to my chemistry teacher, who always had a sci-fi book on his desk for me, I fell in love with Tolkien, and L'Engle, and Asimov with his *Bicentennial Man*. I lived and loved my own world while noting all the pain of others. It was a time of energy and doing. I followed my heart and I longed to make a difference. I didn't have a plan or thought about being an author. I just wrote because it calmed me. But always, someone guided me on my path to writer. The biggest intervention came in the form of a simple question by those two teachers: "Why aren't you going to college?" It took tenacity, and elbow grease, but I graduated from college and swayed into teaching. College was the new edge that grew me more than I could've ever imagined. It was an immersive lifting edge which I almost lost hold of many times. The writer in me gathered every experience. In summary, I was born on an edge. I'd embraced my writer purpose. I'd allowed guides to help me and overcame obstacles. Still, I slipped off the edge anyway.

The Razor's Edge
It took me decades of wrong turns, pleasing everyone, ignoring myself, and of allowing my heart to be silenced and emptied before I collapsed into a green chair and remained there for a year doing nothing. I was a rich yuppie, an empty nester, unemployed, and no one seemed to notice how empty I'd become. What saved me was writing. Over the decades of doing life, I'd lost myself. I'd lost the writer. It had been my personal fall even though many good things happened. I lived in a golf course house, had dinner with the rich side, enjoyed vacations and golf, and raised two boys and taught. But my soul haunted me until it tangled my brain and settled me into mandated listening time. That is when the rise came. The edge that caught me and raised me higher and higher.

The Edger Rises
One day out of nowhere a story fell into my head. I wrote like a madwoman twelve hours a day for months. There was no hesitation,

no overthinking, no lack of energy. It was (most of the time) pure calm. Happiness. If you haven't found your purpose, this is how you know when you've found it.

Then I realized I had no idea what to do with this... thing I'd created. I'd read about Michener and Chandler and Morrison who started late in life with their writing. I decided I could too. I found writing groups and did a lot of how-to reading. A learning-edge. Thanks to college and those early guides I knew how to learn. I reached up and grabbed onto a hold and pulled myself into a new adventure. People helped me every step of the way. Writing partners kept me going, encouraged me, and gently taught me. Editors fanned my sparks and made them flames. Everlasting gratitude is a small drop of what I feel for these authors who reached down and lifted me up. You know who you are, and I thank you. Now, in four short years, I'm a contributor to *ICW Magazine*, listed in Who's Who of Emerging Writers, published multiple times, have novels and collections ready to launch. I'm on a rising edge, still grasping. I enjoy the edge of creation—peering into dimensions and the future.

The Rejoicing Sacrifice

When you're on an edge take a moment to admire the view. I'd started life in a dresser drawer; I rose to hobnob with the rich, an edge filled with as many lessons as the poor times, *The Great Gatsby* comes to mind. With a small nudge, I lost it all. Everything material gone. But I gained the only thing that was ever mine. My voice. My path. My purpose. I'm happy as an Edger.

C.L. Steele, an internationally published speculative fiction author, enjoys creating future worlds. In addition to numerous publications, Steele has been a contributor to literary journals/ magazines and finished fifth in *ICW Magazine*, Great Writing Contest. Listed in the *Who's Who of Emerging Writers*, Steele holds many publishing credits. A Poetry Collection and a novel are due out in early 2021.

She currently has three novel-length manuscripts seeking publishing homes. Steele lives in the Great Lakes Region of the USA. Her cats, Magic and Eclipse, watch, play, and do their best to distract her.

I, SUE MARIE ST. LEE

My mother was a devout Catholic, being raised in the time of hellfire-and-brimstone preaching and beliefs. When she and my dad started the family, Mom diligently studied her menstrual cycle for when to avoid sex during her fertile days. She was successful for the first four children of which I was the fourth and planned to be the last. We four were born exactly three years and three months after the previous birth. Mom's cycles must have been very regular, until child number five came on the scene four years and four months after my arrival and yet another, one year and seven months after the fifth. From that point on, I do not know what form of birth control was used except maybe a permanent, "No!"

The family became equally balanced in gender, three sons and three daughters. Of course, if birthing had stopped after my planned birth, the balance would also have been maintained with two sons and two daughters. The reason I tell you all of this is to give you an idea of the family dynamics in which I was raised. In the span of those four years and four months after my birth, I became the "middle child," surrendering any possible benefits of being the "baby" (or last one born) in the family.

There are many speculations about the trials and tribulations of "the middle child," and in my experience, the horror stories are true — at least in my case.

Another dynamic of the family is that my parents were both first-generation Americans. Their parents immigrated from Poland, and in those days, women were considered chattel— males held the utmost importance in the family. Monies were saved in order to give the boys college educations.

As time went on, my middle-child status took on greater and greater responsibilities—serving as a constant babysitter for my younger brother and sister. If they did something wrong, I suffered the corporal punishment...and they were always doing something wrong. I hated Mom's house slippers, her favorite tool to use in whipping me. The slippers' heels had fallen off, the tacks which were intended to hold the heels on the slipper were exposed. They hurt when being pummeled.

Corporal punishment was not the only penalty. My body healed from the physical, not so much the emotional abuse. Among the destructive words my mother flung my way are: "...we didn't take photos of you because you were so ugly," "...you big dummy....," "...you bad girl...," "...you're dating a boy from Olympia Fields? His parents are both surgeons? What would he want with a peasant girl like you?" As a result of that last comment, I broke up with the boy, my ego absolutely deflated into a negative abyss.

Her character assassination continued throughout my childhood, until after high school, and an embarrassing accusation of having premarital sex with my then, boyfriend. I had had enough and accepted that boyfriend's proposal of marriage. After graduating high school, I worked full-time in downtown Chicago for an elite Certified Public Accounting firm as a private secretary to the owner and the corporate Vice President. I bought a hope chest, stored it in the family's basement and began filling it with pots and pans, items needed to start a new life away from the prison which held me for so many years. When my mother noticed the hope chest and looked inside, she asked me what I was doing. I told her that I was going to be married and move away. Her response was typical, "You're pregnant! You bad girl!"

That's when I learned not to argue with someone of her flawed character and gave no response.

"You can't elope! What will people say? They'll all laugh at me because you got pregnant. No! I won't have it! We'll throw you a wedding."

One week before the wedding, as I drove her and my younger siblings to Sunday Mass, out of the blue she declared, "I cried at your older sister's wedding, I know I'll cry at Cheryl's (anonym) wedding but, I know I won't cry at yours."

Gee, thanks, Mom, I won't be crying either.

So, what does all this have to do with me as — I, The Writer? Everything!

Through that childhood filled with fear, tears, forbidden to have friends because Mom was embarrassed by our lower-class house, loneliness, bullied by my brothers, broken by my mother, I found my saving grace — my imagination. I began writing. Writing was cathartic, I cried through my words, stories and poems that no one would ever read because my voice mattered not, especially in the all-encompassing universe of my birth home.

I wrote stories of hope, love, forgiveness. I wrote my heart out, even if I would be the only person to read my words, it gave me some validation of my existence. "I" mattered to me, even if I was ugly and dumb.

In retrospect, perhaps the universe in its divine wisdom set me in *that* home with *that* mother to strengthen me for the life which stretched ahead for me. I would need all the strength that little girl who cried herself to sleep begging God to die garnered to survive not only every day, ordinary calamities, but the death of my husband, the death of my son, the years praying for my son's safety while serving multiple tours in Iraq in war zones, breast cancer and much more.

My best writing is borne from my heart and is yet to come.

Sue Marie St. Lee writes tales that challenge your imagination and poems that touch your heart — one way or another. She has featured in several international horror anthologies. Her poems and prose can be found on *Spillwords Press*. She is also published on *The Paper Djinn*. Her most recent work features in an anthology inspired by Edgar Allan Poe. This latest publication is by invitation only. Beyond this time-frame, many more tales are in progress, including her late son's Memoir.

I, A. STUMP

I didn't start writing because I had talent or thought that I would be a good writer. I really started writing because in my day job, I'm a pastor. I had absorbed so much pain and hurt from my daily interactions with people going through tragedy that I needed an outlet for that negativity. I needed therapy—I needed catharsis. When we just hold bad stuff inside, we can't decide when and where it will come out. Instead, it seeps out like a poison. So, I decided to open the valve and let some creep out through a controlled medium—writing. The first story I wrote was about the loss of innocence as a group of boys discover a murder victim in a storm drain. It's actually based on a true story from someone I know, and it turned out to be a bit of an analogy of my own life. So, in many ways, my writing career began as an expression of absorbed trauma. This impetus was coupled with a healthy infusion of the dystopian sci-fi that I had read throughout my childhood and adolescence. Influenced by *Fahrenheit 451*, *Brave New World*, and *1984*, it was only reasonable that I would write dark, depressing narratives that showcased the worst in life.

Even without those literary influences and helping others through their own darkness, I had experienced my own trauma—in the form of dying grandparents, the loss of two children before birth, and the consequences of my own stupid decisions. However, the greatest trauma I ever experienced came after I learned to write, and I'm thankful for that timeline of events. My family of six and I were homeless for eighteen weeks (and three days, but who's counting?) and during that time, my wife had her third miscarriage. I was in a dark place with nowhere to go, and no one to turn to. So, I turned to the written word. I dumped my own horror and trauma onto my computer screen. I wrote some incredibly dark stories and was able to give voice to the despair and grief in my own life without destroying my real-world relationships.

After shipping some of those stories out to publishers, I discovered that they resonated with readers. I found a home for my voice and continued writing tales of despair, woe, and death. I didn't do it because I wanted to promote a culture of death, but because death was all around me and needed to be addressed. The reality is that kids get sick and die. People are attacked and murdered. People lose in life. We have to come to grips with those realities, and one of the ways we do that is through fiction that asks us to think about those harsh realities. Along this weird, macabre journey called "life," I managed to pick up some readers and a few friends. I'm thankful for those relationships along the way with people who encouraged me to think more about my writing.

One of those relationships, and probably the most influential, is with friend and fellow author N.D. Coley. We grew up together and he began writing long before I. When I read his stories, I wanted to do the same thing—transport the reader to a different reality. He has faithfully read and critiqued my work and made it better. Not only that, he has been an encouragement throughout a significantly difficult chapter of my real life. He spurred me on to write more and to critically review my writing. In fact, he has been so influential to my writing that I dedicated my first book to him.

Steve Carr and the members of Sweetycat Press have been a constant source of validation for my writing, as well. I've never before been part of a group that has been so focused on encouraging authors. Steve has become a trusted friend and the group has become like family. Such interactions have allowed me to move from writing dark fiction to uplifting, nostalgic prose. I've found a handful of kindred spirits along this journey of writing, and most of them are members of this group.

Greg Krojac has become another trusted companion along the way. Even though we're separated by nationality, a continent, and a time zone, we've been able to form a bond that has resulted in promoting each other's work, a brand-new podcast, reciprocal appreciation of one another's writing, and a friendship that, in many ways, defies conventional logic.

Originally, I began writing as a way to express my own isolation, the inability to rationalize darkness, frustration, fears, and anxieties. Ultimately, I learned that writing is about shared experience and building relationships. A person is not an island. We are not alone. There is an audience of readers waiting to hear your interpretation of the story of life. There is a sea of authors waiting to tell you their own story.

As a person of faith, I don't think that it's a coincidence that I discovered writing immediately before the darkest chapters of my life. I thank God that I learned that I'm not alone. There are others out there longing for connection on an emotional, psychological, and literary level. There are others out there with similar experiences, dreams, and fantasies. I'm thankful to have connected with them. What started out as a selfish, therapeutic activity has become an expression of the great fellowship of humanity.

I suppose that, if I were to pare my life as a writer down to the most basic fundamental, I would have to say that writing fiction is one of the things that makes me human and has allowed me to appreciate the humanity of others.

A. Stump has always loved all types of fiction, and has had stories published spanning multiple genres, including science fiction, horror/suspense, crime, gamelit, humor, and poetry. He has a particular knack for highlighting the macabre subtleties found in everyday life. His passion lies in telling stories of the mundane, infused by supernatural oddity. He holds degrees in Sociology, Anthropology, and Divinity and is on the editorial team of the magazine *Sci-Fi Lampoon*. He lives near Erie, Pa with his wife and four sons.

I, THOMAS STURGEON JR.

While I was growing up from loving to read as a young boy. I used to pick up the latest of the Goosebumps books by R.L. Stine to bury my nose to get away from a grittier reality that was my home life. Learning how to read and growing up in a harsh space. Mental illness was on both sides of the family, generationally cursed and in books I could escape into an adventure while my parents fought, and my father was an alcoholic.

As I was learning the techniques and even my nearby friends and family didn't believe in my ability as usual, they would roll their eyes at the suggestion of even trying to get published.

I had written my first story when I was thirteen years old after being excited about writing in school and learned how to write haiku poetry and prose.

Some teachers loved the way my writing was done while others didn't take their time, scoffing at my disability. They had even said that I wouldn't make it as a budding author saying that I would never be good enough to be published after repeatedly getting called stupid in the middle of class which had felt awkward. Even people have labeled me as mentally retarded or even a low IQ and I didn't want to believe in that mess. I just started writing because it was my art and I enjoyed writing early on.

Learning the techniques of other writer's in their given craft. I learned on my own way with learning the methods of those teachers that enjoyed what I wrote, not the naysayers. After graduating from Northwest Whitfield High School in 2005 with a special education diploma. I couldn't get into a technical college so I didn't go. I had gotten my poetry published but my family would taunt me and not even agree with me. That was hard. Writing in my bedroom not wanting to be bothered by people who didn't believe in my craft each time trying to drag me down along with them in a pit of despair trying to make me think I was less.

After I had been abused for a couple of years, my father died in 2003 from cancer and overdosing on pain meds. My mother had married an abusive man who would hold me down. Sometimes even hitting me when I was asleep or verbally talk trash. I had once again taken to my bedroom and escaped into my own writing even becoming suicidal and got institutionalized. Writing in journals to get the anger and bitterness out of the fray. I don't have any friends where I am now. It only turned out that nobody believed in my writing when I first began. That was rough.

I had found out at an early age when I was still a teenager that I had a mental illness. That didn't stop me from writing even sometimes I felt like a failure. And years later when I met a friend that believed in me. He was a singer in his forties and we both had traits of being artistic and creative. Eventually becoming my best friend. He had invited me to several of his shows and even sung my lyrics that I had written months prior.

An opportunity finally came for me asking if I wanted to do a poetry reading at Ziggy's Underground Music Bar in Chattanooga, Tennessee. The show had gone pretty good, people were asking for more of my writing and that told me that my dream was indeed possible.

I had to believe in myself no matter the hardships. In 2018, I had written a short story called, "The Dead City" which was published in Weird Mask zine in their October issue 6. After more stories were published and I had started finishing up my book. I was 31 then. After I had found out that several of my friends passed away and I knew that I didn't want to die not leaving anything behind and not being able to say that I reached my dreams had almost devastated me to pursue it even stronger, fighting ever so steadily.

In 2019, even more stories were published and I finally went to the ocean for the first time in my entire life. God protected me throughout the process as I went to Gatlinburg as well truly having an adventure. My dreams were becoming a reality. I had refused to let my dreams die. Even as some people thought it would never happen even with my disability.

With this year alone I had gotten a lot of things done this year, 2020. I had turned 34 and had taken things seriously. After purchasing a tablet for the second time. God was with me every step of the way even though it seemed like nobody believed in me. But people believed in me on Facebook and that made all the difference to me. The important people were noticing my stories and that most importantly helped my dream finally coming true.

On July 21st, 2020, my first book, *Red Carnival* was published despite those that had tried to kill my dreams. Even after all those tears cried and having a special education diploma. Making a lot of great friends along the way on Facebook. I had finally achieved my dream after years of struggling. Now those people that doubted me are seeing my results. God was with me every step of the way. Staying true to my word my dream had come to pass no matter how my family rejected me. With the abuse and I found a knowing now that God had a purpose for me all along protecting me from harm. Happy.

Thomas Sturgeon Jr is a thirty-four-year-old author living in Chatsworth, Georgia. He's been featured in twenty-five anthologies in the horror and poetry genres as well as a sci-fi drabble. He loves his family and friends. He has a cat named Tigger whom he loves dearly with his loving nature. He is the author of the horror short story collection called *Red Carnival*. He is currently at work on another short story collection in the horror genre and a poetry collection as well.

I, ANN CHRISTINE TABAKA

Throughout my life, I was a lot of different things, but I never considered poet or writer one of them. I was an artist/illustrator, an organic chemist, a certified personal trainer, an avid wildflower gardener, and a creative cook; oh, and I wrote. I always wanted to be artistic, but wasn't sure that I had what it took. I was never happy with my attempts at art in any form.

Thinking back, I started writing poems in Junior High School. I wrote about all the things that teenage girls write about, or did I? I did write all the mushy love poems about my boyfriends, and the boys that I could not have. I wrote the sad poems of losing boyfriends, etc. But I also wrote about the war in Vietnam (actually a conflict) since I knew so many boys that were sent there, including my brother. I also wrote about things that ate away at my soul, like homeless street people, the aging process, and stray animals. Back then most, but not all, of my poems rhymed.

In my twenties, I wrote a few short stories to submit to magazines like Lady's Home Journal and McCall's. They were either true stories or human-interest stories. None of them were ever accepted. In fact, even with the prerequisite self-addressed stamped envelope, I never even received a reply nor my stories back from many of the magazines. That was the short-lived history of my trying to be a writer.

Jump ahead forty years. I continued to write the occasional poem when I felt the urge, but I never took it seriously until I shared several on Social Media, and my friends started to encourage me to put them in a book. So, I gathered up all my notebooks and scraps of paper and put them into my first poetry book "Overcast Mind" which read like a diary of my life up until that point. Then I caught the bug, and started getting serious. I started to submit newer work to journals and e-zines. I was hooked.

I started to read as many other poets as I could to see what different kinds of styles and subject matter were out there. I wanted to learn and to grow. I found my life and my family a rich source of subject matter, but I never gave up my love of nature and social concerns. During that period, I sometimes wrote two, or even three poems in a day. I would wake up in the middle of the night with a thought, and immediately the light went on and I grabbed my notebook and pen. I could not seem to stop writing. Then came the dreaded lull. I would go a week or more and not be able to write. It was frightening and upsetting. At times I was afraid that I might never be able to write again. Having writer and poet friends to talk with helped. I was not alone in this ebb and flow of writing inspiration.

I never thought I would try to write a story again, when I was told by a friend that I "had to try" writing drabbles for an anthology. They were fun to write, but a lot harder than I thought they would be. I could always come up with a really solid beginning, and usually a decent middle, but I was not good at thinking a story through to the end before I started to write it, so my ends were often times weak. I found it even harder to get a complete story to fit into exactly 100 words. I finally was able to get a decent number of drabbles accepted and published. I thought that would be the end of my fiction career, when yet another friend started to work on me, to get me to write a short story for an anthology.

Once I started writing, I could not stop. The entire story came out in one sitting. Of course, I learned the hard way to sit on a story, and go back and re-read, and re-read, and re-read out-loud before submitting. Again, most of my stories seem to come out at night when I am trying to fall asleep. It is almost as if they appear to me in a semi-dream state. Even now that I have written dozens of short stories and drabbles, I still write the entire story down in one sitting, sometimes within an hour or two. For some reason, if I go back to an unfinished story, I seem to lose the magic charm. It just doesn't work for me. The strange thing is that when I write poems, I can jot down lines, words, stanzas and go back weeks or even months later and pick them up to work on them again.

My subject matter changes depending on the theme that a journal or anthology is looking for. I do write some stories just because they seem to pop into my head, but the majority of my stories have been written for a specific project. Whereas I do not enjoy writing poems to themes. I prefer to write from whatever I am feeling, seeing, or experiencing at that moment. I do not put aside a certain time to write like most serious writes seem to do. I have to write when the feeling hits me. I also do not have aa office or specific place that I write. I carry a notebook and pen with me at all times, and have been known to pull off on the side of the road while driving, to write down something that I was thinking about.

Like most writers and poets, writing has become a part of who I am now. I never thought the day would come when I would say this, but now when someone asks me what I do, I say "I am a poet and a writer."

Ann Christine Tabaka was nominated for the 2017 Pushcart Prize in Poetry. She is the winner of Spillwords Press 2020 Publication of the Year, her bio is featured in the *Who's Who of Emerging Writers 2020*, published by Sweetycat Press. Chris has been internationally published, and won poetry awards from numerous publications. Her work has been translated into Sequoyah-Cherokee Syllabics, and into Spanish. She is the author of 11 poetry books. She has recently been published in several micro-fiction anthologies and short story publications. Christine lives in Delaware, USA. She loves gardening and cooking. Chris lives with her husband and four cats.

I, CYE THOMAS

Writing was never easy for me, not in the sense that I couldn't write, but that I always wanted to write more than I should. I still remember vividly, those days sitting in English class, listening as my teacher instructed the class to write a short story on a particular subject. I'd stare out through the glass window across the school field and let my mind drift. As my pen began to scribble away on the paper in front of me, my head would wander into some imaginary world and for that brief, beautiful moment, I'd be lost.

My trouble was, that I didn't want to come back. The world I created was always far more exciting than the reality that I found myself trapped in, and as a result I found myself struggling with the constraints of my five-hundred-word straight jacket. I suppose I realized then, that although I enjoyed writing, I didn't have it in me to become an author. If I couldn't keep my stories short, then what hope did I have? But I couldn't write short stories. I just couldn't do it, I had too much to say.

My life as a youngster was a troubled one. My mother and father had split when I was six years old and I spent my formative years moving from one foster home to another. As I grew older, I hid from the world by escaping into books, the real world with its grey faces and dreary, loveless landscapes something that I needed to shut out from my mind. Stories of sunshine and friendships and stunning adventures encapsulated me. Writers like Enid Blyton and C.S Lewis created lands that I wanted live in. I wanted those places to be real because my own world was, at times, so very dark.

At eight years old I moved to a permanent foster home in Borstal in Kent, a place that I was to settle until I reached the grand old age of fourteen and returned home to my mother. Though my new home offered stability, it was a place I came to both love and hate with equal measure. My foster parent, Cynthia Howell loved me and my brother Darren in her way, but she was a very strict with a nonsense approach to life. In those early days I was mentally tortured, the reason, Asperger's Syndrome, a condition that at that time was unheard of.

I was different to other boys my age. I was shy and withdrawn and I didn't make friendships easily. I took things literally and was told constantly that I was thick or backward. I suppose, looking back, you could put the way I acted in part, down to the life that I'd lead, but there was also something different about me. Cynthia, or Aunty Jo as we were asked to call her, (she didn't like her real name and referred to herself as Jo Howell instead of Cynthia) knew it and delighted in, humiliating me in front of the other kids in the home, over one thing or another almost daily. As a result, I withdrew further into myself and my books, desperate to escape.

In those early days, though I loved to read, I never once thought about becoming a writer. I still believed that I needed to be able to tell short stories to succeed. One day, near to my fourteenth birthday, my mother took my brother and I home and we were re-united with my sisters who I'd seen maybe one a year since going into care. What should have been a happy reunion soon turned sour as I realized that my mother didn't really care. The fairy-tale ending that I'd dreamed about, was just an illusion. As my teens rolled on, I joined a band and began writing lyrics, immersing myself in my new passion, anything to escape real life.

It wasn't until many years later that I realized that my lyrics were, in actual fact, stories put to music. I might not be able to write five hundred swords, but I could certainly write eighty. But life my life was still troubled. I had no sense of direction and not a clue what I was going to do with my life. I quit school at fifteen with no qualifications and spent the next few years bumming off the state. At seventeen and increasingly desperate to find a purpose for my existence, I left home and moved into a bedsit. A few years later I joined the forces. It was whist serving that I began to read again. I discovered new authors like James Herbert and Dean Koontz and remembered how much I loved books.

In 1993, after visiting Stonehenge in Wiltshire, the first idea for a real story entered my head and I finally decided that I wanted to put it down on paper. Even then though, I pushed the idea aside, refusing to believe in myself, deciding to leave it for a better day. I finally began to write two years later.

Earth Door was supposed to be finished ten years ago. It was something I wanted to write, needed to write but I honestly didn't have a clue what I was doing. It was a learning curb, but an amazing adventure and an incredible journey that I've loved every moment of. There were times that I really began to believe that it would never be finished. I crashed computers, I lost vital information because and hadn't backed it up, but I wouldn't change a thing.

So what now? Well I'll keep on writing and I'll keep on improving. I have found that child again. Maybe he never went away. I have so much more to give now, so many new stories to tell. The future is exciting. I can't wait to write more. So watch this space. Believe in yourself and you might just find a way to the stars. The only obstacle is your own mind.

My name is Cye Thomas. I am fifty-five years and I live in Kent, England with my long-time girlfriend Helen. I am an Aquarius born on the seventh day of February 1965. I love curry, I hate cottage cheese. I have no formal qualifications, but, after all these years believing otherwise, I know I'm not thick. Yes I am lazy at times, but then aren't we all? My hobbies when not writing are martial arts and music. I am employed as a postal worker, a job I have done for over twenty years.

I, ZACH THOMAS

Your writing is unfit for a college writing class. Those words were the shackles that held me at bay, a mental manipulative that forced me to be the person they wanted me to be, and forsake the writer I was destined to become.

For me, writing was and still is a method I use to escape the chaotic hell of life, and a way to contend with the demons of my past. I have been told by fair-weathered friends and teachers, alike, that there is no lucrative means in the pursuit of being a writer. But what the hell do they know, when they are the same ones who demanded that I get a good job, knock down big bucks, and screw my dreams of ever becoming a writer. Now, eight years and four written books later, I get to have the last laugh.

I tinkered with the idea of being a writer starting at the age of five. Sure, looking back, now, I think my early scribbles are complete trash, but everyone has got to start somewhere. At nineteen, I wrote my first book to cope with being a loner at the pretentious, strait-laced Christian College I attended. At twenty-one, I wrote my second book while sitting, bored out of my mind, in my Creative Writing class at the local community college I had transferred to after leaving the Christian one. It was this same class that I was told, by the teacher, that my writing was unfit and too adult for a college setting. So, over the years, my writing has improved from simplistic, nonsensical scribbling to polished works of literary expression, and having a teacher for a mother only intensified my will to write even more.

Most artistic people are gay and liberal, thus said my mother to me once, so long ago. At the time, I paid her no mind, and let her have her two cents worth. She was and still is a vindictive, manipulative, bible-thumping Christian. Considering the resentment, I hold for her, I still love and do my best to respect her as my mother. It is especially hard to do that, now, that both of those things are true about me. I have been together with the love of my life for almost seven years and I am a moderate liberal when it comes to the bullshit circus of politics. Still, though, I am thoroughly content with the man and writer I have become because of those two realizations.

I am not reading another one of your books until you write something that forces you out of your comfort zone. To anyone new to the game of writing, that statement would prove to be utterly disparaging, yet I am used to critiques and criticism from my fiancée. He is the one who said this to me one day while he was folding towels at the salon he runs in the local mall. Because of his challenge, he is the one responsible for my creation of the book, *The Dock Master's Daughter.* Sure, first, I thought: *What an asshole,* but his words were the catalyst for the book, thus far, that I have enjoyed writing the most. With this book, I broke the barriers of being a liberal and a proud gay man. It also helped me openly express myself as an Agnostic.

Now, lastly, advice for those who want to write but have been told the same shit I was told by a family member or a teacher. First off, write about what you know. This is always a key place to start. Second, realize that no two writers are the same. Third, develop your writing style, one solely unique to you as an individual, because no one likes a copycat, always be original. Fourth, always edit and do rewrites of your current work until you are completely satisfied with what lays before you. Fifth, do not ever be afraid to step outside your comfort zone and write something new, this is the key to growth and maturity as a writer. Sixth, always remember it is just a story and characters are imaginative figments of your imagination, no one wants a literary psycho, as a friend, who lives their life through the lens of the books they write. Lastly, never forget, no matter, to always be yourself.

Zach Thomas is twenty-nine years old and the author of four books and a contributor to Breaking Rules Publishing. He lives and writes in Whitesburg, Tennessee.

I, PETER THOMSON

"Captain! Captain! Sparky sick!"

We were an hour into a voyage from Ecuador, with a petroleum cargo for South Korea. I had set the ship on course, handed the conn to the third mate, and gone down to draft my sailing messages. The electronic squawks of the radio room coming to life accompanied me down the stairs.

Third mate Tsang's strident bellow sent me racing back to the bridge. A wail, from a soul in torment, poured out of the adjacent radio room: a blood-chilling mixture of pain, anguish, and animal anger.

No experience in my shipmaster career provoked such overwhelming change in me, and my writing, as the horror that was to enter our lives inside that radio room. I, the writer, became a person prejudiced against all forms of man's inhumanity to man.

Inside the radio room, Radio Officer Felipe Reyes was beside himself, pacing the floor in distress. This usually quiet, unemotional twenty-three-year-old Filipino had ripped open his shirt to beat his chest with his fists, while howling in Tagalog.

"Oh Rosa, my poor Rosa! Please God, not my little Rosa."

I grasped Felipe, and he fell into my arms.

"What's wrong? Tell me what's wrong!" I inquired in a firm, but fatherly tone.

He didn't reply, but pointed to a message pad lying on his work desk. I drew him closer after reading its content.

"Confidential for Captain. Message for Mr. Reyes. His family informed us they received report from Singapore. Regret to advise, sister Rosa passed away today in boat accident. No more detail at present. Please convey our sincere condolence to Mr. Reyes. – Marinco."

I gritted my teeth at the irony in the message. "The darn agency wants me to break the news to him gently, but Felipe has to read it before me in order to receive it."

"Felipe, you must call your family," I suggested, wishing we had satellite communications.

To occupy the time, while we waited for his turn in the radiotelephone traffic queue, I asked him about Rosa.

"Tell me about your sister, Felipe. What was she doing in Singapore?"

He choked over his words, but managed to talk:

"Rosa is the young one in our family; she is seventeen, and wants to be teacher. She go Singapore earn money for college fees."

Once started, Felipe spoke freely. He told me she had answered a recruitment advertisement from a clinic, asking for girls to work in Singapore as housemaids. The contract lasted for a year, on good money, and she had applied. They invited Rosa to Manila for an interview and medical examination. She had passed, was placed on a waiting list and instructed to be ready to travel on short notice.

Felipe's call came through and his father relayed that Rosa had left home only two days ago. She had phoned to say she had arrived in Singapore, had undergone another medical examination, which she had passed, and was waiting to be taken by boat to where she would live and work.

The clinic said Rosa had tripped on the gangplank when going ashore. She had fallen into the sea, between the boat and the quay, and disappeared. Eventually, they found and recovered her, but Rosa was dead.

Felipe moaned softly as his father talked, but worse was to come.

The clinic insisted on cremating Rosa before repatriating her body. Felipe's father wanted his daughter sent home for burial in the family plot. The clinic argued their contract permitted them to cremate Rosa, and they would do so: regardless of the family's wishes.

"Blackguards!" I yelled, racking my brain for a way to help.

But a quirk of fate intervened.

I remembered Felipe's brother, Andres, was also a seaman

312

working on a ship due to arrive in Singapore's Jurong shipyard for minor repairs.

I poked him. "Felipe, you must contact your brother and tell him what's going on. He will be there. Andres can intervene and stop this travesty."

In this way, the awful truth emerged.

We could do nothing more from here, except be patient, and wait for news. Frustration prevailed.

The next day, we knew it all.

The clinic's manager denied Andres access to Rosa, claiming her body had already gone for cremation. The shipping agent who had accompanied Andres became suspicious over the clinic's handling of the issue. The clinical staff's high level of agitation in response to their questions perplexed him, and he suspected they were lying. The agent asked to see the coroner's cremation order issued on release of Rosa's body. The manager dismissed his request out-of-hand. He waved a death certificate signed by one of his doctors in front of Andres and declared Rosa's death had resulted from a simple accident, and there was no legal requirement for a coroner's inquest.

Again, they demanded to see Rosa, and again were told it was impossible. The manager claimed not to know where her body might be; it had not been brought to their clinic. He became angry, and told them to leave or he would call the police to have them removed. But, Andre's doubting agent called the police instead.

Detectives found Rosa lying in an old freezer container on a remote industrial site – her young body mutilated, and plundered of its organs. Unscrupulous gangsters had recruited her not for work, but to be murdered for her body parts. Wealthy people wishing to jump waiting lists for legitimate transplants drive this horrendous trade. Rosa's wait before leaving home lasted only until the criminal syndicate had pre-sold all of her organs. Then, they sent for her.

She now lies at rest in Olongapo City cemetery, close to her family home.

The wickedness perpetrated on Rosa chilled my core. Its inhumane, evil indifference remains with me today, impelling me to strike-out at human exploitation through my writing. Where I perceive injustice abroad in the world, I raise awareness, by playing it out to my readers, through my characters, as a theme in my stories.

Born in England, brought up in St. Albans, and nurtured in the world as a soldier, seafarer and businessman, Peter began writing novels for publication after winning the 2014 Limousin Writer's competition. *The Stopover* series is set in Nebraska, in a backward facing small-town environment that gets caught up in the ills and avarice of modern corporate greed. The *Drive for Freedom* trilogy tells the story of an Afghan emigrant family to the UK and of their enmeshment in the evils of the ancient Dancing Boy culture. He now lives with his wife and four feral cats in the French countryside.

I, MARGRET TREIBER

I've always been an outsider.

And although I have proof of live birth from a human, I will probably never be convinced otherwise. I am and always will be some kind of alien lifeform trapped in the time and space of this reality.

From the time I was barely aware, I didn't mesh with people. My parents were terrified for my first two years of life, convinced that I was mute, as I wouldn't utter a word. When they finally overheard me speak at the age of two, I was chatting to a dog.

It wasn't that I didn't want to interact with people, I was just shitty at it. And people didn't get me in the slightest. They were mean and I was always the awkward, small kid in class who cried easily. Making friends was tough. I'm not saying I had none. But frequently, I found myself alone and would have to entertain myself.

Since being the weird kid made it nearly impossible to attract any attention from the opposite sex, the safest place to date was within my imagination. Inside my head, I could have a boyfriend who wasn't worried about popularity or which designer jeans I should wear. And while I never hooked up with my sixth-grade crush in the real world, he, unfortunately, died in my arms in my first short story. The tale was madly scribbled in pencil on wide-ruled notepaper, cradled in a plastic, blue, battered, loose-leaf notebook caked in faded stickers. What was particularly tragic about this tale was we never even kissed. I don't remember the details, but the poor dude died saving my life in front of his mother. Her only words in response to her child's untimely death, "It must be love."

I kept this masterpiece on the bottom shelf of the disorganized bookcase in my room, where it constantly slid out onto the floor. But since it was in my room and I didn't feel like reorganizing, I'd just leave it there on the carpet. It wasn't going anywhere.

Soon I discovered my grave error in logic, when my mother, smirking and ever so smug approached me and uttered the dread words "It must be love." I was freaking mortified. When I demanded an explanation of why she would invade my privacy and read my most personal thoughts, her defense was that since she kept finding the thing on the floor, she assumed I wanted her to.

What the frack, Mom?

We never spoke of it again after that day. And I learned a valuable lesson about hiding my shit from prying eyes. But no, the incident didn't inspire me to straighten up my bookcase, ever.

On a side note, I apparently had great taste in fantasy boyfriends because the undead bastard grew up to become a TV actor.

My subsequent writing "career" was still years off. While I wrote haphazardly throughout my teen and college years, it would be decades and take bumping into an old college friend who owned and edited a highly respected magazine before inspiration struck to write seriously. That's right, Neil. It's your fault.

Since then, I've written a few typo-filled science fiction novels, two of which have been pulled out of circulation to be edited, finally. I'm in the process of writing another novel and a slew of short stories that may end up in a collection. My shorts continue to appear wherever people will accept them, although I always shoot for paying markets first, because, well, I like being paid. And apparently, some people think I'm funny, so I currently serve as Editor in Chief of *Sci-Fi Lampoon* magazine.

The inspiration to write that first story is lost in the fog of my memory. I may never know what first drove me to pick up that pencil and compose that proto-romance story. But it was a start. The document itself has disappeared in time and space, but the impact of that craptastic piece is forever enduring. While I'll never be a romance author, I will always write. So yeah, it must be love.

Margret Treiber is a writer and serves as editor in chief for the speculative fiction humor magazine, *Sci-Fi Lampoon*. When she is not writing or working at her day job with technology, she helps her birds break things for her spouse to fix. Her fiction has appeared in a number of publications.

I, MIKE TURNER

I, the Writer
Put these words to page
Endeavoring to express
Inform
Motivate
Irritate
Activate
Inspire

I, the Writer
Hope to bring myself peace
And perhaps you, too, serenity
To conjure worlds only imagined
And have you see them
To travel the far corners of imagination
And have you visit them
That you may hear the colors of dusk and dawn
See the sounds of blues and jazz
Feel the tartness of a ripe lemon's succor
Taste the power of the raging green sea
Fall into the black hollowness of despair
To be enveloped by the soul's warming embrace

I, the Writer
Seek to plumb the depths
Of sorrow, joy
Loss, exultation
Loneliness
Love
Exhuming emotion
So that it may live again amongst us

And whilst I can only write what I know and believe and dream
Through the gauzy haze of my recollection
You may read my musings
Through the prism of your own experience and wonder
And forge your own interpretation of it
Thus combining as a collective existence
What we each have wrought
And what only we two may share
Together

I, the Writer
Humbly offer my yearnings
Brashly present my cogitations
Comforting the disturbed
Disturbing the comfortable
Suffering rejection
Longing for acceptance
Achieving in the end only the realization
That in concealing much
Yet baring all
I have become
I, the Writer

Mike Turner retired to the U.S. Gulf Coast after a twenty-seven-year career as a Federal law enforcement executive, where he took up songwriting and poetry. His songs have received radio and Internet play in the U.S., U.K., Europe and on the US Armed Forces Radio Network and were featured at the 2020 Monroeville Literary Festival. Mike has been featured in Sweetycat Press' books, *Who's Who Of Emerging Writers 2020* and *The Book of Books*. His poetry has been published in numerous journals including *Red Planet Magazine, Spillwords Press* and *GreyThoughts*.

I, PAM VAN ALLEN

You'd think an only child born to middle class parents would have it made. Think again. All the benefits and all the expectations come your way, especially when their parenting philosophy is "spare the rod and spoil the child." Early on, music became my shelter and salvation. Music remained my one true love throughout life. It never betrayed me or hurt me, although it sometimes broke my heart, like when John Lennon was assassinated.

Writing was a chore for the first sixty years of my life. Endless term papers throughout high school, college, and graduate school. A thesis for a Master's Degree, then a ridiculous exercise called a major area paper, next a dissertation for a Ph.D. I cranked them all out at astounding speed and with minimal emotional investment. They were a means to an end, necessary evils for earning an advanced degree that would serve as entrée to a professional career.

During that career, I published a few articles and presented some papers, but never set the world on fire with my brilliant expository skills. Temporary disability prompted an early retirement at sixty-one, and I moved on to what I hoped would be a life of luxury in my California ranch-style home with a swimming pool.

At last I had time to read all the works of fiction that had accumulated in my library. One was *Yours Truly, 2095* by Brian Paone, an adaptation of the concept album *Time* by one of my favorite groups, the Electric Light Orchestra. ELO music had accompanied me through the grueling years of graduate training in the 1970s, and I had listened to *Time* repeatedly while writing my dissertation. ELO had issued another concept album, *Eldorado: A Symphony*, and I searched for a book based on this album. When I didn't find one, I realized I could write it.

The days of my retirement had become repetitive and unexpectedly empty. I longed for a creative outlet. Writing fiction seemed to be the perfect solution. The subject matter inspired me, and I got to listen to music all day.

Over the next year I produced my first novel, a work of Rock Fiction, to use the genre title coined by Brian Paone for describing books and stories based on rock music. I asked Mr. Paone to edit the manuscript, and he pointed out all my newbie fiction-writing errors with respect if not compassion. Writing fiction was quite different from writing professional articles. Show don't tell. Don't use the passive voice. Don't start sentences with "it" or "there" without a good reason. Don't write that a character is starting to do something. These writing guidelines improve fiction and wouldn't have worked for professional writing.

This new journey involved as much learning as the first life voyage I had recently completed, just when I thought I knew everything. Workshops on writing and the Chicago Manual of Style helped me grasp the requirements of good writing. *How Stories Really Work* by Grant Hudson, *On Writing* by Stephen King, and countless other references showed me how to construct a plotline, how to write characters, and how to keep the reader interested. I joined a critique group full of talented writers who were sensitive partners all wanting the same thing I did—to make our writing better. Becoming a writer had satisfied my post-retirement desire for a social outlet as well as channeling my creative impulses.

I would never have started writing fiction if my parents were still alive, or perhaps I would have kept it secret from them. That brutal judgment they shoveled on me my entire life would have been too much to bear for something as personal as writing. I don't know how younger writers with critical family members tolerate it. Perhaps that's one reason I've never had writer's block—fear of criticism by strangers isn't as much of a deterrent as fear of criticism by those close by.

But like most writers, as the completion of the manuscript approaches, the demons in my head cry out, "You think this is good, but what if it isn't? What if you get one-star reviews?" Only the rare writer doesn't have lingering fears. My psychological training taught me to change the "what ifs" to "so whats." "So what if you get one-star reviews? Does that mean you have to stop writing? All that means is a few people didn't like your work."

My critique group provides me constructive feedback with honesty and empathy on the wide range of selections I share with them. Occasionally I struggle to accept their feedback in kind. They gave me feedback on this piece.

My writing colleagues tell me I don't channel enough emotion into my characters. I've heard clients talk about every kind of human despair and had a few hills and valleys of my own. What's my obstacle to writing characters with deep emotions? Has the capacity to feel been trained out of me? I have to level with you, dear reader, I don't miss the highs and lows smoothed by more than thirty years of doing cognitive therapy. But my characters shouldn't all be self-actualized, should they? What else is an imagination for?

Pam Van Allen is a retired psychologist living in Northern California. She uses her psychology background to construct stories of rock and roll intrigue. Protagonists cope with the pain of emotional symptoms. Knowing the importance of humor in a balanced life, she infuses gentle, but at times raucous, touches of the absurd and comic. After having grown up somewhat isolated in the south, Pam responded to the call of the West in the late 1990s. She now describes herself as flourishing like a grape on the vine. She enjoys the antics of her rescued cat, Tasha.

I, WENDY VOGEL

I was forty when they told me I had cancer.

The news caught me in the middle of training for my fifth marathon. No family history. One of my grandmothers lived well into her eighties, and the other lived to be 109 years old, so I assumed I had at least another forty years coming to me. And suddenly I didn't.

A lot of things come into focus when you're diagnosed with a chronic, eventually terminal disease. You start to think about what's really important. For many, that's spending time with loved ones. Some folks write a bucket list and start doing crazy things. But for those of us who always said, "Yeah, I'd like to write a book someday," suddenly that "someday" is now.

So I sat down and wrote a manuscript. With no real idea what I was doing, I conceived a magic system and the vague idea of a plot, and went to town. When it was finished, I realized I had no clue what to do with it, so I joined a local writing group.

My husband knew I was writing a book. He's a full-time IT guy and a part-time chef, and spent a lot of nights working at a restaurant, which is when I banged out all those words. He supported me through the cancer diagnosis and the crazy idea that I should sit down and write that book. But until I went to Cincinnati Fiction Writers, he was the only person who knew.

The writing group made me the writer I am today. I made contacts, learned how to think critically about my work, and eventually landed a small publishing deal. That first manuscript became *Flamewalker*, my first published novel.

And when the publisher that made the book a reality went under, the writing group was there to help me pick up the pieces.

I've since found an agent and publisher who have made my dream of a sci-fi series come true. *The Horizon Arc* is complete at five books, and they also contracted me to write a novel as part of another series set in a board game world. From that project, I learned to write in someone else's universe, which has led to more projects and new opportunities.

Now I teach writing at conventions, along with a friend with whom I co-wrote a book on writing craft. We use what we've learned to inspire and educate new writers full of exciting dreams.

I continue to write, and have several projects in the works all the time.

The cancer, held at bay for eight years, has returned with a vengeance. No one knows how much time they really have, though some of us have a better, less optimistic idea than others.

But that's the point.

We don't know. None of us do.

All the "somedays" we have...someday I'll write that book. Someday I'll travel more. Someday I'll learn to play the guitar, or speak Spanish, or cook a really great fricassee. We all say it. And we think our "somedays" are unlimited.

A few of us know first-hand that they're not.

And that's my message to the world. The legacy I would leave.

People read my books, and some will remember me as the author of whichever is their favorite. Other folks just know me as "Dr. Wendy," their veterinarian. Some people will remember me as a runner, or a SCUBA diver, or as the scary lady that sat at the head of the table at writing group.

Most people won't remember me at all.

But my wish for anyone reading this is that you take a moment and think about your "somedays." I hope you have many of them yet to come. I hope you have years and years to achieve all the things you dream of.

I hope I do, too.

But none of us know.

Our own books are all unfinished, with empty pages at the end. We'll all finish mid-sentence. Very few of us will write "The End" to our own stories. We don't know how many blank pages will still be left, and how the last lines of ink will dry.

So write. Dream. Live.

Don't wait until they tell you it's already almost too late.

Make your "someday" happen today.

You'll never regret going after your dreams while you still have blank pages in your book.

Fill them with joy and adventure, and when the ink finally runs out, whoever closes your book for you will know that you lived your stories. You squeezed out every word you possibly could.

And no one can ask for any more than that.

Wendy Vogel is a veterinarian, board game developer, marathon runner, SCUBA diver, president of Cincinnati Fiction Writers, and a really terrible bowler. Her books include the five-novel sci-fi *Horizon Arc* series, *Super Dungeon: The Forgotten King,* the feminist fantasy *Flamewalker*, and *Five Minutes to Success: Master the Craft of Writing.* She lives in Cincinnati with her husband, Andrew, and a houseful of special needs cats.

I, L. T. WATERSON

Whenever people ask me how long I have been a writer for, my answer is, always.

The first story that I remember writing was about a small dog, I was eight or nine years old. The teacher had given us pictures cut from old Christmas cards and asked us to write a story based on the picture. The other children in my class dutifully wrote a page or two, five pages later I was still going. I have loved writing ever since.

I would spend hours in my bedroom writing stories in little cheap notebooks. In fact, I wrote so much I ended up with a rather large callus on my middle finger where my pen rubbed.

I still write my first drafts out in longhand, although these days the notebooks I write in are a little more expensive and I use a pencil now. I enjoy the sound it makes as it moves across the page and it also means my right hand is no longer almost permanently covered in ink.

Nowadays I write my stories in the hope that they will be published, but when I was a child I wrote to escape.

Socially awkward as I was, writing allowed me a way to get away from the world. I wrote all sorts of stories and I loved to include great sweeping descriptions full of similes and metaphors.

I wrote poetry as well, although that was mostly confined to school, as I have never been a confident poet. Having said that all the poems I wrote at school did seem to end up becoming part of the classroom display.

My teenage years were not easy to say the least. Writing kept me sane. English literature classes introduced me to books that I would not otherwise have read and I found I had a real knack for analyzing and understanding characters. Even now creating distinctive characters for my stories is one of my very favorite parts about writing.

When I was fifteen I wrote my first full-length children's book. I think it was probably one of the very few stories that I actually managed to finish. Now, I try never to leave a story unfinished although inevitably it does happen, although I always tell myself I will go back and finish or rewrite it later.

The story I wrote and finished, which was later thrown away in a fit of disgust and despair, was a *Famous Five* type adventure and I must have liked it a lot at one point because I also wrote a sequel. At about this time I also wrote another adventure story with the Beatles as the main characters. I think that was probably my first piece of fan fiction and it is one of the few stories from my teenage years that I still have. I actually really like it.

Many writers write to be published and, I suppose, to an extent that is what I have become. Knowing that people enjoy what I write is a big motivation in encouraging me to send my stories out into the world. But in those early days I wrote purely because I loved it, because the pouring out of words, even if I was the only one who would read them, seemed a worthwhile exercise in itself.

In many ways writing has saved me from myself countless times. It has given me something else to focus on when life has been at its bleakest.

Writing my first full-length novel, sadly never again to see the light of day, got me through one of the loneliest periods of my life and so, while I cannot say that I was not a little disappointed when it was (quite rightly) rejected, it had by then already served its purpose.

Sadly, though at this point I lost any faith I ever had in my writing and I gave up on the idea of creating my own worlds and my own stories. The one glimmer of hope at this time was my discovery of fan fiction. I still very much had the urge to write, an urge which only goes away when I am deeply depressed, and fan fiction, although frowned upon by many writers, offered me a way to keep writing even when I no longer felt I had the energy for it.

It also gave me an audience for my stories and I found that other people enjoyed my work and it gave me a way to make connections with people that up until that point I had been unable to make.

Getting from first story written to first story published has been a long journey. For an extended period of time my greatest enemy was lack of confidence, these days it is lack of time.

I am working on a novel with the provisional title of *The Truth Seer*, but with children and a house and a husband to look after I find that making time to focus on it is difficult.

Yet despite my time constraints I still write.

Words flow from me; they always have and they always will.

L. T. Waterson lives in a house full of books halfway up a hill in Southampton, England, with a husband and three boys, her house is never quiet. She has been a journalist and an archaeologist and is now just generally curious. Her work has appeared in anthologies from Clarendon House, Stormy Island Publishing, and Zombie Pirate Publishing among others. You can find her on Facebook at Lucy Waterson author.

I, GER WHITE

I, The Writer, was blessed with growing up in the time I grew up in where we got a good basic education. My first school was a two-roomed school (honestly!) with four in my class. So you can imagine the attention we got – it was like being educated by a mother at home –without distractions.

My first teacher played a major part in my education as she had curly red hair like Lucille Ball, and I was committed to be everything she was!

Similarly my lineage and DNA absolutely played a major role. I grew up in Southwest Ireland in the 60s. My Dad and Mum both were writers of plays and stories, but best of all wrote little love notes to each other across the open fireplace at night time! They performed such plays on stage which meant rehearsing in neighboring houses and touring locally and this entertained the entire community during Winter months.

Being part of a farming culture that appreciated the story was a strong influence in my desire to write. For example; my cousin JD would casually visit our home every few weeks, and tell stories of cattle marts, and fairies, of striking deals and pub talk and hardships and how to overcome them – the solution was always – laughter.

Most of my warm life memories center on the written word and writing.

In Ireland of the 1960s most Irish of working age emigrated to America or England for work. My neighbor had four sons and two daughters with only one son at home on the land. She was a sad lonesome woman who longed to hear from her daughters in England. She looked out the window with longing, hoping the Postman would stop with a letter from England. On the day that he did, her world lit up. I watched her face and whole persona change. She got that letter and fondled the writing on the envelope. She then placed it beside the radio for a time admiring it, savoring the moment of reading.

Then after speeding through household chores, she put on the kettle for tea with fresh soda bread. And both of us sat at that large rectagonal table and drank tea and she read. She only read some parts aloud. I was only nine, so she felt I would not understand. I decided there and then that letter writing was a valuable skill and I wanted to bring such joy to others hearts.

In my 30s I had a few dark years in which writing again saved me. The sting of boyfriend betrayal rocked my world. In this instance a boyfriend two-timed me, and the deceit along with the loss – just pulled the rug from under me. So writing was my salvation. I poured my heart out on paper. Rhyming came easily and it was very healing for me to just write and write. I destroyed most of them later but the writing of itself was very healing.

I have had other sensational moments in writing. I had left yet another job! An odd thing occurred a week after I left when I received a letter from a red-haired lad who had sat at the desk next to me in the boring office job. He wrote that he could fully see why I had left the job, as I had way more life to me than what the job offered! I wrote back and thus began regular correspondence between him and me. We wrote 12 pages of hand-written letters back and forth. Exchanged them every three weeks of so. It was such a buzz to see the handwritten letter on the mat, with a letter especially for me. We explored worlds, made up worlds, made up names for bicycles, and typewriters, and the sea and the land. These letters were another life-line for my survival.

John B Keane – international writer from Listowel, Co Kerry was another strong influence. Each week at home on a Friday evening we got the *Limerick Leader.* I have a published poem about this paper called "Newspapers on the Floor" published in a Clarendon House poetic publication – *Cadence.* John B wrote a column in this newspaper each week. He lived only 14 miles from me but each week he came up with some fresh vital story from the street where he lived. This was a curiosity to me and I thought "he is seeing something in life that I am not." That intrigued me.

It is such a joy to see my stories in print in local magazines and each time builds my confidence to continue writing. A big breakthrough in my writing world was being published in four Books by Clarendon House in last few years and also in featuring in *Who's Who* book by Sweetycat Press.

What I love about promoting my poems and short stories, is that it brings all my friends and family together. The love of the written and spoken word seems to be a common bond between me and my family and any friends that I really get along with. Each time I have a published work, I am restoring communication lines with friends of old as well as finding new friends.

I am fortunate also to love the English language. Being Irish, this would one time be a traitorous thing to say - but we have to admit it is one of the major universal languages, so I am fortunate to love it and to be highly educated in it. Every self-development book I read and every forgiveness and healing journey I take improves my writing. I am constantly working on myself.

Finally, from writing I have found many new friends. These are in America, England, Ireland, Canada, Venezuela, Greece and other countries. I love bonding with my fellow man and woman through the spoken word and feel that bond of friendship strongly.

Honestly writing keeps me alive and makes life worth living.

Gerardine White – best known as Ger White grew up in the West of Ireland. Short stories and poems published in *Ballyguiltenane Rural Journal* over several years. Short stories and poems published in four Anthologies from Clarendon House Publications. Poem published in *Spillwords*– an online literary publication, in which she won "Author of the Month" in April 2020. Poems also in *Ingenue* a monthly magazine promoting creative talent of any genre. Writing is her "go to" place for sorting out woes of the world or nostalgic glances at ways gone by. Happily married, currently resides in Sussex.

I, JUSTIN WIGGINS

When I discovered my voice as a writer after a great crisis in my life, and found healing and hope, I still continued to read widely, write every day, learn from other writer friends, be open to constructive criticism, and thrive in an artistic community. I really enjoy promoting my friend's music, podcast, business, books, and experiencing that joy which is part of being in community. I am thankful to have a community here in the mountains of North Carolina, and all around the world through the benefit of social media. It is something which I yearned for, for many years, and now it is a reality, and for that I am immensely thankful.

After having a book, a poem, a play review, and other short works published, and being told by people that they have been moved by my writings in some meaningful way, my zeal for the craft has only continued to grow stronger. Writing has continued to help me heal, and it is something I greatly look forward to every day. I don't have a set formula though. Sometimes I will write in the morning, late at night, on walks, and sometimes it will be 500 words a day, sometimes 100, and sometimes 20. I usually like to brew a good cup of coffee or tea in my Narnia mug, and then sit down, write with my pen in a favorite Celtic writing journal, then type up what I have, edit and revise.

As any writer knows, good writing is very hard, challenging, and often filled with failures, but it is also filled with great joys, triumphs, and things that you never would have expected to happen in this life. Call it a miracle, grace, luck, or whatever word you would like use, these kinds of experiences stay with you for the rest of your life. One such experience was when I got to do a book signing at a Barnes and Noble in Asheville, North Carolina that I used to work at. That day, to me, was a very special day of joy and community. Many people came out to support me, and it reminded me, that out of a dark night of the soul I went through years ago, came an amazing community, a life changing trip to Oxford, England, a strengthened faith and renewed passion for writing, literature, and art; a move to the mountains of North Carolina, graduating from Montreat College, my book *Surprised by Agape*, and other incredible experiences that I marvel at. I thank The Great Artist for His amazing agape love.

Justin Wiggins works and lives in the primitive, majestic, beautiful mountains of North Carolina. He graduated with his bachelors in English Literature from Montreat College with a focus on C. S. Lewis studies in May of 2018. His first book was *Surprised by Agape*, published by Grant Hudson of Clarendon House Publications. He has also had a poem, and other short pieces published by Clarendon House Publications, the *C. S. Lewis Sehnshuct Journal*, and by Sweetycat Press. Justin has a great zeal for life, work, community, writing, literature, art, pubs, bookstores, and coffee shops.

I, G. ALLEN WILBANKS

Where do writers come from? Are they born, or are they a product of their environment? I have no idea, and I'm fairly confident the following information will offer absolutely no enlightenment to the question.

My writing career started at a very early age. I was in first grade when the elementary school I attended decided they wanted to compile a book of drawings, poems, and short stories created by the students at the school. At just six years old, I composed a poem and submitted it to the reading committee.

The poem was quite advanced, and the school staff could see right away that I was a prodigy whose work of creative genius absolutely must be included in the school publication. The poem was about a bunny, named Sunny, who was very funny, and other similarly complicated verbal imagery. I was quite proud of it and felt its inclusion in the book was an accomplishment of the highest magnitude.

It wasn't until a few years later that my mother explained to me that any child in the school who could stop eating paste long enough to drag a crayon across a piece of paper was going to get published. Absolutely nobody who submitted was rejected. That disappointing bit of information came much too late, however. The first stone had already been firmly set to pave the path that I would follow from that day forward.

All through high school, I read books voraciously, and I wrote my own stories during any free time I had between studying and hanging with friends. I wrote fantasy, science fiction, and horror, as those topics interested me the most. When I graduated from high school and was accepted into college, it therefore seemed only natural that I should major in computer science.

You see, my parents thought writing was a hobby, and weren't about to send their child off to college to study how to improve his skills at wasting time. So, instead, I spent my first two years almost failing out of school because I drank too much and rarely went to classes, a very writerly thing to do.

When I convinced my parents that I had zero interest (or ability) in the field of computer science, I was finally allowed to change my major to something more fitting to my personal interests. I changed my major to ... genetics.

At least it was an improvement, as I did find the subject to be interesting and worth attending classes to learn more about. I graduated with a B.S. in genetics a few years later and quickly discovered that there was absolutely no job market in my field for anyone with less than a Master's degree and five years previous experience. I was stuck.

So, what did I do with a college degree I couldn't use and a lifelong love of writing? You all know what comes next, so say it with me: I went into law enforcement and got a job as a police officer.

What? You didn't see that coming? Well, neither did I, really.

I spent the next ten years of my life honing my writing craft by creating little gems of prose that went something like this:

"The RP stated he last saw his vehicle parked in his driveway at 10:45 PM the night before. At 5:15 AM this morning, he discovered his vehicle was missing."

Or:

"While traveling northbound on Ralston Avenue, V1 failed to stop at the posted stop sign, entering the intersection of Ralston Avenue and Hayne Road. V1 struck the driver's side, rear quarter-panel of V2 who was traveling westbound on Hayne Road."

It was riveting reading. All my supervisors told me so.

After many years of focusing solely on my current career, I finally started writing fiction again on my free nights and weekends out of boredom and a desperate desire to stay sane. I am not sure it worked. If you ask my family, they would advise you that my sanity is an ongoing work in progress. I did find some limited professional success however, getting a few of my stories published.

I decided to publish using my middle name while I was still working as a police officer. I made the decision because I didn't want to use a pen name, but I still wanted to separate my writing from my job. I didn't want anyone to confuse my fictional life with my work on the streets.

I could imagine being in court and having an attorney question me about a recent arrest.

Attorney: "Officer, you arrested my client because you say you found a gun in the pocket of his coat?"

Me: "That's correct."

Attorney (holding up a magazine in his hand): "Officer, did you write the story in this magazine about a police officer that planted a gun in the pocket of an innocent man in order to frame him for a crime he didn't commit?"

Me: "Uh…"

Fortunately, that particular nightmare never came to life. Mostly because I was publishing very few stories at the time rather than from my clever attempt at altering my name.

In 2016, I finally took the plunge. I retired from real life and decided to live full time in a fantasy world of my own making. I am happy with the change, and I believe I made the right decision. To date, since retiring from law enforcement, I have published two short story collections and two novels, as well as another two hundred short stories in magazines, anthologies, and online venues.

I believe six-year-old me would be proud of what we have accomplished.

Or not.

He might be more concerned with whether or not he got a cookie in his lunch that day. I really have no idea how a six-year-old thinks.

G. Allen Wilbanks is a retired police officer living in Northern California. For twenty-five years he wrote crime and collision reports to pay the bills, while writing horror and fantasy fiction during his off-time to stay sane. He is a member of the Horror Writers Association (HWA) and has published over 200 short stories in *Daily Science Fiction, Deep Magic*, and many other magazines and online venues. His work has also appeared in several internationally best-selling anthologies. G. Allen's most recent novel, *A Life of Adventure*, was released in July, 2020.

I, BRYANT WILEY

I was a junior in high school when I fully realized the power of the written word. The year was 1997. I lived in a small city outside of The Bronx, called Mt. Vernon. Perhaps small is too big a word to use for a city that is only four-square miles. Despite the size, the high school I attended is known for producing such notable alumni as Dick Clark, E.B. White, Denzel Washington, and many others.

The house I lived in at the time was a three-family home, owned by my aunt and uncle. My room, a shared space with my brother and two of my cousins, was the entire basement. Being secluded from the rest of the house, we stirred up quite a bit of trouble down there. As anyone who has raised teenage boys can attest, not a single day passed without incident. We were like young animal cubs, driven to test the boundaries of the world surrounding us. At the best of times, the four of us could put our heads together and solve any problem we turned our collective attention to. At the worst, well, let's just say I wouldn't be surprised if there's still a Bryant-sized hole in the drywall near the basement steps.

If there was ever any semblance of peace in the basement, I can guarantee you that kung fu flicks were responsible for it. We were obsessed with them, worshiping The Shaw Brothers as though they were the second coming of the messiah. The simple plots are what drew me in, but the fight scenes, choreographed to perfection, are what held my attention. To this day, I remember watching one of the most brutal scenes—a man side-stepped a flying kick, grabbing the assailant's testicles as he did so, and tearing them from the attacker's body as he fell—and realizing that nothing was impossible.

In school, I was taking an SAT prep class. It proved to be one of the most valuable classes of my scholastic career. Having gained a small amount of notoriety amongst my peers as a rapper, I'd already had a way with words. However, studying for the reading and writing portion of the test unlocked a world of vocabulary that I hadn't yet realized I was capable of wielding. I wrote tons of essays for that class, navigating my way through the art of rhetoric. I noticed, with a small measure of shock, that my expanded vocabulary began to spill over into my everyday life. Soon a knack for stringing words together, and my love for martial arts films would converge.

One evening, out of sheer boredom, I wrote a short story about an evil shogun, Zhang Ti, defending his shogunate against a nomadic Mongol tribe, led by Crowal The Savage. Both were cruel leaders, thirsty for power. The hero of the story was a mysterious figure named—please don't hate me for this—The Drive By Samurai. The plot was cringeworthy, full of sword fighting, magic, kung fu, and even time travel. The story ended on a cliffhanger; the shogun was about to discover the samurai's identity. I let my brother and cousins read the story, and they enjoyed it enough to want to know what came next. I hadn't thought that far ahead though. It was just an attempt to see if I could write scenes worthy of The Shaw Brothers. I didn't have anything else to add to the story, but I didn't want to let the only readers I had down. That's what led me to write the letters.

I was sitting in my room watching TV, thinking of how I modeled the shogun after my oldest cousin. He was working at the time and wouldn't be back until long after I fell asleep. I wanted to try and make The Drive By Samurai a deeper character, so I wrote an antagonizing letter to the shogun, and left it on my cousin's bed where he could easily find it after returning home. My hope was that I would garner some insight, via his feedback from the letter. I was not expecting a reply. It seemed that the samurai's words had incensed the cruel ruler. What followed was a week of correspondence between the two characters. Both calling for the other to back down, in a series of escalating threats. I enjoyed the back-and-forth between the two, but the shogun took it too far.

I awoke to the sound of my cousin stumbling in after a night out with friends. The glow of the light from his side of the basement cast eerie shadows around the living space. I lay there for an indeterminable amount of time, before seeing my cousin lumbering across the room. As he approached, something glinted in the light. He drew closer and I saw that it was a screwdriver. The way he held it brought one single thought to my mind, someone was about to get stabbed. The meager light was not enough to read the expression on his face. I had no clue what was about to happen. He reached my bedside and produced a piece of paper, noticing that I was awake. My cousin was close enough now, that I could see the coldness in his eyes. I'm pretty sure I stopped breathing when he forcefully slapped the paper onto the side of a large moving box at the head of my bed and stabbed the letter with the screwdriver, pinning it to the cardboard. He then turned and walked away, muttering something ominous like, "I await your reply."

I did read the letter in the morning. I'm certain I replied to it too, but for the life of me I can't recall a single word. Eventually the world of the Drive By Samurai faded into obscurity. All these years later, I regret that I didn't hold on to those letters, if only for a comedic look back at a time when I used words to drive a man insane.

Born in The Bronx, NY and residing in Atlanta, GA, Bryant is a world-traveling author. His unique life experiences have given him a fresh perspective on the horror genre. He is a loving father of four, avid reader, and a huge music lover. When not writing, you can usually find him out at a music festival or concert. Bryant cites authors Joe Hill, M.R. Carey and Stephen King as a few of his many inspirations.

I, KAVITHA YARLAGADDA

My childhood was more about playing and going to school. I was mostly an average student in academics. When I was in the fifth standard I think, we were introduced to the library which opened up a totally new world to me. I used to look forward to the library period which was once a week, we couldn't yet borrow books, but the reading part made me happy and content. I started off reading the basic stuff and gradually took a liking to some serious fiction thrillers. I used to borrow books from the school library and another library in our neighborhood, I used to devour books.

But then academics caught up and my reading had taken a back seat, it was much later that I found that I had a knack for writing. It started off with me writing letters to my family and friends during my university days and helping out friends with their college essays. Then marriage and kids happened and I was helping other kids with their essays but serious writing did not happen. It was in 2005 that I started writing essays because I loved to write, which gradually went on to me starting my blog and writing something daily. Ever since I have never stopped, writing is a passion for me, when people are unfair with me, I write, when I feel the society is filled with injustice and corruption, I include that in my writings, anything which makes me happy goes straight into my writing. My everyday experiences and feelings reflect a lot in my writings.

The more I read the more I wanted to write, it was like an urge that I wanted to satisfy, I was always restless, wanting to do something, clamoring for more. It was this urge of mine that made me publish my first e-book on fitness in 2015. It was a short read with some tips and diet to follow, nevertheless I was excited and happy that I was an author. My writing journey continued with me adding blogs and writing for every essay writing competition that I chanced on, but without a single one being accepted, then I started publishing all of them as guest posts. It was in 2017 that I joined a book group wherein we had word prompts and the enthusiasm of the group members motivated me to write more regularly.

Poetry happened by chance in 2019 when I was very upset about trees being chopped off for development in our city. I penned down a short four paragraph poem about the importance of trees, I loved the way it turned out. This was one crazy phase when I used to write a poem daily and later published an e-book of twenty poems in February 2019. I continued the habit of writing poetry and later updated my book to sixty poems and marketed it and got myself a few printed copies and even showcased it at a literary festival. This book consisted of poems about social issues, environment, feelings, objects, nature and everything that I felt strongly about. My daily poetry went down to penning quotes and posting them on my social media handles.

This is a poem on "writing" from my e-book of poetry:

Writing is like music to me, words roll out on my keyboard like I'm playing a rhythmic note

Writing is therapeutic to me it taps my subconscious self and relaxes me like nothing else

Writing makes me happy; I have the power to make others happy through the stories I weave

Writing taught me to be patient, when I struggled to put down even a single word

Writing gives me the power to dream, and take my readers on a trip to faraway land

The saying 'the pen is mightier than the sword' is so apt.

Now I had so many untold stories inside me, I felt very strongly towards people abusing laws, being unfair to others and causing inconvenience to many, this made me write to the concerned authorities frequently, and many of my friends started asking me to write with their concerns. This sort of gave me an idea and I started writing short stories, and this time I wanted to approach traditional publishers and have a printed version of my book. I had a completed manuscript of fifteen short stories, and in June 2020, I sent in my synopsis and sample chapters to five well known traditional publishers and eagerly waited. By August ending one of them had rejected and I didn't receive any response from the other publishers, so I added a couple more stories and had decided to self-publish my book of short stories which is scheduled to be live by this month ending. Though my book was not accepted by any traditional publishers I was happy that my book, which was very close to my heart is coming out this month.

For me writing is therapeutic, it is more like a solace to me, I write when I feel stressed and angry, writing soothes me and helps me relax. And more recently I have started writing articles as a freelancer for some news publications and have written short stories for a couple of anthologies which have been published. My family members especially my sons and my niece are my best critics and they help me be sane and encourage me to continue writing. Writing gives me the power to make an impact on others by giving my readers enlightening and insightful information through my writings. Writing has the power to make a change and create a sense of curiosity to a reader. As a writer I want to impart knowledge, entertainment and create a sense of anticipation in my reader.

I see myself writing till the fag end of my life, writing keeps me active and keep my brain cells kicking with life. My school library, reading and my education played a major role in seeing me as a writer today.

Kavitha Yarlagadda is a Civil Engineer by profession. Her passion for writing since the past fifteen plus years made her take up writing. She published her first e-book of poetry collection *Profound Thoughts* last year. Apart from being a contributing writer at a couple of online forums, she loves writing essays, poetry and short stories. When she is not writing, you can find her reading, watching movies and listening to music. Apart from writing, her passion towards the environment and her Facebook groups keep her occupied. She currently resides in Hyderabad, India and not a day goes by without writing.

Made in the USA
Coppell, TX
27 October 2020